FOR THE LOVE OF ART

LEGENDA

LEGENDA is the Modern Humanities Research Association's book imprint for new research in the Humanities. Founded in 1995 by Malcolm Bowie and others within the University of Oxford, Legenda has always been a collaborative publishing enterprise, directly governed by scholars. The Modern Humanities Research Association (MHRA) joined this collaboration in 1998, became half-owner in 2004, in partnership with Maney Publishing and then Routledge, and has since 2016 been sole owner. Titles range from medieval texts to contemporary cinema and form a widely comparative view of the modern humanities, including works on Arabic, Catalan, English, French, German, Greek, Italian, Portuguese, Russian, Spanish, and Yiddish literature. Editorial boards and committees of more than 60 leading academic specialists work in collaboration with bodies such as the Society for French Studies, the British Comparative Literature Association and the Association of Hispanists of Great Britain & Ireland.

The MHRA encourages and promotes advanced study and research in the field of the modern humanities, especially modern European languages and literature, including English, and also cinema. It aims to break down the barriers between scholars working in different disciplines and to maintain the unity of humanistic scholarship. The Association fulfils this purpose through the publication of journals, bibliographies, monographs, critical editions, and the MHRA Style Guide, and by making grants in support of research. Membership is open to all who work in the Humanities, whether independent or in a University post, and the participation of younger colleagues entering the field is especially welcomed.

SELECTED ESSAYS

Each title in *Selected Essays* presents influential, but often scattered, papers by a major scholar in the Humanities. While these essays will, we hope, offer a model of scholarly writing, and chart the development of an important thinker in the field, the aim is not retrospective but to gather a coherent body of work as a tool for future research. Each volume contains a new introduction, framing the debate and reflecting on the methods used.

Selected Essays is curated by Professor Susan Harrow (University of Bristol).

Managing Editor
Dr Graham Nelson, 41 Wellington Square, Oxford OX1 2JF, UK

www.legendabooks.com

For the Love of Art

❖

Peter Dayan

LEGENDA

Selected Essays 10
Modern Humanities Research Association
2021

Published by Legenda
an imprint of the Modern Humanities Research Association
Salisbury House, Station Road, Cambridge CB1 2LA

ISBN 978-1-78188-476-8 (HB)
ISBN 978-1-78188-480-5 (PB)

First published 2021

Copy-Editor: Charlotte Wathey

CONTENTS

❖

FRAMEWORK

❖

I am a one-trick academic pony. In everything I have written, in every conference paper I have given, and in most of my teaching, I have always pursued a single specific idea. It is about the nature of art as it has been perceived over the past two centuries, and its relationship with the truth. I find this idea quite simple and coherent. However, I know that it cannot be explained or expounded in general, abstract, or philosophical terms. It can only reach us, as do works of art, as a process, an unfolding. I must give to it each time the form of a story, which turns out also to be the story of how I discover it, wherever I happen to be looking. To me, all the stories I have told are variations on this one theme.

But because my stories have been populated by so many different characters, this single-mindedness has never been visible from the outside. I have published, lectured, and organised workshops on music from the eighteenth to the twenty-first century, including that of Rameau, Beethoven, Nielsen, and Jean-Claude Risset; on Picasso, Braque, Whistler, Ian Hamilton Finlay, and a brace of Turner Prize winners; on Romantic novels and post-structuralist theory, concrete poetry, shadow puppets and Wagner, Symbolism, Dada, Merz, and Darwin, not to mention my original home territory: nineteenth-century French poetry. My work tends to be read by people interested in the particular subjects I am writing about, not in the singular idea that for me is the heart of the matter.

This used to bother me when I thought about it, but no solution presented itself — until one day in October 2018, when, quite out of the blue, an e-mail arrived in my inbox from Susan Harrow in Bristol, inviting me to put together a volume for the Legenda 'Selected Essays' series. My first reaction was a blend of astonishment and gratitude. My second was elation. Both feelings grew as I corresponded with Susan and with Graham Nelson at Legenda. I realised that they were giving me the opportunity to do what I had always wanted to do, but hadn't known how to.

My *Selected Essays*, I thought, were going to enable me at last to put on display the hitherto unseen coherence of my intellectual life. I would join together essays on very diverse topics, to bring out what they all had in common. It would be my chance, for the first and only time, to write a book that would explicitly be about the idea itself, about the pony's one trick, and not about Mallarmé, or George Sand, or Dada, or even the relationships between the arts. By means of an introduction, a postscript, and introductions linking the essays, I would build them into an achronological intellectual autobiography out of which would emerge the force of my obsession with that idea. Shortly before he died, Mallarmé had written: 'suffisamment, je me fus fidèle, pour que mon humble vie gardât un sens' [sufficiently, was I faithful to myself, for my humble life to keep a sense or direction].[1] My life and work are infinitely more humble than his, of course, but I would allow myself to imagine that I share his sense of faithfulness, both to oneself and to a single direction.

There is one small academic pond within which I am already seen as a fish with a certain obstinate sense of direction: the pond known as Word and Music Studies, which is part of a network of ponds recently mapped as constituting the orographic system of Intermediality. I have been honoured to work with the Word and Music Association almost since its inception in 1997, and I honestly think I have been to more conferences with 'word' and 'music' in the title than anyone else in the world, which is fitting since I remain the world's one and only Professor of Word and Music Studies. There are conflicting currents beneath the surface of that pond. To put it simply: one current likes to look for ways to understand how words and music work together, borrow from each other, exchange with each other; it seeks a common terminology for examining the relationships between the arts. I swim with the opposite current: the one that looks for the refusals to work together, the stubborn separations, the impossibilities of exchange, how each art remorselessly turns the other into something it cannot be. The Word and Music Association biennially publishes a volume, in its series *Word and Music Studies*, of essays based on papers given at its conferences; most of those volumes contain an essay by me on this topic, investigating the way the arts keep each other at a distance. Meanwhile, I have published three books since 2006, the last of them pompously subtitled 'A Lesson in Intermediality for Our Times', in which I turn that kind of analysis into a general principle underlying artistic intermediality in the nineteenth and twentieth centuries. That is the trick, indeed, for which this pony has become known, the trick which gets me invited to conferences and has brought me a steady trickle of wonderful postgraduate students. However, for me, though it does seem a good trick, it is really only one of the costumes in which the original trick can be performed. I would like, in this volume, not to remain dressed in that costume. So, dear reader, if you are after my theory of intermediality, please look for it in those volumes of *Word and Music Studies*; in *Music Writing Literature*; in *Art as Music, Music as Poetry, Poetry as Art*; or in *The Music of Dada*. In *For the Love of Art*, my aim is rather to allow the fundamental principles behind that theory to emerge.

Those principles (like my theory of intermediality) do not concern discourse in general, or literature in general, or the arts in general. They have to do specifically with the arts as they have existed since the nineteenth century, and continue to exist, in Western Europe. They lead rapidly to the disagreeable conclusion that if we want to understand how we really receive art, even today, we should actually listen to what artists have been saying at least since the days of Flaubert and Baudelaire: art is not in the service of social progress. Its importance cannot be measured by, or correlated with, any kind of usefulness. It is not naturally democratic. As Richard

---

1   Stéphane Mallarmé, *Œuvres complètes*, ed. by Bertrand Marchal, 2 vols, Bibliothèque de la Pléiade (Paris: Gallimard, 1998–2003), II, 672. All translations in this book are my own, unless otherwise indicated.

Taruskin tells us in the title of a belligerent and salutary book, music is dangerous.[2] So are the other arts. If you allow yourself to ask what purpose they serve, what they are for, and pursue that question with real academic rigour, you risk finding yourself stuck with some very uncomfortable answers. Authoritarianism, elitism, reactionary politics, and misogyny often appear where they are least wanted. Our contemporary notions of 'impact' ask us to presume that the arts, by their very nature, lend themselves to a mutually beneficial synergy with democratic society, which we academics should try to strengthen. Perhaps for some kinds of art, this is true; but for the arts as I have found and worked with them, in the tradition that stretches at least from Chopin and Poe to Ian Hamilton Finlay, it is not true. For the same reason as art rejects the critical argument, it rejects the most fundamental tenet of democracy, which is that everything of importance is open to rational debate — debate that takes place in words. We often desperately try to hide from this fact, but the artists themselves did not. That helps to explain why so many of the artists mentioned in this book, including Chopin, Poe, and Ian Hamilton Finlay, as well as Baudelaire and Nerval, Apollinaire and Stravinsky, Whistler, Verlaine, Mallarmé, Henri Rivière, and even Tristan Tzara were in so many ways profoundly antidemocratic thinkers. A worryingly high proportion of them had sympathies, or at least a fascination, with aristocratic, monarchic, war-mongering, or fascist regimes. This is one reason for our persistent difficulty in decolonising the curriculum. It also explains why, especially at the end of the nineteenth century and in the first third of the twentieth, the forces of social reaction often found it disturbingly easy to turn art to their own ends.

The art produced by women in this period does not generally have the same kind of relationship to the authoritarian. That is one of the causes of (or excuses for) its marginalisation. George Sand's correspondence with Flaubert, and her relationships with Chopin and Delacroix, demonstrate this magnificently. She refused to divorce her own writing from her socially progressive agenda. But precisely for that reason, she also refused to consider her novels as great art, within the tradition to which, for her, Chopin, Flaubert, and Delacroix belonged. I am not sure she ever thought that a woman could produce works of genius within that tradition, which she loved. Sand admired Pauline Viardot as a magnificent artist when she performed works written by men; but did she consider Viardot's value as a composer in the same way as she considered Chopin's?[3] Similarly, Sand's character Consuelo, in the

2   Richard Taruskin, *The Danger of Music and Other Anti-Utopian Essays* (Berkeley: University of California Press, 2010). Taruskin's has long been the most effective voice in challenging us to face up to the implications of the fact that many of our musical heroes of the twentieth century, including Stravinsky and Webern, had fascist sympathies. I see the phenomenon as even wider than he does, and more organically rooted in the aesthetics of the time.

3   Chopin rated the compositions of Pauline Viardot (née Garcia) very highly. In July 1847, Chopin and Viardot were both staying in Sand's country house at Nohant. They played and sang to and with each other, shared their compositions, and admired each other's work. Chopin wrote in a letter to his family: 'Elle m'a chanté les chansons espagnoles qu'elle a composées l'an dernier à Vienne [...]. Je les aime beaucoup et je doute qu'on puisse ouïr ou rêver quelque chose de plus parfait en ce genre [...]. Je les ai toujours écoutés [ces chants] avec ravissement' [She sang to me the Spanish songs she composed last year in Vienna [...]. I like them very much and I doubt that one could hear or dream

novel of that name (discussed in the fourth part of this book), is recognised by all as a true artist when she sings; her musical compositions, on the other hand, have a status, and a relationship to judgement, that remain problematic. As Naomi Schor demonstrated more than three decades ago in her magnificently honest *George Sand and Idealism* (as did, in a different but no less pertinent way, Christine Battersby in *Gender and Genius*), the question remains of exactly how in practice we appreciate women's writing, music, and painting in its ambiguous relation to the values of the art we love. My own opinion is that this is the key question for our time. It requires a profound interrogation of what we mean by love, for which we are perhaps not ready. I have to admit that I have skated round this question for many years, and I am not proud of this.

Meanwhile, it is a moot point whether it is possible to translate a Chopin prelude into a poem, or a painting, or a symphony. But concerning whether it is possible to translate a Chopin prelude into any kind of rational, critical argument — that is not a moot point. We know it cannot be done. If, one day, we cease to know that, if we come to believe that the discourse of art is transparent to the democratic discourse of our rationality, then art as Chopin knew it and as I have always loved (and mistrusted) it will be dead. I see no sign of that happening, though. The love of art, in the twenty-first century, mercifully preserved by a monumental duplicity, persists.

★   ★   ★   ★   ★

None of the essays in this book is a straightforward re-publication. Several began life as conference papers aiming to make a polemical point (including the second essay in the volume, and my hectoring of Darwin in Part III). Since I extemporise quite a bit when talking at conferences, what you have here is a writing-up from notes with the benefit of hindsight, not the text of what I actually said. Others are more or less revised versions, or translations, of previously published papers. One, composing Part II of the book, has been put together from three published articles. Susan Harrow kindly encouraged me to allow myself to revise and update my work; I have taken advantage of that encouragement.

The first of the book's five parts, 'Against the Standard of Criticism', shows where I stand in relation to the academic critical tradition. Inspired by Mallarmé,

---

of anything more perfect of their kind [...]. Whenever I have heard these songs, they have ravished me] (*Correspondance de Frédéric Chopin*, ed. and trans. by Bronislas Edouard Sydow and others, 3 vols (Paris: Richard-Masse, 1953–60), III, 202, letter no. 587, originally in Polish). This is exceptionally high praise, coming from Chopin, who was generally undemonstrative. I do not remember coming across such enthusiasm for any other living composer in his letters. But Sand, who certainly heard the songs too, had, as far as we know, nothing to say about them. I think we often underestimate the extent to which now famous male cultural figures, in the nineteenth century, could appreciate the quality of the work produced by women at the time — work which generally vanished from view by the end of the century, and often remains almost unknown today. The positive opinion of the male artist was invariably framed, as Chopin's is here, by an indication that the female artist's work has to be considered within the context of a specific limited genre. This corresponds, of course, to the social limitations placed on women, and is part of the dynamic that excluded women from full participation in the central canon. But that framing did not necessarily diminish the admiration.

Derrida, and some courageous younger colleagues, I have allowed myself to believe that criticism, if it is to be lucid about its intrinsic flaws and to recognise its true potential, has to feel the gravitational pull of the style of the artworks on which it feeds. This inevitably leads to tension with the natural assumptions and house style of academic institutions; a tension which has doubtless already made itself felt in this introduction.

Part II locates the fundamental reason for this tension in and around the word 'truth'. The academy enjoins us to tell the truth. That is supposed to be a fundamental value, for us. But what if art turned out to be precisely that discourse in which the concept and value of truth are disqualified? Beginning from Satie's bald affirmation that there is no truth in art, I show how and why artists in all media have refused to be bound by the criterion of truth as we, today, in the academy, are supposed to accept it.

What one cannot deny is that science, since the nineteenth century, has developed by following that criterion of truth. How, then, can the discourse of science relate to that of art, if there is no such truth in art? Are they destined to pass as ships in the night? The third part of this book hinges on a rather impassioned lecture which I imagine myself giving to Charles Darwin. He had an unshakeable faith in the scientific method, and the truth it led to. But he could also see how difficult it was to reconcile this truth with our sense of beauty. This bothered him, because he placed the appreciation of beauty at the heart of his demonstration that we all evolve from the same origin. I believe he really meant it when he wrote, in *The Descent of Man*, that for him, the female Argus pheasant's appreciation of the beauty of the male was the most wonderful fact he knew in natural history; wonderful, perhaps, in the old sense, that it was something he could only wonder at. In what time could that appreciation have evolved? Or had it, somehow, always been there? Is the sense of beauty coeval with life itself? In assessing beauty, Darwin always had a problem with time. Conscripting Derrida to help me, I try to show him, indirectly at least, and far too late, how there might be different times for different truths.

There is one criticism of my method which I have repeatedly encountered, and never parried with a clear conscience. As I said at the outset, when I write about what I call 'art', I am usually, really, only talking about one limited artistic tradition, which began in Europe at about the beginning of the nineteenth century. Paris soon became its intellectual centre, its capital. (Hence it has always felt natural, to me, that French culture should dominate in my subjects of study.) But even in Paris, and even in the nineteenth century, other ways of creating music, poetry, and novels were being practised, especially by women; for me, in the first place by George Sand. Those alternative forms of artistic practice provide a challenge to the canon. They do not dispute its force, but they do expose its de facto links to patriarchy and social conservatism. As they do so, they give us both a second tradition which deserves our attention, and a unique perspective on the patriarchal canon itself. I give them a small voice in the fourth part of the book; smaller than I should have done. The re-discovery of women's creativity over the past two centuries is an ongoing process, for me as for many others I think, and I find it belatedly opening my eyes.

However, I conclude the book with a return to what, for me, figures the core, the heart of the great patriarchal tradition. Cores and hearts, like souls, do not become visible until the living body around them is violated. The artist's book embodies this condition like no other genre. What matters is hidden. The artist's book cannot be displayed, like a painting. It cannot be performed to an audience of hundreds, or printed in thousands of copies. It is itself. It is in itself. Its values are enclosed, privately, within it. Perhaps they should stay there. Still, they refuse to.

PART I

❖

Against the
Standard of Criticism

As usual with academics, the first book I published was a revised version of my doctoral thesis, and it made an attempt to obey reasonably well the rules of the academic game. My second book was very different. It was about the French Romantic writer and translator Gérard de Nerval. It had an in-your-face title: *Nerval et ses pères, portrait en trois volets avec deux gonds et un cadenas* [Nerval and his Fathers, Portrait in Three Panels with Two Hinges and a Padlock]. It was a quite violent polemic against the literary critical tradition. The subtitle was a pitch to buy out of that critical tradition, by describing the book as a painted triptych. With its intermedial reference to visual art, it aligns the book with creative, rather than critical work. The style reflects that alignment, often hinging on stories, puns, and parables. No wonder the book was not much appreciated by academic *nervaliens*.

The second of the book's three panels is intended as a demonstration that the mindset of criticism, its common sense rationality and paternal authority, quite literally killed Nerval. He committed suicide, in 1855, at the age of forty-six. According to my account, he was driven to it because his psychiatrist, whose authority over him was very much that of a critical father figure, demanded of him that he 'talk sensibly', or suffer physical as well as mental torture.[1]

But talking sensibly, for Nerval, meant betraying his art; and that was worse than death. So he took himself off. I unrepentantly maintain, in the book, that traditional academic criticism has exactly the same destructive mindset as Nerval's psychiatrist. Both are fatal to the workings of the literary mind.

What I did not know when I wrote the book, in 1990–91, was that twenty years later, I would come to assert that there was an essential tendency, from Nerval's time on, for artworks to effect their escape from criticism by defining themselves intermedially: they would claim an identity in a medium different from their physical medium. So by describing my book as a painting, I was buying in to an intermedial artistic tradition I was to spend much of the rest of my academic life explicating.

---

1   Among this psychiatrist's routine methods of persuasion were the use of metal shackles, and throwing buckets of cold water repeatedly over the patient's head. All correspondence was censored, and visits were only allowed if the patient could demonstrate loyalty to his doctor's views.

Since *Nerval et ses pères* is an undisguised assault on the scholarly critical mindset, I was pleasantly surprised that the conservative Swiss academic press Droz agreed to publish it (though the editor did veto one of my more outrageous puns), and less surprised that it found few echoes in the scholarly critical community. I knew it was thoroughly unfashionable. However, two decades later, the concept of 'creative criticism' became current. I recognised in it what I had been trying to do, and felt profoundly grateful to those who had propounded it. I gave a lecture to the conference of the Society for French Studies in 2015 in which I defended that notion, and allowed myself once again to take a polemical stance against the idea that there is any sensible, rational way to judge the literary mindset. It turned out to be quite a crowd-pleaser, in a way that would have been unthinkable two decades earlier. That lecture was the basis for the second piece in this part. I am grateful to Professor Dinah Birch for her permission to quote in it the document she wrote on the assessment of creative writing, for REF 2014.

Creative criticism has found a niche, today. Still, it is by no means welcome everywhere. The history of the first piece in this part demonstrates this. I wrote it in 2017. I had been invited to submit something for a forthcoming volume to be entitled *The Routledge Handbook of Music Signification*. I sent to the editors an abstract, preceded by this warning: 'I propose to write a piece that is not a traditional academic article, but rather an essay in the style of what has recently become known as "creative criticism" (references on request!)'. The piece in question was an autobiographical account of my relationship with the birds that Beethoven himself names in the second movement of his Pastoral Symphony: the nightingale, the quail, and the cuckoo. The editors initially expressed themselves 'thrilled' and 'eager'. But when I sent in the essay a few months later, their eagerness waned. To put it simply: they wanted me to engage with Beethoven's symphony as a work around which there is a critical tradition. I, on the other hand, was pursuing, as I had been in my Nerval book, a kind of truth about art which can only be told through the unfolding of personal stories, respecting always a limited personal perspective. The two requirements were incompatible. After a short exchange, they accepted this, decided not to include my essay in the book, and wrote to me:

> You are absolutely correct: you indicated from the beginning that you would be offering a 'creative critical' focus, and your abstract was perfectly clear on that point.
> We believe the merits of your original article and the points you make, including your framework for making them, deserve to be appreciated in a more appropriate home. It should be published as *you* envision it, without [us] trying to shoe-horn it, as it were, into our conception of what you are saying to suit our conception of what we need for the volume. Therefore — and with a great deal of regret — we need to let it go, and we are looking forward to reading it in another, more fitting, venue.

I have taken them at their word.

The final essay in this part is the only one based on previously published material. It appeared in the journal *Dix-Neuf*, in an issue on the theme of ecopoetics, in 2015. Its subject matter, an article by Mallarmé, is completely different from that of 'What

Beethoven's Nightingale Means to Me'. But I note a number of similarities between the two essays. Both carefully avoid citing an immense critical tradition. Both are concerned with the relationship between nature and art, and how we perceive it. And both have at their hearts the same quotation from a letter by Beethoven, which expresses a sentiment I have been pondering for years, concerning the origin both of nature and of art.

As I read through 'Which Came First? Nature, Music, and Poetry in Mallarmé's "Bucolique"' to prepare it for this volume, I realised that it was quite dense, and would be hard going for anyone not familiar with Mallarmé's prose. So I revised it, with Susan Harrow's kind encouragement. The version you have here is longer and, I hope, more reader-friendly than the original. Nonetheless, I fear it remains, of all the essays in this volume, the least accessible for anyone without an interest in the text being analysed. Mallarmé has never been easy.

CHAPTER 1

❖

What Beethoven's Nightingale
Means to Me

For Martin

Yet nature is made better by no mean
But nature makes that mean: so, over that art
Which you say adds to nature, is an art
That nature makes.
　　　(Shakespeare, *The Winter's Tale*, iv.4)

What follows is the record of a personal journey. It has helped me to learn that there are things that only stories can explain, and that those things are what I value most, in music and elsewhere.

It begins in an unpromising setting: a sprawling unspectacular town in the north-east of England called South Shields, in the early 1970s. It was a ship-building and coal-mining town, declining steadily. (Over the following thirty years, all the heavy industry closed, and the town acquired one of the highest unemployment rates in the country.) My family lived there. It was not a musical environment. I heard hardly any music when I was small, and no classical music at all. Nonetheless, for reasons which I have never understood, when I was six, I asked to play the violin. By the time I was fourteen, I was competent enough, by local standards, to participate in a performance of Beethoven's Pastoral Symphony, which was organised at the local Marine and Technical College.

My memories from that time are fragmentary, and not numerous. But they are extremely vivid. None is more vivid than my memory of the first bars of that symphony, played at the first rehearsal. I remember the very grain of the paper of the second violin part from which I played, and the colour of the walls (peeling grey paint with a yellow undercoat). I remember the slightly mouldy smell of the room. And one of my most powerful auditory memories is of the sound of the first violins, dedicated and dogged amateurs, playing the opening tune, with a vibrato and a predominance of cheap metallic strings that would, like the deliberate tempo, now be considered picturesque. As with all my early vivid memories, I now realise that what made it stick in my mind was a violent frustration caused by incomprehension.

That frustration arose from the opening phrase, played by the first violins. Its

FIG. 1.1. Beethoven, Pastoral Symphony, opening of the first movement.

sheer simplicity and brevity, heading to a pause on the dominant, left me with an underdetermined yet overwhelming impression I have never been able to shake off. Was this simplicity actually, really, for the restless adolescent that I was, boring? Was I bored? Or was it something that I could appreciate as a necessary building block for a great work of art? Could I appreciate it? How? What should I do with it? I was stumped. I knew Beethoven was a Great Composer, but I couldn't see how. I thought that probably what I ought to do was something that I now know might have been called 'structural listening' (though I had no term for it then): to take the patterns of intervals and the patterns of rhythms, and see how the symphony used them, constructed grand designs out of them. I tried. For example: apart from one rising third, one descending fifth, and one rising fourth, all the intervals in that first tune, and in my second violin part when it entered, were seconds. Why? What, if anything, did that mean?

The feeling of frustration was compounded, much later in the schedule of rehearsals, by the famous passage in the slow movement where the orchestra stops, and the flute, oboe, and clarinet play the parts, according to Beethoven's annotation, of nightingale, quail, and cuckoo. I had never heard the symphony before. I had no idea that these birds were meant to be heard there. My second violin part contained only rests at that point; no names of birds. The first time we got to it, what I actually heard in that passage was this: the flute played repeated major seconds, at first slowly, then increasingly rapidly; then the oboe came in, and disputed the major second, by obstinately playing a repeated note; finally, the clarinet played a major third, and refused to stop playing a major third, until the first violins came in and played a tune in which all the intervals were seconds. That struggle between repeated notes, seconds, and thirds continued until the end of the movement, the last two notes of which were, for my ear, a falling major third, the same notes as the clarinet had played. So thirds won in the end. And so they did at the very end of the whole symphony — or did they? For the final two chords of the symphony, like those of the slow movement, seem dominated by a falling major third; but the flowing semiquavers in the cello part lead into the very last chord with a second followed by a repeated note. So depending on whether one's ear catches the cellos' semiquavers, or the quavers in the rest of the orchestra, one will hear either a second then a repeated note, or a third.

Was all this calculation of intervals of any interest at all? I was not convinced. But how, if not through such calculation, might I find the meaning of the music? Only one alternative occurred to me. It had been suggested by another formative musical experience I had had not long before.

My first violin teacher, Marjorie Hall, was the headmistress of a local primary school. She was playing the viola in that performance of Beethoven 6. She had earlier taken me to an orchestral concert at the City Hall in Newcastle. It was the first concert I had ever been to. I tried to listen carefully. (Again, I now know that what I was trying to do was what we might call 'structural listening'.) I failed. I couldn't concentrate on the notes of music. My mind wandered in a strange daze; a sensation which I have ever since associated with the colours (cream, gold, and dark brown varnished wood), penumbra, and smells (dust, polish, and other people's posh concert clothes) of that concert hall. I wondered whether I should feel guilty at this. My teacher had gone to the trouble of taking me to Newcastle for the concert; my parents had paid for the ticket; the orchestra had rehearsed, and was now playing; and I couldn't repay them with my concentration? Was that not proof that I was unmusical, or idle, or both? The answer I eventually gave myself was determined by my feeling at the end of the music. Although I did not know the piece (and cannot now remember what was played), I felt my drifting mind going with the shape of it, and somehow I knew when its end was nigh; and after the end, I had that strange tingling feeling which I have ever since associated with the experience of great works of art. Somehow, then, although I had paid no conscious attention, though I had been daydreaming (I spent a lot of my life in those days being told off for daydreaming, by teachers and parents), the music and I had been in contact with each other. That gave me another model of listening: one that entirely escapes conscious control. Perhaps the real meaning of Beethoven's symphony, similarly, was one to which I could only gain access by not bothering to try to understand. In which case, all my calculations about intervals would be pointless and misguided.

But soon, those two models were disrupted by a third, which I could not make mine. In a break in one of the rehearsals, I overheard the wind players talking about birds. What birds, I wondered? I soon understood that the falling third in the clarinet was meant to be a cuckoo. What about the others? I heard mention of a quail and a nightingale: where were they? I had never heard either bird, and had no idea what I was supposed to be listening for. I was too embarrassed by my ignorance to ask, but over the course of the rehearsals I found out. Taking this in conjunction with the descriptive titles of the movements, I found myself frankly annoyed. Beethoven, apparently, followed happily by all the musicians who had played the work (including those in the room), had pinned the form of the work to a description, a specific scene, which he had had in his head — and worse still, specific sounds imitated from nature. I rebelled against this, quite violently. No, I thought: the music, if it is music, must have its own logic. My other two models of listening, which I might now call 'structural' and 'unanalysable', seemed to me, somehow, morally acceptable. But the explanation by description or imitation of an external scene seemed to me morally wrong. It could not be right for music to be a mere imitation of something outside it. And yet Beethoven had seemed to assert this by his annotations. How could he?

The answer, of course, is that he didn't. No one has ever known better than Beethoven what he was doing, and he was certainly not telling us that his music was simply an imitation of three birds. But it took me several decades to understand this.

Meanwhile, on 21 April 1993 — the night before my oldest son's fourth birthday — just after nightfall, in a small bush at the edge of a vineyard, not far from the sea, in the Massif des Maures in Provence, I heard a nightingale sing. I knew it had to be a nightingale; what else could it be? I never saw it, but I stood there in the dark, under the stars, listening, alone (the rest of my family was in a little holiday house isolated among the vines, about half a mile away), as so many people have done

FIG. I.2. Beethoven, Pastoral Symphony, second movement, bars 129–32.

before; as I am sure Beethoven, who loved to be alone in the countryside, must have done in his youth; listening in endless astonishment to the richness and variety of its song, which contained so many complex phrases, so different from each other, separated often by careful pauses, and including crescendos and tone variations such as no other bird I have ever heard can manage (except perhaps the lyre-bird of Australia). It was unforgettable. It sounded nothing like the nightingale in the symphony, which repeats endlessly the same two notes, played by the instrument, of all those in the orchestra, with the most limited range of dynamics and of tone colour. I wondered what Beethoven had been up to. Surely he must have known that he was betraying the most musical of non-human creatures. Perhaps, after all, I thought, the pattern of notes in that passage really was dictated more by some arcane logic of contrasting intervals than by imitation of birds.

Another ten years later, I read George Sand's *Lettres d'un voyageur*, and I discovered I was by no means the first person to hear the Pastoral Symphony without initially realising I was supposed to be hearing birds. The narrator of that work, written in 1834, tells us that the first time he heard the symphony, he did not know the programme, and heard no birds. As he listened, he imagined that the symphony told a Miltonian tale of a rebel angel; and for him, the trills of the flute were no nightingale, but rather the fallen angel's final cry to heaven. When, later, he was told of Beethoven's titles and annotations, he had no trouble, on re-hearing the symphony, adapting his vision to one of an idyllic countryside. This was my introduction to a fourth kind of listening, to which I am not personally inclined, but which my research gradually led me to realise was extremely common, and frequently held to be universal, in the nineteenth century: when people heard instrumental music, they always imagined a story or at least a series of visual images to go with it. That story could be directed by the composer, if a programme was provided; but in the absence of such a programme, one would naturally be invented by the listener. This led me to realise that I had been unfair to Beethoven in being angry with him for inserting the birds' names, and indeed the titles of the movements. Why should he be different from anyone else, when listening to his own music? Why should I expect him not to hear stories and see pictures? And why should he not have the right to tell us what his personal stories and pictures were? They did not need to constrain us. I learned that many other composers, including Brahms, Stravinsky, and Schoenberg, admitted in private that they, too, associated particular images with particular pieces of instrumental music, though they were reluctant to say what they were, because they did not want to give the impression that their own images somehow defined the meaning of the music. I understood and respected their point of view, and surmised that generally Beethoven shared it, since the Pastoral Symphony remains an exception in his work. I also learned to respect composers such as Berlioz and Debussy who, like Beethoven in the Pastoral Symphony (or so I now thought), were not averse to suggesting programmes that would allow concert-goers to glimpse the composers' narrative and visual thought processes, while always ensuring there were plenty of clues to the music's fundamental independence of those thought processes.

What I still could not respect was any kind of approach to musical meaning that accepted words or pictures could encapsulate the essential signification of the music. It was becoming increasingly clear to me that very few composers made this mistake. All the composers named above were well aware of the gulf between musical signification and the signification of programmes. Even Wagner, I discovered, was closer to that opinion than was generally thought. Audiences, however, it seemed to me, were frequently not so aware. They heard the Pastoral Symphony as if it really expressed the essence of the countryside, and Beethoven's birds as if they were really there to represent birds. So I was no longer annoyed with Beethoven, for telling us what his music meant; instead I was annoyed with his audiences, for believing he had told them what his music meant.

I was, by this time, becoming a 'word and music studies' scholar. I found myself, over two decades, writing books and articles following the evolution of ideas on these matters from the time of George Sand up to the 1980s. I always retained a nagging sense that the fount of all these ideas was Beethoven, whose thought I had not investigated. I felt I should. Eventually, I spent a few days looking through his correspondence, and reading the standard English potted versions of his writings. I acquired a powerful sense that here was a man who was not in the habit of expressing publicly his thoughts on the question of music and signification, but who in fact had thought through in advance all the questionings that would exercise the next century and a half — and me. The key seemed to me a well-known sentence in a draft letter of 1825: 'Wie denn in der Kunst die Natur, <gegründ> u. sie wiederum die Natur in der Kunst gegründet ist' [Inasmuch as Nature is founded in Art, and, again, Art is founded in Nature].[1] Art is founded in Nature; but then, Nature is also founded in Art. What we call nature — the natural, as opposed to the artificial — does not pre-exist our arts; it is called into being by them. It is a natural illusion, doubtless, to suppose that nature came first. In fact, it did not. The two are co-creative. Beethoven, as one of the privileged band of true creators who could appreciate this, always expressed the relationship between nature and art in terms that allowed travel in both directions: through art to nature, or through nature to art; and the solidarity between the two was at the heart of his concept of composition. He did not compose after or before nature, but with nature.

His biographer Schindler reported being taken by Beethoven to the spot in the countryside which Beethoven associated with the birds evoked in the symphony. Beethoven, he records, told him: 'Hier habe ich die Scene am Bach geschrieben und die Goldammern da oben, die Wachteln, Nachtigallen und Kukuke ringsum haben mit componirt' [Here I wrote the scene by the brook and the yellowhammers up there, the quails, the nightingales, and cuckoos all around composed with me].[2] It is ornithologically difficult to believe that he could have heard those four birds together in the same place at the same time. One might also note that by that stage in his life, Beethoven was already quite deaf. But he did not need the birds to be physically present, or physically audible. After all, he did not tell Schindler that he had heard the birds at that spot. Rather, he said that this was where he had written the scene, while the birds composed together, or with him. The nature of that composition between Beethoven and the birds is the key to his art. One could just as well say: the art of that composition between Beethoven and the birds is the key to his nature.

Ordinary mortals, however, always seem to have been unable to accept Beethoven's sense of reciprocity between art and nature. Our natural (or is it artistic?) tendency is to assume always that one of the two is original, and the other is imitative and derivative. Either Nature is beautiful, and the work of art is beautiful because it imitates Nature; or Art is beautiful, and Nature only seems so when she happens to conform to the demands of our artistic sense. Both these non-Beethovenian attitudes, I discovered, are to be found in the nineteenth century. The former, certainly, is more common among lay people, but the latter is by no means rare among artists. The painter Whistler provides an extreme example. He also supplied the best evidence of how the bourgeois public will always default to the former position: to the belief, which he loathed, that a work of art is valuable because it represents something valuable in nature. He painted a portrait of his mother (of whom he was not fond), and called it *Arrangement in Grey and Black*. But it became popular under another title: *Whistler's Mother*. It has been widely received as an icon of motherhood.[3] Certainly, this is not how Whistler conceived it. Yet he

1   Ludwig van Beethoven, *Briefwechsel Gesaumtausgabe*, ed. by Sieghard Brandenburg, 7 vols (Munich: G. Henle, 1996–98), VI, 96; *The Letters of Beethoven*, coll., trans., and ed. by Emily Anderson, 3 vols (London: Macmillan, 1961), III, 1224.
2   Anton Schindler, *Biographie von Ludwig van Beethoven* (Münster: Aschendorff, 1860), p. 154.
3   For the entertaining history of this reception, see *Whistler's Mother: An American Icon*, ed. by Margaret MacDonald (London: Lund Humphries, 2003).

did allow it to be known that the sitter for the portrait had been his mother (even though this was, in fact, only half true), in the full knowledge that his public would seize on this — and give him both a good cash price, and the opportunity to berate them for their stupidity in believing that the subject of the painting was the source of its value. I also discovered that throughout the nineteenth and early twentieth centuries, these contrasting views were often expressed, precisely, in relation to Beethoven's Pastoral Symphony, which inspired uniquely passionate reactions. Some loved it for its representation of nature; but many, including Debussy, mocked and despised it, for precisely the same reason. However, this polemic, I noted, died down from the 1960s. After that, as I had found when I first encountered the work, no one except, it seemed, for me was surprised or shocked or bewildered to find birds represented in the symphony. It was felt to be quite natural. It made this symphony neither better nor worse than, nor even essentially different from, Beethoven's other symphonies. Apparently, some questions which used to be asked were no longer being asked, about how music signified. Both Whistler's perspective, and Beethoven's careful ambiguity, had vanished from the cultural scene.

Another decade later, I happened to be listening to the Pastoral Symphony, on a CD, with my youngest son, then aged five. We got to the birds. I told him about them. He listened. Then I became angry with myself. Why was I, I asked myself, foisting on him the naive interpretation ('those are birds') which I had myself been mercifully spared on first encountering the symphony? Why had I not let him discover for himself the richness and complexity of the relationship between music, nature, and meaning? Having led him astray, it was now my duty to let him see the truth. To arm myself with that truth, I returned to my reading of Beethoven's writings, to those annotations on the symphony, and to the score. I also read David Wyn Jones's book on the Pastoral Symphony in the 'Cambridge Music Handbook' series, and discovered that, according to him, the nightingale motif had in fact begun as a purely musical structure. Looking at Beethoven's drafts of that movement, he finds:

> One ending is based on quaver motion in fifths and sixths [...]; another, marked *Ende*, alternates the same figure with a single bar of trills on the tonic. These trills and the recognition that they occur throughout the movement, as already notated in many pages of sketches, seem to have prompted the decision to include the imitation of birdsong.[4]

That might seem to explain the plain fact that Beethoven's nightingale does not sound like a nightingale. Wyn Jones adds that Beethoven appears, in his decision to evoke the sounds of nature, to have been following the well-known example of Haydn, who had done similar things in his popular oratorio, *The Creation*. Haydn's nightingale, however, was different in two vital ways.

First, as Wyn Jones tells us, it sounded different: 'Haydn and Beethoven [...] have a different perception of the nightingale'.[5] Indeed they do. Haydn's (to be heard

4   David Wyn Jones, *Beethoven: Pastoral Symphony* (Cambridge: Cambridge University Press, 1995), p. 67.
5   Ibid., p. 11.

in the aria of the angel Gabriel 'Auf starkem Fittige', in Part 2 of *The Creation*) sounds significantly more like a real nightingale, at least to the extent that its song (represented, as in Beethoven, by solo flute) is extended, highly varied, and has quite a tessitura. Beethoven, in contrast, confined his poor nightingale to a single repeated interval, a second; surely we can only understand this, as Wyn Jones does, as a result of his compositional process. Second: as Haydn's nightingale is introduced, the singer, the angel Gabriel, actually mentions the bird, so that a live audience would know what it was; whereas Beethoven merely writes the bird's name on the score, so that a listener may remain in ignorance of it.

That space left for ignorance is encoded in many of Beethoven's comments on the symphony's programme, including the most famous, which appeared on the performance parts, as it did on the handbill at the first performance:[6] 'Mehr Ausdruck der Empfindung als Malerei' [More expression of feeling than painting]. Of course, not much is changed by this if one interprets 'Empfindung' as meaning the specific feelings associated with, for example, storms, country dances, or hearing nightingales. But I had by now realised, through working on the history of words such as *Empfindung* in German and 'emotion' in English, that a very different interpretation was possible. What if *Empfindung* is taken to mean, not particular sentiments necessarily attached to particular images or events, but rather, more generally, the way in which we feel or receive such sentiments, the movement of the soul that they occasion? It was widely accepted in Beethoven's time that art occupied an intermediate, and mediating, space between the realm of specific perceptions, always accessible to precise verbal or pictorial representation, and the mysterious realm of the soul, which cannot be thus represented. As we have lost our sense of the real existence of that mysterious realm, we have acquired the unfortunate habit of pinning all kinds of feeling to specific perceptions, to events in the real world. That is not how Beethoven thought. His nightingale did not have to sound like a living nightingale because the *Empfindung* that he personally associated with it could exist, at the level of the soul, independently of all nightingales, and, through music, be sensed by a listener without needing to be mediated by any bird.

A year later, as I was to begin working on the essay you are now reading, I rewarded myself in advance by buying another CD of the symphony: Carlos Kleiber's uniquely passionate and driven performance. When I put it on, my son, now six, made himself a nest out of a pile of my pullovers, buried himself in it, and listened with me. He had no comment to make about what it might or might not represent. I do not know if he remembered what I had told him of the identity of the birds. He came away, as I did, singing the tune from the beginning of the first movement: that little motif that wanders to the dominant. The birds, I thought, had, for him, been absorbed back into the music.

I felt somehow absolved. After more than forty years, one of my initial frustrating incomprehensions had dissipated. I now knew that the birds could be a translucent, passing presence in the music: that they didn't have to be heard as birds for the music to be what it is; that Beethoven knew this from the beginning, which is why he could

6   Ibid., pp. 42–43.

allow himself to write 'Nachtigall' by a motif which, as he knew, sounds nothing like a nightingale; and that conversely, they did not, either, have to be received (as Debussy received them) as an obstruction to musical appreciation. Certainly, they were not real birds, not birds imitated from nature, but were founded in art, as nature is. At the same time, there is no point in fighting the illusion, so universal in the nineteenth century, that music conveys images and portrays meaning. It is an illusion; this we know, because different people will not see the same images upon hearing a given piece of music, unless they have been given the words to direct their imagination. But it is not an illusion that can or should be banished, because art has to create nature, just as nature has to create art. We are making a dangerous mistake if we demand that music have a stable signification. We are not making a mistake if we accept that music will generally be received as if it naturally signified something. The most intrepid and alert composers enjoy walking on the tightrope of that 'as if', and giving us the evidence both of our compulsion to see things, and of the ambiguous existential status of what we see. At the age of fifty-nine, I felt a great deal happier with the symphony than I had been when I was fourteen. I also felt tremendously privileged to have been able to spend so much time, over so many years, working towards the understanding that I now had.

None of the above, however, addressed the other frustrating incomprehension of my first encounter with the Pastoral Symphony. Should I try to understand it by what I would now call 'structural listening', beginning, perhaps, from the simplicity of the birds' contrasting intervals? Or should I use my developed intelligence of the nature of musical meaning to persuade me that the right way to listen was, indeed, the daydreaming which had been my response to that first orchestral concert? I have often, in conferences and seminars, found myself, without having meant to, defending the view that there is something in the value of a piece of music that of right escapes analysis. I know, now, that many composers have said this; and that structural analysis has often seemed to them something that should come only after listening, not before or during. I know, also, from personal experience, that such analysis is a natural part of getting to know and love a piece of music; though I cannot explain why. And then it occurred to me that perhaps the second frustration can be resolved in the same way as the first.

Nature is founded in art, as art is founded in nature. Perhaps, in the same way, the structure of a piece of music is founded in those aspects of it which we can only receive without analysis, just as those aspects we can only receive without analysis are founded in its structure. That peculiar reciprocity is the true root of our faith in the individual work of art, as it is the root of our faith in art and in nature themselves; yet it is something we are extremely reluctant to accept, for the simple reason that we cannot understand it, and we do not like to accept that there are truths we cannot understand.

In one way, there is, as many people have sensed, an edifying similarity with our difficulty in swallowing certain truths of general relativity and of quantum theory. To quote Richard Feynman: 'We choose to examine a phenomenon which is impossible, *absolutely* impossible, to explain in any classical way [...]. We cannot make the mystery go away by "explaining" how it works. We will just *tell* you how it works'.[7] The same applies to signification in music, as it does to the relationship between nature and art. We can show you how it works, but we cannot make the mystery go away. However, there is also an essential difference between quantum theory and the question of art and nature, music and signification. The truth about quantum theory demands to be accepted because on it is based much science of practical importance to our modern world. The truth about musical signification, on the other hand, has no such need to be accepted. The experience of the last two centuries, and especially of the last fifty years, appears to show that it can be safely ignored. People have always loved Beethoven's Pastoral Symphony, whatever their opinion of the status of his nightingale. Who has ever, in the past, bothered to ask the obvious question: why does his nightingale sound so little like a nightingale? No one that I know; people just accept that it *is* a nightingale. Very few listeners do what David Wyn Jones did, and understand its motif in terms of the use of intervals in the musical construction of the movement. I am sure Wyn Jones is right; but his truth, it seems, does not need to be known by concert-goers or CD buyers; perhaps not even by conductors.

Having reached that point in my reflections, I realised that it explained a great deal about my life. From an early age, I had been frustrated by my incomprehensions. This frustration drove me, as it did not drive anyone else I knew. Another peculiarity of my way of thinking was that I was far more willing than most people to accept there are truths which escape our understanding. I see now that throughout my academic life, I have been attracted to writers who similarly embraced the mystery, the incomprehensibility, that flows from accepting the reciprocal relationship between nature and art, and between music and meaning: Nerval, George Sand, Marceline Desbordes-Valmore, Mallarmé, Marie Krysinska, Cécile Sauvage, Virginia Woolf, Francis Ponge, Samuel Beckett, Jacques Derrida. Conversely, I have been repulsed by those who see nature as a given, prior to art, and art as an expression of a truth about that prior nature: Victor Hugo, Maupassant, Dickens, Zola, Breton, Houellebecq, and the tribe of 'common sense' literary critics who reject Mallarmé or Derrida simply on the grounds that what they say is too obscure and oxymoronic to be convincing. It is not surprising, then, that over the years, my own writings have often been received as obscure and unconvincing — but above all, as simply unnecessary. In a world where academic writing, like cultural activity in general, is valued according to its impact in real life, why should anyone bother with an investigation of a kind of truth which is neither in harmony with our normal ways of thinking, nor very useful to the cultural industries? I am not under the illusion that the story I have just told will persuade anyone to go to a concert or buy a CD.

And yet, I tell my story; I tell it to you. I tell it because I believe, however foolhardy and immodest that may be, that there is truth in it, a kind of truth without

---

7   This celebrated sentence, dating from the early 1960s, is to be found in Richard Feynman, *The Feynman Lectures on Physics* <http://www.feynmanlectures.caltech.edu/III_01.html> [accessed 30 June 2020].

which Beethoven's symphony would not exist (though I accept the symphony can be received without conscious knowledge of that truth); a truth that he knew, that others have known, that runs counter to our instincts but that deserves to be unfolded. Beethoven himself could not make it known other than by connecting his music in carefully complicated ways with stories, stories that mattered to him personally. He loved the countryside. His memories of the countryside formed stories that permeated the meaning that his sixth symphony had for him personally. The fact that such memories are not necessary to enjoy the symphony neither validates nor invalidates his stories; it merely proves that everyone, including its creator, lends meaning to a work of art. Music signifies. We may figure that signification in stories, or in structural listening. Both those figurations may be thought valid. Neither is necessary. Every story and every structure are no more than a co-creation, between the music and the listener. It never *is* the meaning of the music; any more than the flute's trills *are* a nightingale. What the music *is* remains beyond our words, our stories, and anyone's structures. Let's leave it there, when all's said and done.

CHAPTER 2

❖

French Studies and the Assessment of Creativity

Can one assess creative writing? I am going to offer you two very different answers to this question. One I will present as having its origins in France in the nineteenth century; the other, as British, and defined in 2014. I will be suggesting that in the field of French studies, our values are distinctive, and it will not serve us well to try to bypass this fact. Those distinctive values have given us a different history from our colleagues in English departments, in our relationship with the assessment of creativity; a less comfortable one, in many ways. But if we look back to, and learn from, a French tradition of creative criticism, we can turn this to our advantage.

2014 was, for British universities, the year of the first Research Excellence Framework, or REF. One of the REF's main remits was to assess the quality of publications, referred to as 'outputs', by UK academic staff. A radical innovation over previous British research assessment exercises was that the REF signalled it would accept and assess 'creative outputs' in the same way as more traditional academic critical outputs; so one could submit for assessment a poem or a novel in the same way as an article in *French Studies* or a monograph published by Peter Lang.

Assessment for the REF was carried out by four Main Panels: one, roughly speaking, for science, one for medicine, one for social science, and one — known as Main Panel D — for the arts and the humanities. Main Panel D was divided into ten sub-panels. One of these sub-panels was entitled 'English Language and Literature'. Another was called 'Modern Languages and Linguistics'.

All sub-panels were expected to apply the same assessment criteria. Since the assessment of creative writing was a new departure, the chair of the 'English Language and Literature' sub-panel, Professor Dinah Birch, of the University of Liverpool, put together a document which went to both sub-panels.

This is how that document began:

Notes on the Assessment of Creative Writing

The REF definition of research includes creative outputs among those that can be submitted for assessment:

'research is defined as a process of investigation leading to new insights, effectively shared ... It **includes** ... the invention and generation of ideas, images, performances, artefacts including design, where these lead to new or substantially improved insights'.

Creative outputs are not assessed differently from other outputs submitted to the exercise. If the output cannot be identified as a process of investigation that has demonstrably led to the sharing of new or substantially improved insights, then it will score a zero on the grounds that it cannot be included within the REF definition of research.

A few paragraphs further down, the document tells us how Shakespeare's plays might have been considered, if they had been submitted to the REF.

It may be helpful to note that when we are assessing creative writing as research, we are not assessing the research that might have gone into the project, but the creative project as research. If (to give an example) *The Merchant of Venice* were submitted to the exercise, it would not be assessed in terms of the accuracy and depth of Shakespeare's research into mercantile practices in Venice. Nor would *The Winter's Tale* be downgraded for setting a scene on the seacoast of Bohemia, or for its misleading representation of 16th-century approaches to the husbandry of sheep. The work would be assessed in terms of the new insights generated by Shakespeare's exploration of ideas, in conjunction with the dramatic forms and poetic language that express and develop these ideas.

This has the singular virtue of giving us a very clear and functional distinction between creative writing and non-creative writing. Non-creative writing has to tell the truth about the world outside it. A non-creative research paper has to get its facts right. But a creative writer can invent fictions, such as a Bohemian seacoast. I will call this, in a very old-fashioned way, the criterion of objective truth.

That criterion is central to the assessment of critical writing, but not, or at least not in the same way, to the assessment of creative writing. What, then, takes its place, in the assessment of creative writing? We might begin by noting that the REF assessment would not aim to address equally all the features of Shakespeare's plays which have traditionally been considered important. In assessing creative writing *as research*, it establishes a hierarchy of values. The primary qualities it looks for are 'ideas' and 'insights'. Other features, such as dramatic form and poetic language, are taken into consideration only to the extent that they 'express and develop these ideas'.

This, I am sure, for most people in the UK today, inside and outside universities, would seem a perfectly sensible way of proceeding. It is normal, now, to suppose that ideas and insights are what literature is about. But I have an abnormal perspective on all this, because of a certain French literary culture which I have taken to heart. I shall now try not only to share that perspective with you, but to suggest that perhaps, in a way, it is the common inheritance of French studies.

I began my academic career working on French authors from Sand and Baudelaire to Lautréamont, Rimbaud, Mallarmé, and their many twentieth-century admirers. I found that if there is one thing that they all have in common, it is the fundamental principle that the singular value of art is very precisely and distinctively not in its ideas, in its insights, or in what expresses and develops them. This principle can usefully be observed at work in, for example, Mallarmé's lecture 'La Musique et les lettres' [Music and Letters].

Mallarmé carefully separates out two different kinds or functions of language. The contrast between those two functions is made manifest in the way the word *idée* [idea] appears in the text. It is conspicuously used in two different senses. One corresponds, doubtless, to the sense the word has had up to this point in the present essay, which is the sense given to it in the REF document; that is, the ideas that lead to insights, doubtless into a world taken to exist before the insight came along and saw into it. The other type of idea, which Mallarmé systematically distinguishes with a capital I, is the Idea of art, the Idea of the work, which cannot lead to an insight because it does not point us to anything that exists in the tangible universe outside or prior to the work. This artistic Idea is tellingly always in the singular. Our insightful ideas are multiple, being a reflection of the richness and complexity of the world we live in; but the artistic Idea is always unique, in reflection of the unique character of each work of art, and of art itself.

In the printed text of Mallarmé's lecture, we find the word *idées*, in the plural and without capital, twice. Both occurrences are in the introductory section entitled 'Déplacement avantageux' [Useful journey], which concerns itself with the contemporary political and institutional circumstances of literature, in England and in France: 'Je confesse donner aux idées, pratiques ou de face, la même inattention emportée, dans la rue, par des passantes' [I confess that I give to ideas, practical or facing me, the same inattention as passers-by, in the street, take away with them]; 'Le génie, du reste, se servit de la langue, et des idées en cours, avant d'y mettre le sceau' [Genius, one might say, made use of our language, and of the ideas current at the time, before imprinting its seal thereupon].[1] Genius uses current ideas; but it uses them *before* it imprints its seal.

After that, in the main body of the lecture, the word *Idée* comes back four times, always in the singular, and always distinguished by that initial capital. I cite below all four occurrences. They are noticeably less easy to read than the above sentences containing *idées* in the plural. The singular Idea of art is never open to direct understanding. It leads us towards a thickening, an obscurity of meaning, rather than towards insight. This is one of the reasons for which, in every one of the four sentences, music is evoked. Music, after all, at least as far as Mallarmé is concerned, is the art which affects us without making direct use of current ideas; the art which proves that ideas, as expressed in language, are not the fundamental matter of art:

> Quelle agonie, aussi, qu'agite la Chimère versant par ses blessures d'or l'évidence de tout l'être pareil, nulle torsion vaincue ne fausse ni ne transgresse l'omniprésente Ligne espacée de tout point à tout autre pour instituer l'Idée; sinon sous le visage humain, mystérieuse, en tant qu'une Harmonie est pure.

> [Whatever agony, also, the Chimaera may agitate pouring out through its golden wounds the proof of the equality of all being, no conquered torsion falsifies or transgresses the omnipresent Line spaced out from each point to each

---

1   Mallarmé, *Œuvres complètes*, II, 57, 60. All page references to Mallarmé's work will be to this edition. The word *passantes* being here in the feminine, one could take this sentence as a rather unpleasantly sexist assertion that Mallarmé pays no heed to the women he sees in the streets, whereas he might well pay attention to men. However, an alternative interpretation would hinge on the fact that the word *idée* is itself feminine: Mallarmé pays no heed to passing ideas seen in the street.

other to institute the Idea; unless, mysterious, in the form of the human face, to the extent that a Harmony is pure.]

Par contre, à ce tracé, il y a une minute, des sinueuses et mobiles variations de l'Idée, que l'écrit revendique de fixer, y eut-il, peut-être, chez quelques-uns de vous, lieu de confronter à telles phrases une réminiscence de l'orchestre [...].

[On the other hand, following this outline, a minute ago, of the sinuous and mobile variations of the Idea, which the written text claims to fix, perhaps there was, for a few of you, room to set up a comparison between certain sentences and a reminiscence of the orchestra [...].]

Je pose, à mes risques esthétiquement, cette conclusion (si par quelque grâce, absente, toujours, d'un exposé, je vous amenai à la ratifier, ce serait pour moi l'honneur cherché ce soir): que la Musique et les Lettres sont la face alternative ici élargie vers l'obscur; scintillante là, avec certitude, d'un phénomène, le seul, je l'appelai l'Idée.

[I pose, aesthetically at my own risk, this conclusion (if by some grace, absent, always, from an exposé, I led you to ratify it, that would be for me the honour sought this evening): that Music and Letters are the alternate faces here stretching out towards obscurity; there scintillating, with certitude, of a single phenomenon, the only one, I called it the Idea.]

Je l'infère de cette célébration de la Poésie, dont nous avons parlé, sans l'invoquer presqu'une heure en les attributs de Musique et de Lettres: appelez-la Mystère ou n'est-ce pas? le contexte évolutif de l'Idée —[2]

[I infer it from this celebration of Poetry, of which we have been speaking, without for almost an hour invoking it in the attributes of Music and Letters: name it Mystery or might one not say? the evolutive context of the Idea —]

Mallarmé's singular Idea is not an idea of or about anything. It is itself a phenomenon, indeed the only one. It appears to us through a process, not of insight or understanding, but of institution, ratification, fixation, invocation. Note also the key role of mystery, 'Mystère' and 'mystérieux', in the first and last of these four sentences. The reason for the necessity of mystery is given in the parenthesis in the third quotation. No exposé, we are told, can convince us of what Mallarmé wants us to believe. Only grace can do that. (There would be much to say here about the theological concept of grace, and how it intersects both with mystery, and with Mallarmé's path to the Idea.) Correspondingly, Mallarmé does not suggest that Music and Letters are in any sense expressions of, or insights into (or proceeding from), the Idea, convincing us of its truth. Rather, they are directly, mysteriously, identified with it; they actually are the face of the Idea itself. They are materially the only form the singular Idea can have.

We have, then, in Mallarmé's text, a clear opposition between on the one hand a practical and plural idea, of use in life and politics, and on the other hand the singular Idea of art. This opposition is not Mallarmé's alone. It was very common in the second half of the nineteenth century, and lasted well into the twentieth. It always, quite logically, leads to a powerful, principled rejection of the values

2   Mallarmé, *Œuvres complètes*, II, 68, 68, 69, 73–74.

of academic criticism; because criticism is about ideas, useful and practical ideas, which it pursues in the plural, through graceless exposés. Criticism is therefore not, by definition, interested in the Idea. Endless examples could be given of this rejection of criticism. Sand, Baudelaire, Mallarmé, Ponge, Debussy, Satie, Braque, Schoenberg, Stravinsky, and their ilk all say the same thing: criticism reduces art to the wrong kind of idea, to the plural ideas of bourgeois thought, it brings art down to the level of what can be discussed, and for that reason criticism is totally irrelevant and totally contemptible. As Whistler, American by birth but French by aesthetic conviction, put it: 'No! let there be no critics! they are not a "necessary evil", but an evil quite unnecessary, though an evil certainly. Harm they do, and not good'.[3] Am I, as a critic, to consider myself crushed by Whistler's condemnation? Perhaps I can find a way to wriggle out from under it. The critics that Whistler is spitting on here are the critics who assess creative works, who judge painters, who (like Ruskin) think that their reasoning gives them the right to say what is good and what is bad. This might conceivably leave in the clear modern academic critics like me, who wouldn't dare to judge works of art. We don't assess art, we merely appreciate it, as we try to teach our students to appreciate it. It is tempting, though not entirely reassuring, to cling to that distinction between acceptable critics who appreciate, and evil critics who judge and assess.

★   ★   ★   ★   ★

David Evans's recent book on Théodore de Banville, a poet who is appreciated much less than he deserves, has a splendid subtitle: *Constructing Poetic Value in Nineteenth-century France*. The whole book demonstrates magnificently how Banville sails deliberately close to the wind of conceptual emptiness, how he writes poetry that one could easily take as meaningless and pointless, in order precisely to insist on the point that the real distinguishing character of poetry is not its meaning or its point. Poetry's value is not to be sought in the ideas or insights that it expresses, nor indeed in the way it follows any rules or principles that can reasonably be discussed. The quality of poetry is *something else*, something that by definition escapes definition. And that *something else* is therefore also precisely what escapes the judgement, the assessment, of all the politically or academically sanctioned institutions of our democratic times, whose focus is of necessity on what they can debate, discuss, and understand as ideas plural. I quote Evans quoting Banville:

> Ni les gouvernements, ni les académies, ni les directions des beaux-arts, ni aucun des personnages officiels qui agissent en leur nom, ne sont et ne sauraient être juges en fait de poésie, et les œuvres de cet art divin passent leur compétence.[4]

> [Neither governments, nor academies, nor the directors of conservatories and schools of art, nor any official persons acting in their name, are or can be judges of poetry. The works of this divine art are beyond their sphere of competence.]

3   James McNeill Whistler, *The Gentle Art of Making Enemies* (London: Heinemann, 1994), pp. 30–31.
4   David Evans, *Théodore de Banville: Constructing Poetic Value in Nineteenth-century France* (Oxford: Legenda, 2014), p. 13.

For Banville as for Mallarmé, poetry is a kind of activity whose values have to be understood separately from those of society at large. It is a divine art, and not a social practice. That separate, asocial status of art is signalled by a specific vocabulary, of which the key markers are the word *art* and the word *poésie*.

Do we, today, continue to recognise that separate status of poetry? As we shall see, the answer is: in some ways yes, and in other ways no. The extent to which the answer is 'no' is clearly visible in the vocabulary of Professor Birch's 'Notes on the Assessment of Creative Writing'. The word 'poetry' does not occur anywhere in that document. Nor does 'poem'. Nor does the word 'art' (though 'artefacts' does). Nor does 'aesthetic', nor, indeed 'beauty' or any of its cognates. The word 'literature' only occurs in the expression 'previous literature', to which the creative output must make 'informed reference'. 'Creation' does not occur. And this is the only occurrence of the word 'creativity': 'a novelist might extend the limits of contemporary thinking about cloning and creativity through formal experimentation with narrative structure (as Kazuo Ishiguro did in *Never Let Me Go*)'. The REF, in assessing creative writing '*as research*', looks to reward, not creativity itself, but the extension of the limits of 'thinking about' creativity.

Seen thus, the available perspectives on the openness of creative writing to critical judgement could, in fact, be said to have evolved surprisingly little since the nineteenth century. Then as now, there was an official discourse that did accept (in spite of appearances) the unique status of the creative arts, a status which gave them the right to use fictions to tell their truths; but at the same time, that official discourse established ways of subjecting the creative to democratic debate and rational evaluation. Then as now, there was an alternative, which differed from the official democratic discourse in that it rejected absolutely any evaluation of art that depended on rational, critical methods. This alternative, incarnated in the Mallarmé-Banville definition of poetic value, was not the only discourse available then, and is not the only discourse available now. Nonetheless, it was and remains strangely powerful. It has a long history of resistance to its critical other.

That resistance has not made itself felt in the same way on both sides of the Channel, or of the Atlantic.

★   ★   ★   ★   ★

As we have seen, in the 2014 REF, the 'English Language and Literature' sub-panel and the 'Modern Languages and Linguistics' sub-panel both made it clear that they would accept creative outputs. However, whereas the former received a large number of these, the latter received very few. Why? Two possible explanations seem to occur spontaneously when I put this question to colleagues. The commonest response is that those of us who teach foreign languages can't be creative. We are too close to the normative values of language teaching to allow ourselves the spontaneity and rule-bending that characterise creativity. Perhaps ... but as we shall see, that doesn't really stand up in the face of the fact that people who teach English as a foreign language seem to have relatively little difficulty with creative writing.

The other explanation that emerges is that we are faced here with a contrast between two traditions. One is anglophone. It conceives quite naturally of creativity in terms of insights, and therefore accessible to reasoned assessment. The other tradition is French, or more broadly continental European. It longs to keep the value of creativity beyond the reach of reason, and particularly academic reason; therefore, it refuses to submit creative writing to assessment as if it were composed of ideas.

The more I have looked into this question, the more convinced I have become that the latter is the true explanation. To begin with: as far as I can ascertain, while many other European countries have their systems for assessing academic research, the UK is the only one that allows creative writing to be assessed as research in the same way as criticism. Certainly, France doesn't allow this; nor does Germany, or Austria, or Italy, or Denmark, or Holland. And that fundamental divergence between British practice and Continental practice in the assessment of creative writing is paralleled in the teaching of creative writing.

Creative writing as a subject taught and assessed at university began in America between the wars, and it largely stayed confined to America for thirty or forty years. In the 1960s and 1970s it began to spread; but that spread was always very uneven. As a university subject, it has always remained disproportionately postgraduate, disproportionately concentrated in anglophone countries, and above all disproportionately concentrated in *English* departments.

All over the world, creative writing as a university subject tends to be something that English professors are happier with than professors of other languages. This does not mean, of course, that they are blind to the theoretical difficulties. The English Literature department at Edinburgh University has a magnificent and flourishing creative writing section. I put to one of my colleagues in that section, Allyson Stack, who teaches on their creative writing MSc, the point that the writers we most admire, the great writers of the past two centuries, have generally been sceptical about the notion that creative writing can be taught at all, and often violently hostile to the idea that creative writing can be legitimately assessed by professional critics, or indeed evaluated on objective grounds. She agreed with this. She also agreed that it is in theory a serious problem that in the academy, where creative writing is taught, it has to be assessed. But she gave a simple answer to the implicit question. I'm not aiming to train sculptors, she said; I'm aiming to train carpenters. I'm teaching a craft, not an art. You can't teach art, but you can teach craft.

This distinction between writing as an art and as a craft is also one that can be found in the nineteenth century, and continues to flourish today. It figures among those gathered together in a most amusing article on the subject of creative writing courses published in the *Guardian* in March 2014.[5] Hanif Kureishi is quoted as saying that creative writing courses are a 'waste of time', Lucy Ellmann that they are 'the biggest con-job in academia', and August Kleinzahler that teaching creative writing is telling a 'lie to young people'. But Matt Haig, like Allyson Stack, asserts that creative writing also contains an element of craft which can be taught, while

5   <http://www.theguardian.com/books/2014/mar/04/creative-writing-courses-waste-of-time-hanif-kureishi> [accessed 10 October 2021].

Jeanette Winterson says, 'My job is not to teach my MA students to write; my job is to explode language in their faces'. None of these ideas, again, is new. None shows any sign of giving way to the others. We have here, not so much grounds for a debate, as a constellation of contrasting ideas about what literature is.

The stars composing this constellation really have not moved much, it seems to me, since the nineteenth century, though their relative brightness may have waxed and waned, and they indubitably appear differently depending on which country one views them from. Certainly, in the nineteenth century, there were no university courses in creative writing, nor indeed courses in literature as we know them. However, there were academies that claimed to teach musical composition, and painting. The great French artists of the time whose work we admire today all expressed, at some point, scorn in principle for these institutions. The conviction that creativity cannot be taught was a fundamental article of faith for painters including, of course, Whistler, as well as for composers such as Satie and Debussy. Writers shared that conviction. Debussy and Whistler were among Mallarmé's soulmates, as was Manet, one of the great initiators of the principled rejection of academicism. All would certainly have agreed that any institution that claimed to teach creative writing would be a 'con-job' and a 'lie'. They might well also have had some sympathy with Jeanette Winterson's view. Mallarmé more than once described literature as a bomb. But I cannot see them having much sympathy for Matt Haig and Allyson Stack's concept of creative writing as to some extent a craft that can usefully be taught in academic institutions.

In France, the story of creative writing courses only really begins in 1968. A few enterprising spirits who had encountered creative writing workshops in the USA, and liked the way they gave a voice to the student, tried to do similar things back home in France, notably in Aix-en-Provence, then in Paris. It was not easy. It was never easy. From the very beginning, they had to find ways round the fundamental problem that no one, including them, believed it was possible to teach students to be Great Writers; but the Great Writers model was the dominant one, the one with real cultural capital, for French students as for lecturers; whereas in America, the dominant model, what students were aiming to be, was not the Great Writer, it was the Published Writer. The way round this problem was to avoid anything that designated literature or creativity in the description of what the students were being asked to produce. 'Creative writing' remained a term used in English. There was no direct translation of it. French universities came up with a different term for their own version of the American creative writing workshop: 'ateliers d'écriture'. Now compare that to the American original: 'creative writing workshop'. You can see that the French simply crossed out the word 'creative'. This is because they may believe you can teach people the craft of writing, you can teach them to write like published writers, but they don't believe you can teach or assess creativity itself. A Google search reveals that 'atelier d'écriture créative' does now exist, but it is much more recent, still rare compared to 'atelier d'écriture', and not widely used in universities.

Similar things may be noted in Denmark.[6] The expression 'creative writing' doesn't translate happily into Danish. Departments of Danish know it exists, but they don't like it and they don't teach it. There is a famous state-funded national academy in Copenhagen whose title literally translates as The Author School; but it is completely outside the university system, it doesn't give university-style degrees, its 'outputs' are never assessed as research, and its title conspicuously avoids the word 'creative' and its cognates. Departments of English in Denmark, on the other hand, are relatively happy with the teaching of what they call 'creative writing'. Meanwhile, the South Gate School of Creative Writing has recently opened in Aalborg. It aims to tap into a demand for creative writing courses which is currently not being satisfied by Danish universities. Most of its tutors are Danish. But its website is in English. And while people taking its courses are allowed to write in their own language, which is usually Danish, the language of tuition is English. The principal of the school is an American, LeAnne Kline, who studied Creative Writing in Pennsylvania.

★   ★   ★   ★   ★

I shall now offer an intermediate conclusion. In the world of letters, there are two opposing traditions. One operates on the assumption that creative writing can be taught and assessed, though it acknowledges (more or less openly) that there are limits to the reach of that assessment. This tradition was born, like the notions of conceptual art and creative industry, in the USA, and it remains predominantly anglophone. The other tradition sees the only true value of creativity as something that cannot be taught or assessed; any aspects of writing that can be taught and assessed will be by definition not creative, and will not deserve to be called art (or poetry, or perhaps literature). This second tradition was born, actually, I suspect, in Germany, but I will swerve around that history here; the point I have to make is that France, and more particularly Paris, is where it grew to dominate a certain self-defining international literary and artistic universe. It continues to loom over the vernacular cultures of continental Europe. The distinction between the two traditions manifests itself most obviously in one's instinctive response to the question: can a novel or a poem be subject to reasoned academic judgement? But behind that question lurks the more fundamental one: can literary works legitimately be read for their ideas, insights, and expression, so that we can rationally debate and objectively assess them?

To that latter question, the great French tradition answers no, and continues to answer no. To that same question, the anglophone academic establishment, in creative writing departments as in the REF, answers yes.

Does this mean that we in French departments are destined either to remain on the wrong side of academic institutional history, or else to be traitors to our cultural heritage, and cave in to an anglo-saxon agenda? Have we missed the creative

---

6   I cite the examples of France and Denmark for the simple reason that I have friends there who teach creative writing, whom I can ask about these things. I am grateful to Anne Roche, Sara Greaves, LeAnne Kline, and Steen Christiansen for their advice.

writing boat? Are we condemned to watch in dry critical frustration as our English Literature colleagues across the corridor have fun writing novels and producing plays which create impact as well as making those REF stars twinkle, bringing in money to their viable departments? My honest answer would be: in many ways, yes. But in one way especially close to my heart, no. In fact, our French heritage points us along a path towards the confluence of the creative and the critical.

★   ★   ★   ★   ★

Creative Criticism, presented and edited by Stephen Benson and Clare Connors, is a wonderful anthology, published in 2014, containing fourteen pieces by fourteen different critics. Eleven were originally written in English. The other three are all translated from the French. They are, unsurprisingly, by Roland Barthes, Hélène Cixous, and Jacques Derrida. One can quite well read into the volume an appreciation of the fact that the great French tradition is the original source of the very notion of the creative that underlies creative criticism. But the book begins squarely in the anglophone university world. Here is the beginning of the Introduction:

> Here is your final assignment:
>
> *Write an essay on any two of the set texts you have read for this course. [...] Your argument should be supported by quotations from your texts and by a close analysis of these. It should be clear in its theoretical methodology, and demonstrate knowledge of critical debates in the field. You will want to consult the department style sheet for information on how to present and reference your essay, and the general marking criteria document for further advice on what is expected of you at this level. Please make sure you are also aware of the university's plagiarism policy.*
>
> *Word count: between 2,000 and 2,500 words.*
>
> *Deadline: 3pm, 1 May 2014*
>
> If you are a student, or a teacher, on most higher education literature and arts courses, a version of this rubric will be — predictably, or heart-sinkingly, or gut-wrenchingly — familiar to you. [...] Such conventions are at work, too, in academic and literary journals [...]. There is nothing — necessarily — *wrong* with them. [...]. But oh, how achingly distant they seem, in their language and their assumptions, from the very 'texts you have read' and about which you are being asked 'to write'. Where, here, is the recognition of the passion and lostness and wonderment of reading, or of the mutable matter of reading as event or encounter or happening? Where is any intimation that *what* 'you have read' might make a quite different claim on you, enjoining you to respond to it — to write, and to live — in ways the 'general marking criteria' will not and perhaps cannot register?[7]

Note the centrality of the reader in this account, of the encounter between the reader and the text. Traditional criticism claims to be objective in that it supposes its object exists. Without that supposition, the criterion of objective truth could

---

7   Stephen Benson and Clare Connors, 'Introduction', in *Creative Criticism: An Anthology and Guide*, ed. by Stephen Benson and Clare Connors (Edinburgh: Edinburgh University Press, 2014), pp. 1–47 (pp. 1–2).

not operate. But creative criticism does not claim to tell us what the literary work is, certainly not to assess it; it claims only to tell us what happens to the creative critic as she or he encounters the work. Benson and Connors are extremely careful never to imply that this means creative criticism is free personal writing. On the contrary, they constantly stress the values of responsibility, respect, and faithfulness to the texts we read. But the fidelity they value is not fidelity to objective fact. It is fidelity rather to the specific way in which the work refuses to settle into fact. That fidelity must always be creative precisely because it does not have an object which can be securely pegged to any ideas or insights. Hence the striking definition proposed by Connors: 'Creative criticism registers the way works of art don't just passively lie there, all before us, as the world did to Adam and Eve, but come at us in some way'.[8] Note her use of the expression 'works of art'. That is the heart of the matter. Creative writers, in this view, whether they self-identify as poets or as critics, believe in the distinctive force of art. For them, artistic writing, which is synonymous with creative writing, does not function in the same way as other kinds of writing. It does not give us ideas or insights; in fact, perhaps it does not give anything. Rather, it comes at us.

Note also that Connors does not confront this distinction head on. She never tries to give a direct definition of 'works of art'. Instead, she brings the category to life by persuading us that we, like her, like the student depressed by the standard essay rubric, know in our bones, from our experience, what it is, and that it has a unique value as well as a unique force. As critics we cannot pin it down. Rather, it pins us down, when we let it. Whatever we maintain in public, when we are watching our words and trying to conform to what we have learned it is acceptable to think, the fact is that we still believe in works of art, even though that belief is beyond the reach of general marking criteria. Furthermore, our definition of art remains squarely where the nineteenth century left it. Art is what cannot become an object of knowledge. It is what escapes ideas and insights. As Braque put it: 'Il n'est en art qu'une chose qui vaille: Celle que l'on ne peut expliquer' [There is in art only one thing of value: the Thing one cannot explain].[9] The work of art refuses to lie down quietly while we come at it with our critical methodological tools, threatening to extract from it ideas and insights. Whatever we can explain about it is precisely that which is of no artistic value. Art overwhelms our critical capacity. As creative critics, all we can do is to register the process of being overwhelmed; we cannot judge the thing itself.

★   ★   ★   ★   ★

The REF's distinction between creative and non-creative writing does not map neatly onto the categories of writing we find in *Creative Criticism*. As we have seen, it rests on the criterion of objective truth. Creative critics write about art, while knowing that art refuses to lie down and be an object; therefore, they cannot really tell an objective truth about it, about what matters in it. It rebels, and they allow that

8   Ibid., p. 37.
9   Georges Braque, *Cahier* (Paris: Maeght, 1994), p. 21.

rebellious quality to contaminate their own writing. This inevitably leads them to being accused of lacking critical rigour, as Baudelaire, Mallarmé, Barthes, Cixous, Derrida, and many others found to their cost. That accusation is in one sense perfectly fair. Creative criticism does indeed always create, not only a commentary, but its very object; therefore it is not objective, it is respectfully creative.

To quote Professor Birch again: 'It may be helpful to note that when we are assessing creative writing as research, we are not assessing the research that might have gone into the project, but the creative project as research'. One would have to be able to say the same about creative criticism. Like creative writing, it would have to be allowed to escape from the criterion of objective truth. But that would have difficult institutional consequences.

The essay rubric which opens *Creative Criticism* is clearly designed to require students to write with scholarly rigour. That is not incidental. It is precisely what allows the 'general marking criteria' to be objective; which is, surely, something that all assessment criteria ought to be. At the same time, that requirement to write with scholarly rigour is also what causes the heart to sink, and the gut to be wrenched. The creative urge pushes us to refuse the criterion of objective truth. Without that criterion, scholarly rigour cannot be assured. So, it would seem, we, as academics who have to give marks and confer degrees, are faced with an unpalatable choice. Either we ask our students and our colleagues to write with scholarly rigour and a due regard for objective truth, in which case we squash their creative urges; or we allow them to be creative, and we lose our access to objectively justifiable marking criteria. Can we really allow the sacred cow of scholarly rigour thus to be confined to a corral with a variable perimeter? As peer reviewers, should we accept critical articles whose value is in the way they themselves work, and not in their objectively demonstrably sound relationship to 'the literature'? articles that begin, not from the assumption that the literary object exists in the way that sheep husbandry or the borders of Bohemia exist, accessible to analysis using crafts that can be learned, but rather from the lived experience of the way the work of art comes at us, and as it does so, unbalances our methodologies, leaving us not with ideas, but in search of the Idea, the Idea of art itself, which does not objectively exist?

Can we give ourselves that freedom? Have we the courage to do so? For it would certainly take courage. We are constantly required, not only to assess work (that of our students and of our colleagues), but to justify our assessment. This is easy enough to do where ideas and scholarly rigour are what we are judging. Can we do it for work that proclaims its allegiance to a tradition that has always refused critical judgement? I think we can; but only if we are bold enough to take the decisive steps that Clare Connors took in *Creative Criticism*: to admit our belief in the distinctive force of the work of art, and then to allow ourselves to aim to give that force to our own critical writing. We must reunite the concepts of creativity and of art, and we must not exclude ourself from the community of artists. Mallarmé invented the 'poème critique'; Derrida spent his entire career pushing textual analysis towards literature. Let us reclaim this inheritance.

It is true that as modern linguists, we spend much of our time working with language in its unexploded state. We teach our students to obey grammatical rules, and to express ideas and insights using those rules; that is part of our job. But need it be all our job? What about the insight, which I have been trying to share here, that there is a value in creativity to which insight has no access? which can be appreciated, but not assessed? That insight is certainly untimely. It sits ill with a fundamental, necessary, unavoidable presupposition of the REF, which is that excellence can be pinpointed and certified. It tells us that if we allow our students to be critically creative, we will have to confess our inability to justify objectively any bad marks we may feel moved to give. How could we cope with this? It seems unthinkable. However, it is equally true that the values of art and of creativity have survived their untimeliness for two centuries now. They have refused to give up the ghost and open themselves to our insights. They continue to come at us, and to defy our reason. That is as true in Britain today as it is anywhere else. I would indeed maintain that if one thinks about the way the arts are received and appreciated now, beginning from the undiminished popularity of precisely those painters and composers who first rebelled against the academy, it is as true today as it has ever been. We have all met (I hope!) the restless student evoked by Benson and Connors, who knows in her bones that there is something about literature which objective criticism tries to squash. It is time to bring that hidden truth to light. And the mission to do so is ours.

We are the inheritors of the French creatively critical tradition. Fortunately for us, we work within an academic system that, while it cannot fully sign up to a concept of art which would threaten its ability to justify objectively its assessments, nonetheless has the honesty and openness to allow for the existence and distinctiveness of creativity, as well as to allow it into the academy. This is a rare conjunction in academic history. Let us seize the opportunity. We will find allies in unexpected places, including among our students, as those of us who have experimented with the assessment of creativity have found. Let us not deny the existence of contrasting value systems, nor the claims of the objective; but let us resist, more explicitly than we have done, the claim that ideas and insights are all that matter. We, in French studies, know different, and we are the people who can bring that difference into the light.

CHAPTER 3

❖

Which Came First?
Nature, Music, and Poetry in
Mallarmé's 'Bucolique'

'Ecopoetics' was the topic of the special issue of the journal *Dix-Neuf* for which this essay was originally written. The word draws together two terms: the ecological and the poetic. Neither, to put it mildly, corresponds to a concept with a clearly defined perimeter. In any rational analysis, the slipperiness of each can only too easily compound the slipperiness of the other. I would like to show how Mallarmé can help us to knot them firmly together. From the perspective he builds, the ecological and the poetic have a symbiotic relationship. Neither can thrive without the other. Or rather, better: each provides the only sound definition of the other. If you want to know what ecology is, ask poetry. And if you want to know what poetry is, look to nature.

Mallarmé's critical poem 'Bucolique' was published in the section 'Grands Faits Divers' of his volume of collected prose works *Divagations*, in 1897, the year before his death.[1] It lets us see that permanent and necessary bond between poetry and nature. Ecopoetry here becomes the only possible poetry, and poetic nature the only possible nature. But the shared roots of nature and poetry are hidden deeper than our language normally allows us to go. Only poetic writing can trace them.

Mallarmé had a unique genius for combining the poetic with the intellectual. In his 'poèmes critiques' [critical poems], he manages to express things that in almost all other circumstances remain of the order of the unsayable. I will attempt to show how he does this in 'Bucolique', explaining, or perhaps rather mapping the creation of, the notions of nature, music, and poetry — unless it be nature, music, and poetry themselves, rather than their notions, that are here created. That attempt will take me to the limits of my powers of exposition and analysis. In fact, in some ways, those powers will turn out to be insufficient. Anyone used to savouring the subtleties of Mallarmé's prose will see that I artfully dodge many ambiguities that

---

[1]   'Faits Divers' is (as is typical of Mallarmé's favourite locutions) highly ambiguous. A *fait divers* is a trivial story, most often a crime story, in a newspaper. But literally, *faits divers* are merely diverse facts. Given that 'Bucolique' is less than five pages long, I do not provide, in this article, page numbers for my numerous quotations from that essay. It can be found in: Mallarmé, *Œuvres complètes*, II, 252–56.

academic rigour would require me to unpack. I cannot undertake this task within the span of an academic essay, except by promising myself that my only guiding principle will be a desire to trace as faithfully as I am able how those notions interact in Mallarmé's text. They certainly do not compose a linear or rational argument, or any pattern that can easily be represented. The best image I can give of the form they appear to me to take would be of three snakes, inextricably entwined, each simultaneously eating and giving birth (viviparously) to both the others.

★   ★   ★   ★   ★

Mallarmé presents himself, in 'Bucolique', as a peculiarly fortunate person; fortunate because he has had the privilege of access both to nature, and to music:

> Témoignez comme la destinée [...] me choya. Le double adjuvant aux Lettres, extériorité et moyen ont, envers un, dans l'ordre absolu, gradué leur influence.
>
> La Nature —
>
> La Musique —
>
> Termes en leur acception courante de feuillage et de sons.
>
> [See how fate [...] favoured me. The double adjuvant of Letters, exteriority and means have, for an individual, in absolute order, gradated their influence.
>
> Nature —
>
> Music —
>
> Terms in their everyday sense of leafiness and sounds.]

Let us begin by noting that Nature, here, is not to be taken as synonymous with everything that exists. Nature is not coterminous with the universe. It means the world of the leafy. We might call this the unbuilt environment; a world informed, like leaves, by forces that do not appear to proceed principally from the hand of man. The word *musique* also has, here, a carefully limited initial sense. It is not that universal, that abstract, ideal, mythical or mystical, and eventually silent concept, which one so often finds evoked under the name of music in the poetry of the time, from Poe to Ponge (and quite often by Mallarmé himself). Here, music is sound. Music almost throughout 'Bucolique' refers us to audible sound, and usually quite specifically and concretely to what Mallarmé has heard at concerts in Paris.

These two, leafy nature and sounding music, are 'le double adjuvant aux Lettres'. What might this mean? An *adjuvant* is, in its primary meaning, a secondary medical treatment designed to improve the efficacy of the primary treatment. Nature and music would, then, be, according to Mallarmé, secondary to Letters; their function would be to help Letters to work as they should. This should seem bizarre. According to all our traditional notions, it is putting the cart before the horse. Has it not always been said that nature comes before culture? And must music not be at least as old as poetry? After all, we generally believe that poetry was born as song, and song depends on music. Furthermore, music, as we commonly define it, occurs in nature, in the song of the birds if nowhere else, and that certainly predates any written language. So it is safe to say we normally think that music and nature both came before Letters. Therefore, it seems at the very least peculiar to say that their purpose is to assist Letters. Is Mallarmé trying to imply that in fact, Letters came first? Or is he trying to slip past us a novel kind of reasoning according to which the purpose of music and nature might have been defined post facto by the upstart Letters? As he so often does, Mallarmé has hidden a provocation in a syntactically subordinate position that allows it to pass almost unnoticed, and to insinuate itself into the reader's mind without receiving the questioning that reason would say it deserves.

The point of hiding it is that it would be a mistake for us to try to resolve the question, to pierce the enigma. In fact, that would, as we shall shortly see, be the most fundamental mistake of all. The secret must be there, and we must feel drawn to it, but not as if it were destined to be resolved; it must evade, not only resolution, but assimilation to the status of a problem to be addressed. Nature, music, poetry, and humanity itself all depend on a secret created, kept, defended, and inaccessible to our rational faculties. That secret needs a hiding place. It finds that hiding place in the folds of anteriority. All the interest of the tale I have to tell, here, stems from the question of what came first. Before returning to the question of the absolute ordering in time of nature, music, and Letters, let us examine the order in which they appeared, according to 'Bucolique', in Mallarmé's personal experience.

When Mallarmé says that nature and music have 'gradué leur influence' [gradated their influence], he may well mean that one came before the other, chronologically, in his own life. He came to know nature before music:

> La première en date, la nature, Idée tangible pour intimer quelque réalité aux sens frustes et, par compensation, directe, communiquait à ma jeunesse une ferveur que je dis passion comme, son bûcher, les jours évaporés en majestueux suspens, elle l'allume avec le virginal espoir d'en défendre l'interprétation au lecteur d'horizons. Toute clairvoyance, que, dans ce suicide, le secret ne reste pas incompatible avec l'homme, éloigne les vapeurs de la désuétude, l'existence, la rue.

> [The first in date, nature, tangible Idea to intimate some reality to primitive senses and, in compensation, direct, communicated to my youth a fervour which I call a passion as, its funeral pyre, on days evaporated in majestic suspense, it lights with the virginal hope of forbidding the reader of horizons from interpreting it. All perception that, in this suicide, the secret does not remain incompatible with man, pushes away the vapours of obsolescence, existence, the street.]

The secret clearly plays a key role in this passage. Exactly what that role might be is less clear. What Mallarmé tells us directly about it is complex enough. It is that the secret does not remain incompatible with man: that double negative (again, lurking in a syntactically subordinate position) is what dispels the vapours. But what was the secret?

Rather than telling us what it was, Mallarmé points us towards the place where it is kept. If one reads back to the previous sentence, one comes to suspect that nature herself assumes the role of its gatekeeper. She lights a nightly funeral pyre in the hope of preventing the reader of horizons from interpreting it; that, indeed, seems to be the very reason for the glory of the sunset. This anthropomorphises nature. It gives her an intention: the intention to keep a secret.

We had earlier discovered that nature does not include the built environment. That exclusion of human civilisation from nature might seem to imply a fundamental opposition between the natural and the human. However, we now see that although nature in one sense excludes the human (indeed, is defined by her exclusion of the human), in another sense, she is nonetheless not simply inhuman; she has properties which we normally consider reserved to humanity, notably the ability to feel hope, and to keep a secret — not to mention the ability to commit suicide nightly. And it is that secret of an animate nature, a nature with her own life and hope, the hope that she can keep her secret, that we must see as compatible with man.[2]

Mallarmé is not asking us to unravel this strange secret of nature; on the contrary, he is asking us to allow her to create and defend her secret, as if she were human. That is the condition of 'clairvoyance'. Already it violates two of our rational principles: that only sentient beings, and not nature as a whole (certainly not nature considered in a sunset), can have hopes; and that secrets are destined to be pierced. Why should we accept this as 'clairvoyance', rather than obscurantism?

But before he answers this question — or, perhaps, in order to answer it in the only possible way — Mallarmé moves on to the second, 'dans l'ordre absolu', of his destiny's blessings: music, in which he immediately recognised the glory of that sunset in which Nature repeatedly dies to hide her secret:

> Aussi, quand mené par je comprends quel instinct, un soir d'âge, à la musique, irrésistiblement au foyer subtil, je reconnus, sans douter, l'arrière mais renaissante flamme, où se sacrifièrent les bosquets et les cieux [...].
>
> La merveille, selon une chronologie, d'avoir étagé la concordance ; et que, si c'est soi, un tel, poursuivi aux forêts, épars, jusqu'à une source, un concert aussi d'instrument n'exclue la notion : ce fantôme, tout de suite, avec répercussion de clartés, le même, au cours de la transformation naturelle en musicale identifié.
>
> [And so, when led by an instinct I well understand, one evening in ageing, to music, irresistibly to the subtle fire, I recognised, with no doubt, the late but ever reborn flame, in which skies and spinneys sacrificed themselves [...].
>
> The marvel, following a chronology, to have tiered the concordance; and that, if it is oneself, an individual, chased through the forests, disseminated, to a wellhead, an instrumental concert similarly should not exclude the notion:

---

2   I use the word 'man', rather than a gender-neutral term which would encompass the whole of humanity, because it reflects what Mallarmé does, and I am attempting to clarify his arguments, not to set them in a critical context. This gendering of humanity clearly deserves a critique — as does the parallel gendering of nature and music as feminine. (One might ask whether poetry somehow escapes such gendering.) In consistently giving the name of Mallarmé to the first-person narrator of this essay, I am similarly inviting a critique which I do not provide, concerning the identification of the biographical author with the protagonist of a text. I am, I might say, uncritically adopting some nineteenth-century perspectives. My justification is that without them, Mallarmé's nature is impossible to elucidate; and it is worth elucidating, though its gender politics are of its time.

this phantom, the same, immediately, with repercussion of clarities, identified in the course of the natural transformation become musical.]

This chronology, in 'Bucolique', the chronology of the appearance of nature and music in Mallarmé's personal times, is double. On the one hand, Mallarmé evokes a linear chronology, the story of his life in which the appreciation of nature preceded that of music as heard in concerts. On the other hand, at strategic points throughout the essay, he also invokes a chronology as cyclical as the daily birth and nightly death of nature: the annual cycle of the cultured Parisian bourgeois (including himself), who goes to concerts in the winter, then, as the concert halls fall silent, leaves town to spend summer in the country. In both chronologies, what Mallarmé never does is to meditate on the appearance of nature or music without simultaneously introducing the point of view of the human witness. Neither music nor nature exists, it appears, until it is seen. But they only come into existence when seen by the right kind of eye. Nature, the nature that seems to have preceded music, is only visible to the witness 'si c'est soi, un tel, poursuivi aux forêts, épars, jusqu'à une source' [if it is oneself, an individual, chased through the forests, disseminated, to a wellhead]. And the immediate result of this self-pursuit, which enables one to see nature, is that one becomes a ghost, a 'fantôme'.[3] It is only a phantom of the self that remains the same, identifiably the same, before music as before nature. But is a ghost not normally the spirit of one already dead? Who or what had died in order to give birth to this ghost? Mallarmé himself? Or the notions of nature and music? No chronological answer is offered.

After the paragraph quoted above, Mallarmé turns his attention back to the city, to tell us why, without concerts, it is not worth staying there: 'A quoi bon tarder aux palais — ce dont, aujourd'hui faute d'histoire, ils peuvent disposer est un orchestre; j'ai, pour mon usage individuel, confronté à sa chimère le délice' [Why hang around these palaces — all they can have at their disposal, today for want of history, is an orchestra; I have, for my individual use, confronted the delight with its chimaera]. 'Faute d'histoire'? This can only mean one thing: that if there had still been history in the palaces of Paris, Mallarmé could have found in them the qualities that he now prizes only in nature or music. But according to what definition of history is the Paris of the Third Republic devoid of history? We are soon given a negative clue:

> Y penser ou invinciblement chanter, au gré d'un bondissement allègre intérieur, quoique bas, en vers: on constate que le commun des murs réverbère l'écho par des inscriptions qui ne sont pas en rapport, proclamant l'annonce d'ustensiles, de vêtements, avec les prix.

> [To think or invincibly to sing, at the inspiration of a joyful interior leaping, though sotto voce, in verse: one notes that the common surface of walls reflects the echo by inscriptions which have no connection, proclaiming the advertisement of utensils, of clothes, with their prices.]

It is advertising that has chased away history. The consumer economy blocks

---

3   Unless it is 'la notion' rather than 'un tel' which gives rise to the 'fantôme' evoked here. This is one of the many syntactic ambiguities which, as I warned in my opening, I fear I have dodged.

history, blocks what history used to have in common with the music that now, in the city, remains alone 'en rapport', connected to poetry, for the poet. The reason is, plainly enough, in the relationship to time of the consumer economy. We see something advertised; we want it; we buy it; end of story, and end of history. What is missing (or perhaps repressed) here, what is essential to true history, is the irresolvable question of anteriority; the secret of what came first. Capitalism does not care for that.

Neither, however, quite probably, does the mineral world, in and of itself. Two paragraphs later, we read: 'La mer dont mieux vaudrait se taire que l'inscrire dans une parenthèse si, avec, n'y entre le firmament — de même se disjoint, proprement, de la nature. Quelque drame d'exception, entre eux, sévit qui a sa raison sans personne' [The sea of which it would be better to say nothing than to inscribe it in a parenthesis if, with it, the firmament does not also enter — is similarly to be separated, properly speaking, from nature. Some drama of exception, between them, rages which has its reason without anyone]. The idea that the built environment is not natural is a familiar one; but it is quite extraordinary to present the sea as similarly separate from nature. Mallarmé might seem to be ignoring, here, the great French nineteenth-century poetic tradition of presenting the sea as the very emblem of the majestic natural world, opposed to the pettiness of modern society. However, the explanation Mallarmé gives here for the sea's removal from nature is not only simple and perfectly clear; it also allows us to appreciate why that separation between nature and the sea need not apply in all circumstances. The sea in 'Bucolique' is unnatural because the drama in which it is caught up, with the sky, needs no witness. It 'a sa raison sans personne'.

Baudelaire's poem of the sea in *Les Fleurs du Mal* shows perfectly how the sea might be reintroduced into nature. Its very title is 'L'Homme et la mer' ['Man and the Sea']. He begins his poem, not with the sea itself, but with man: 'Homme libre, toujours tu chériras la mer!' [Man, if you are free, you will always cherish the sea!].[4] Man's perception of the sea frames the poem. (Baudelaire's purpose is also to point out similarities between man and the sea; we might note that one of these similarities is the jealousy with which they keep their secrets.) Thus Baudelaire ensures from beginning to end that the sea in his poem never has 'sa raison sans personne' [its reason without anyone]. Mallarmé's exclusion of the sea from nature might therefore legitimately be said to depend on point of view; or to be more precise, on the absence of a point of view. Once again, the boundary of nature is determined not by what is, but by what is witnessed.

★ ★ ★ ★ ★

'La première en date, la nature, Idée' [The first in date, nature, Idea] ... let us remember that nature had become an idea for the young Mallarmé (and of course, it does not exist unless it is an idea), when he saw the sunset, when it 'communiquait à ma jeunesse une ferveur que je dis passion comme, son bûcher, les jours évaporés en

4   Charles Baudelaire, *Les Fleurs du Mal* (Paris: Poulet-Malassis, 1857), p. 40.

majestueux suspens, elle l'allume avec le virginal espoir d'en défendre l'interprétation au lecteur d'horizons' [communicated to my youth a fervour which I call a passion as, its funeral pyre, on days evaporated in majestic suspense, it lights with the virginal hope of forbidding the reader of horizons from interpreting it]. Certainly, the sea has sunsets, too, if one joins it up with the firmament; but it is more difficult to figure them as burning up the sea itself; and that burning-up is all-important. For the burning, here, cannot be taken simply as a visual impression or illusion. It must be a holocaust, a funeral pyre, a 'bûcher'; in the following sentence, it is said to be a 'suicide'. Nature is not nature unless she destroys herself regularly, immolates herself in a sacrifice. Nothing is more crucial, at this juncture, than to think through the implications of this. The dynamics and rationale of the sacrifice are not obvious to our modern minds (my students have great difficulty appreciating them); but they were fundamental to nineteenth-century poetic thinking.

A sacrifice is not merely death or destruction. It is the offering of something to a higher power, which exists on a higher plane. The thing offered is destroyed in this world; but with the hope that it will be taken as a gift in another world. It travels in the smoke of its destruction, from our world towards the divine. It would therefore be meaningless, it would not be sacrifice, without belief in the existence of that divine realm.

Let us remind ourselves that Nature, according to Mallarmé, sacrifices herself nightly, committing suicide on the funeral pyre of the sunset. It was, indeed, that nightly sacrifice of woods and sky that Mallarmé remembered when he discovered music. The fire of music is, for him, the same as the fire of nature; both are the flames of sacrifice. But where does the smoke of this sacrifice go? What divinity takes it up, and gives us grace in return? The answer to that question was always clear in the Bible, as in many other religious traditions. It was to God. For Mallarmé, however, there was no such simple answer. Indeed, there could be no answer. The destination of the sacrifice had to be a secret; and that secret had always to be generated anew, in the coils of nature, music, and poetry.

It is, as we have seen, the sacrifice, the holocaust, that Mallarmé initially recognises in music as the quality which makes it analogous to nature:

> Aussi, quand mené par je comprends quel instinct, un soir d'âge, à la musique, irrésistiblement au foyer subtil, je reconnus, sans douter, l'arrière mais renaissante flamme, où se sacrifièrent les bosquets et les cieux; là, en public, éventée par le manque du rêve qu'elle consume, pour en épandre les ténèbres comme plafond de temple.

> [And so, when led by an instinct I well understand, one evening in ageing, to music, irresistibly to the subtle fire, I recognised, with no doubt, the late but ever reborn flame, in which skies and spinneys sacrificed themselves; there, in public, fanned by the lack of the dream which it consumes, to spread forth its darkness as the ceiling of a temple.]

This immolation leads us not to light, but to darkness. The key image of Mallarmé's critical poetics is not dawn, but sunset. That darkness is here figured as a temple's ceiling, doubtless analogous to the ceiling of the concert hall, defending us from the inhumanly and unnaturally light sky.

Music's sacrificial flame is, we are told, 'éventée'. That word has two possible meanings. Either the flames are being fanned; or something is being revealed that would have liked to remain hidden, as a fox in its earth is *éventé* by the hounds that sniff it out. Music, like every sacrifice, both sniffs out the divine secret, and feeds it.

One of the most obsessive themes of French nineteenth-century literature is the increasing immateriality of divinity. Over the course of history, the gods have steadily retreated from our sight, fleeing from the materiality of that which is sacrificed to them, into ever more impalpable abstraction. This retreat of the gods gives rise to a human drama repeatedly played out, from Nerval's 'Christ aux oliviers' to Banville's *Exilés* and Flaubert's *Un cœur simple* and *Tentation de saint Antoine*. We moderns cannot believe, as our ancestors did, in a divinity with a material form. But how can we adore what we cannot figure or imagine? What becomes of divinity when its material form is lost? Is divinity lost, too? Perhaps not. Perhaps we can no longer imagine the denizens of the other world, whose noses might have breathed in the smoke of our burnt offerings; but the direction of the immaterial remains, and our sacrifices can point the way:

> Esthétiquement la succession de deux états sacrés, ainsi m'invitèrent-ils — primitif, l'un ou foncier, dense des matériaux encore (nul scandale que l'industrie, l'en émonde ou le purifie): l'autre, ardent, volatile dépouillement en traits qui se correspondent, maintenant proches la pensée, en plus que l'abolition du texte, lui soustrayant l'image.

> [Aesthetically two successive sacred states, thus they invited me — primitive the first or earthly, dense still with materials (no scandal that industry, should prune it of them or purify it); the other, ardent, volatile stripping down to traits that correspond with each other, now close to thought, in addition to the abolition of the text, subtracting the image therefrom.]

The value of nature is not to be found in leaving her unchanged. On the contrary: nature as she materially exists must be sacrificed. This sacrifice can be of three orders. There is the sacrifice that we see in nature herself, every time the sun sets (and every autumn). There is the sacrifice of material parts of nature, as they are transformed on the altar or in a factory. And finally, there is the sacrifice of nature to music, in the order of aesthetic succession. For aesthetics are closely related to religion, and follow its historical development; but in the last resort, aesthetics can survive where religion cannot, aesthetics provide the last resort of the sacred, because they can figure the process by which the secret of the idea survives when no material form can be attributed to it, and when its relationship with human thought can no longer be one of unambivalent anteriority. Religion makes the mistake of trying to tell us that nature, and the gods, must have existed before us, and demand a tribute. In the succession of aesthetic states, we are learning not only that this is not true, but that its lack of truth need not mean that nature or divinity cease to exist. They live on, thanks to music, and to the reciprocity which is the truth of their time. They are to be sacrificed to us, as much as we to them.

What is the place of poetry in this aesthetic succession? Music, as Mallarmé hears it, tends towards what we would today call 'abstraction', without text, and reducing the role of the image. It is that very abstraction, that bonfire of the materialities, that gives it the right of succession to nature. Does this not bypass poetry? And yet we were told, from the beginning of the passage I have been discussing, that nature and music are but the supplement of Letters, 'le double adjuvant aux Lettres'. Their purpose is to help Letters to work. Once again, we are caught in the folds of the undecidable anteriority. Letters must have come before Music, and Music must supersede letters, because music abolishes the text and the images that letters convey; writing sacrifices itself for music. But music comes before letters, poetry comes after music, because this text is a poem which, like every poem, could only have been written after the poet had witnessed what music can do. Indeed, the chronology is here doubly inverted. Not only does poetry come after music; nature comes after music (and before poetry). For the story that 'Bucolique' tells is of the poet who, after the end of the concert season, goes out to his beloved countryside, then writes. Nothing comes stably first; nothing comes stably last; everything depends on its anteriority and its posteriority to everything else; and the human, in this, is merely another participant in the counterdance.

'Bucolique' begins, in fact, with a human — a human divided in two, like the self and the ghost we have already met: 'Le Monsieur, plutôt commode, que certains observent la coutume d'accueillir par mon nom, à moi esprit, là-haut, aux espaces miroitant' [The Gentleman, reasonably easy to deal with, whom certain people observe the custom of greeting with the name that belongs to me, me, a spirit, in elevated spheres, shimmering in space]. This spirit and its associated gentleman are moved to leave the town for the country. The voice of a 'raisonneur', a reasonable man, is heard, telling us that a poet has no place in the modern town, for reasons which will be familiar to us: the town, as it exists today, does not recognise the importance of the divine, of art, of the timeless; it brings out the wrong side of human nature, not the ghost or spirit, but the 'Monsieur'. The implication is that it was not ever thus, that once upon a time, towns had art (and as usual, this chronology is doubled: it is both historical — until the advent of the consumer society, town life had artistic meaning; and an annual cycle — in winter the town has art, in summer it has none); in those good old days, doubtless, poets had their place in Paris all year round. This might appear to take us back to the opposition between a world where the spirit is at home, and a world where it is not. In nature as in the town that possesses history and art, the spirit is at home. In the consumerist town, it is not. As usual, the world of the spirit appears not only more timeless than, but also chronologically prior to that of consumer society. Mallarmé, quoting Horace, takes the poet's love of nature back to ancient times. But, again as always, the order of things turns out not to be so simple.

Silence au raisonneur —

Il profère, pour marquer ses griefs pas sans déprécation —

Que l'artiste et lettré, qui se range sous l'unique vocable de poëte, n'a lui, à faire dans un lieu adonné à la foule ou hasard; serviteur, par avance, de rythmes
—

Que, cependant, nécessaire d'y être venu et même d'avoir tenu bon; pour s'en retourner, docte et, n'importe où, enfouir comme inutile, précieux son tribut, avec la certitude d'aucun emploi.

[Let the reasonable man be silent —

He proffers, to mark his grievances not without deprecation —

That the artist and lettered one, who classifies himself under the sole term of poet, has for his part, nothing to do in a space occupied by the general public or chance; servant, in advance, of rhythms —

That, nonetheless, necessary to have come thither and even to have pulled through; to return whence he came, learned and, it matters not where, to bury as useless, precious his tribute, with the certainty of no employment.]

Why write poetry if it is sure to be useless, 'inutile'? The answer can only be that, while it may be useless in this world, there is a higher point of view from which that does not matter. That higher point of view depends on the logic of the sacrifice. The word of the poet is a sacrificed word, a word that has lost its value in the material world. But one cannot sacrifice that which originally had no value in this world. The poet must take the currency of the town — the language of the crowd, of the general public — and turn it into a treasure with no exchange value beyond its appeal to the sacred (just as the priest of ancient times took the currency of his time — a lamb, perhaps — and turned it into something that could no longer be sold). That would be impossible if the town and its currency did not exist. Therefore, for the poet, common language must come before poetry, and the town must come before the country. And indeed, in 'Bucolique' we are always shown the poet moving from the town to the country, never the contrary. The reference to Horace supports this; for Horace, too, is describing a poet who lives in the town, and dreams of going out to the country. Perhaps, then, nature has always been something which poets have seen elsewhere, not where they originally lived. Perhaps nature always came after, not before, an unnatural civilisation. And yet nature is also always felt to have existed before. Are not the rhythms that the poet serves present in nature before him, before he finds them, before he leaves the town to discover them? One could continue indefinitely with these inversions of anteriority, and it would get one nowhere. That is, doubtless, why Mallarmé places the whole passage under the invocation: 'Silence au raisonneur'. The reasoned condemnation of the town is something to which we should not listen, because it threatens the undecidability of the anteriority of nature. We should not listen to the voice of reason, exactly as we should not try to pierce the secret of nature; the secret that she protects from us by sacrificing herself.

And yet, in 'Bucolique', the voice of reason is not silenced. Mallarmé writes: 'Silence au raisonneur', and then he lets the reasoner speak. This is the true privilege of poetry. The reasoner speaks; he tries to reason. His reason, however, as soon as he speaks of poetry and of nature, betrays itself. He would like to tell us that the town is no place for poets; that nature is where poets should be. In fact, he also tells us the opposite. The very function of poetry is to use the language of reason to defeat reason; to use the language of anteriority to render anteriority undecidable. Poetry alone, it turns out, can tell us where nature really is. Nature is neither before us, nor after us, nor with us; she did not invent us, and we did not invent her; yet we would not exist without her, nor she without us. Exactly the same is true of music, and of poetry. But only poetry can say this. Nature and music share the condition; they do not share the ability to impart it. I could not have written this essay about a piece of music, or about a sunset in a forest.

'Bucolique' begins with the question of how a human is seen. It ends with the same question. Between the beginning and the ending, there is, one might say, a distance of 'quinze lieues', about thirty-five miles, or a ninety-minute train journey, the distance from Paris to the forest of Fontainebleau. At the beginning, our guide, the easy-going gentleman, 'le Monsieur, plutôt commode', appears to be in the capital; at the end, though his journey is not explicitly described, we have the clear impression that he is in the countryside, in the great forest, alone. Who will see him there? Or will he suffer the unnatural fate of that which has its 'raison sans personne', its reason without any human presence required? No need to worry: it is sufficient for him to perceive himself, and this is what he does. As ever, he divides himself into a perceiver and a perceived. And again as ever, the distributed roles are not stable. For humanity to be what it must be, the perceived must be caught in the folds of the undecidable anteriority, with music and with nature. It must make them, and they must make it. It cannot simply be in the time of the urban story; it must be in the process of escaping from that time.

The last paragraph of 'Bucolique' is a single rich sentence which describes the escape from Paris, the arrival in the country, the rejection of the 'miasme' [miasma] of urban life, the joy of finding nature, and the feeling that our own magnificence is to be seen in nature herself. But we need not have forgotten that nature, in 'Bucolique', has a secret to defend, for which she daily immolates herself. And if one reads the sentence carefully, one will see that secret well defended. One might suspect that in fact, nature, inscrutable, gives nothing of herself away. She gives us back only what we give to her — which is, perhaps, our own music. Nature, we discover, reveals our magnificence only when she hears that music. It is only the person who in imagination cuts and plays a flute who, escaping from the noise of the town, can hear the voice of nature. Does nature, then, come before music, and before the human who makes it, as the reed comes before the pipe? Or does the pipe-player create the music and, through that music, nature? As ever, the anteriority is undecidable. But in the end, 'undecidable' is not the right word. Rather, both directions of the anteriority are necessary. There is no music, no poetry, and no true humanity without nature both before and after; and vice versa:

> Combien, véritablement, une capitale, où s'exaspère le présent, restreint, dehors, la portée de ce miasme.. il ne traverse l'atmosphère de quinze lieues, au-dessus d'herbes et de feuilles.. nul intérêt ne rappellerait sur le coup — combien de la forteresse construite, par les gens, exprès, contre leur magnificence comme la répand la nature, sauf un recours à la musique dont le haut fourneau transmutatoire chôme, ces mois — je dis combien, sur les remparts, tonne, peu loin, le canon de l'actualité: que le bruit puisse cesser à une si faible distance pour qui coupe, en imagination, une flûte où nouer sa joie selon divers motifs celui, surtout, de se percevoir, simple, infiniment sur la terre.

[How far, in truth, a capital, in which the present pursues its own exasperation, limits, beyond itself, the reach of this miasma.. it travels not fifteen leagues through the atmosphere, above grass and leaves.. no interest would remind us at the time — how much from the fortress constructed, by people, on purpose, as a defence against their magnificence as nature lavishes it, with the exception of a recourse to music whose transmutatory blast furnace is idle for the current months — I say how much, from the city walls, the cannon-noise of the news carries little: that its sound may cease at so scant a distance for he who cuts, in imagination, a flute wherein to tie together his joy according to divers motifs that, above all, of perceiving oneself, simple, infinitely on the earth.]

Let us not lose sight of the fact that this flute is imaginary, not real. Up to this point, all the music in 'Bucolique' had seemed to have sounded; it was the music of concerts earlier heard in Paris. Now, we have the inaudible music of the poet in the country. That music born of poetry, which comes (does it not?) after the music heard in concerts, is what allows the poet to see himself out of time, 'simple, infiniment sur la terre'. No one, in Mallarmé's post-religious world where the sacred cannot be material, can actually be infinitely on the earth. The earth itself cannot be infinite; nor can nature. The infinite has no physical place here. Nor does the simple. But in our imagination, we can perceive ourselves as both simple and infinitely on the earth, provided that we can allow music, nature, and our own sense of our divided humanity to retain the secret of their infinitely reversible anteriority; and the means to that perception, which creates human spirituality just as it creates nature, is called poetry.

Can we stop there? No. What I have just said might seem to imply that poetry comes first; that it appears — from where? — to give birth to nature, to spirituality, perhaps to music, and to our perception of ourselves as simple, infinitely on the earth. That chronological priority, if we allowed it to stand, would put an end to the undecidable anteriority, and kill poetry itself. Nature founds and limits poetry as much as poetry founds and limits nature. Poetry must always also appear determined by an absolute, prior, chronologically anterior, principle — whether we call that principle the divine, or nature, or music.

I have so far, in accordance with the method I set out in my first three paragraphs, with the exception of one line from Baudelaire, refrained from quoting any text other than 'Bucolique'. But I would not like to give the impression that it is itself an absolute source. So I will allow myself to end by quoting the man who was the key figure in the creation of the musical tradition which gave rise to the Parisian concerts which Mallarmé attended, and which, in 'Bucolique', represent the echo of nature in civilisation. Beethoven wrote, in a draft letter of July 1825: 'wie denn in der Kunst die Natur, <gegründ> u. sie wiederum die Natur in der Kunst gegründet ist' [inasmuch as Nature is founded in Art, and, again, Art is founded in Nature].[5]

5   Beethoven, *Briefwechsel Gesamtausgabe*, VI, 96; *The Letters of Beethoven*, III, 1224. The terms of this sentence clearly went round in Beethoven's head, as they do in mine. The editors of his correspondence cite a notebook in which he appears to rehearse in advance the argument of the letter, writing (in that mixture of German and semi-grammatical French he often used): 'la vrai nature [...] trouve toujours ses principes dan[s] l'art [...] wiederum dasselbe von der Kunst in die Natur' [true nature always finds its principles in art [...] and again the same is true of art in nature] (*Briefwechsel Gesamtausgabe*, p. 98)

PART II

❖

Truth in Art

There are three French male writers of whom I remain in awe: Lautréamont, Erik Satie (better known as a composer), and Tristan Tzara. I constantly and gratefully admit intellectual defeat at their hands. Whatever I find myself thinking as I read their work, they always turn out to have thought it before me — and to have thought it through to the point where they pull the rug out from under my own cogitations. They prove, for me, that the creative can and does run rings round the critical.

This explains why none of them has ever been very fashionable in critical circles. Anyone who wants to write an academic monograph that makes sense is well advised to avoid them. They have been better served by editors and critics who know how to admire them from a safe distance, whose strategy is to present rather than to explain (Henri Béhar and Ornella Volta, especially). But they are the most valuable of allies if what one wants to do is to conduct an enquiry into the strange things that happen to the concept of truth, when it is evoked in the context of art.

I spent several happy years working on Satie. I wrote a number of articles, for different occasions, in which I cited his opinions on the question of truth in art. In accordance with my usual strategy of trying to imply that such questions are perceived in a remarkably consistent and stable way by artists in all media, I often related his pronouncements on the subject with those of other composers, painters, and poets. I have taken three of these articles and amalgamated them into a single long essay. It begins with Satie; then it meanders through the works of Braque, Lautréamont, Derrida, Mallarmé, and one or two others in passing, showing how their thoughts on the subject of truth in art are fundamentally the same as those of Satie.

Those thoughts, for reasons I have already touched on, have their limits. Every single one of the authors, composers, painters, and poets cited here is a man. To state the obvious: this is not because there were no women writers, painters, or composers at work in the period I am examining. Nor is it because no women had anything to say about the relationship between art and truth. It is because, as we will see more clearly in Part IV of this book, the artistic tradition about which I am writing here is essentially a masculine one. The masculine 'genius' tradition depends on a concept of creativity which turns its back on women. It excludes the maternal, apart from anything else. (And of course there is plenty else. To begin with, it thrives on a kind of social freedom of movement which was physically denied to women.) This becomes plain enough if one reflects on the list of qualities that are ascribed to great artists by Satie and others. The most consistent of them is immortality. And deathlessness mirrors itself in a quality one might call birthlessness: the genius is not of woman born. The truth of art has no known birth parent.

Parallel to this androcentric creativity was another tradition, known to me largely through the work of writers such as George Sand, Marceline Desbordes-Valmore, Marie Krysinska, and Cécile Sauvage, and composers including Fanny Mendelssohn, Pauline Viardot-Garcia, Clara Wieck, and Germaine Taillefer. That parallel tradition was always kept separate from the male-dominated cultural mainstream. It always had, as we know, a lower cultural status. In France at least, it was also subjected to a thorough campaign of intellectual repression towards the beginning of the twentieth century, after which it remained in academic limbo for decades. When I was a student (in Oxford, between 1976 and 1985), it was completely invisible. (As far as I can remember, I got my degree without ever reading the work of a single woman author.) I did not begin to understand its distinctiveness until the 1990s. My greatest academic regret is that I have not spent more time on it. I have never become enough of an expert on it to feel able to bring out its central truths, as I have been able to bring out those of the androcentric great art tradition (though I do believe one could). Sometimes I have felt myself so burdened by the weight of stale pale maleness that I have felt quite ashamed of returning to the old canon. Still, it retains its power, and it is worth understanding for that reason. One must know one's enemy — especially when one cannot help admiring him.

CHAPTER 4

❖

Is There Truth in Art?

Il est d'usage de croire qu'il y a une **Vérité** en Art. Je ne cesserai de le répéter — même à haute voix: '*Il n'y a pas de Vérité en Art.*' Soutenir le contraire n'est qu'un mensonge — & ce n'est pas beau de mentir... C'est pour cela que je n'aime pas les *Pontifes:*★ ils sont par trop menteurs — de plus, je les crois un peu bêtes (si j'ose dire).   — Erik Satie, *Pensée pour* **Fanfare.**

★ J'entends par Pontifes tous ces beaux messieurs qui 'pontifient'. On les reconnaît à leur air sérieux. (46)[1]

[It is the done thing to believe that there is a **Truth** in Art. I shall not desist from repeating — even out loud — that: '*There is no Truth in Art.*' To maintain the contrary is but a lie — and it is not nice to tell lies... That is why I do not like *Pontiffs:*★[2] they tell too many lies — and furthermore, I think they are a little stupid (if I may say so).]

★ By Pontiffs, I mean all the fine gentlemen who 'pontificate'. They may be identified by their air of seriousness.]

It is certainly true that Satie, in his later years, did not tire of repeating that there is no Truth in Art. In saying so, he was doubtless very much in tune with the spirit of his artistic milieu, which included such aesthetic anarchists as Picabia and Tzara, as well as the great artistic revolutionaries of the time, Picasso and Stravinsky, for whom he had unbounded admiration. And every time he repeated this point, he was careful to attribute the erroneous belief that there is a Truth in Art to that class of writers whom he variously called 'critiques', 'pédagogues', 'Pontifes', 'pions': people of the serious persuasion, who think it is possible to teach or describe what makes a piece of art good or bad.[3] Attacks against this tribe are, in fact, the staple of Satie's writings. It might appear sensible to infer from this that it would be foolish for a critic to look for any kind of truth in Erik Satie's writings about art.

1   All such references in brackets within the text of this essay are to: Erik Satie, *Écrits, réunis par Ornella Volta* (Paris: Champ libre, 1981). Many of the texts in Volta's invaluable collection of Satie's writings have been published in English translation, for example in: Erik Satie, *A Mammal's Notebook*, ed. by Ornella Volta, trans. by Antony Melville (London: Atlas Press, 1996); or *The Writings of Erik Satie*, ed. and trans. by Nigel Wilkins (London: Eulenburg Books, 1980). However, there is no volume in English that includes all the texts I quote. I have, as usual in this volume, provided my own translations. All italics and bold in quotations are in the originals.
2   The French noun *Pontife* has both a religious sense (the Pope as Pontiff), and the derogatory meaning corresponding to the English verb 'pontificate'.
3   More on the word *pion* below (n. 11).

Nonetheless, that is what I am going to do. I shall argue that while there may, for Satie, be no Truth in Art, there are truths about art, susceptible of at least indirect expression, which Satie himself maintained with remarkable adroitness.

It is so rare to find in Satie's public writings an argument of traditional, rational, positive form, maintained and repeated apparently without irony or antiphrasis, that one cannot but be struck by his echoing of one of the key concepts of late nineteenth-century aesthetics: that a historical study of music proves there is no unchanging definition, accessible to criticism or to pedagogy, of what music is. Satie uses this relativist argument in order to deny the right of critics to measure new music by old yardsticks. It can be found in almost all his writings about contemporary composers; and it becomes most insistent precisely when he is most concerned to assert that there is no Truth in Art. An example from an introduction he wrote for a concert of new music in Vienna in 1922:

> Or — (et je ne saurais trop le répéter): ... il n'y a pas de Vérité en Art... Vis-à-vis de Beethoven,... Bach n'est pas la Vérité;... vis-à-vis de Chopin... Rameau n'est pas la Vérité... L'Immortalité les a unis,... fondus,... associés...
> Tous sont dans la Vérité,... au même titre,... au même degré...
> ... La Vérité???
> Ils ont la leur... la leur propre... Ce qui n'est pas trop mal... pas mal du tout.
> En Art ...s'il y avait une Vérité...Vérité Unique... depuis longtemps,... elle serait tellement fixée,... qu'il serait impossible à l'artiste d'employer une autre technique,... d'exprimer d'autres sensations,... de traiter d'autres sujets que ceux monopolisés par cette Vérité. (96)

> [But the fact is — (and I cannot repeat it too often): ... there is no Truth in Art... Compared with Beethoven,... Bach is not the Truth;... compared with Chopin... Rameau is not the Truth... Immortality has united them... blended them... associated them...
> Each has attained the Truth,... in the same sense,... to the same degree...
> ... The Truth???
> They have their own... each has his own... Which isn't bad... not bad at all.
> In Art... if there were a Truth... a Single Truth... it would have been so well established,... for a long time now,... that it would be impossible for an artist to use any technique,... to express any sensations,... to treat any subjects,.... other than those monopolised by this Truth.]

But is Satie saying, here, that there is no truth in Art, or that there are multiple truths? The bald statement 'il n'y a pas de Vérité en Art' seems to imply the former. However, the following lines suggest, rather, that each composer only seems not to be the Truth when judged by criteria appropriate to other composers. Considered in himself (for all the composers Satie lists, here and in comparable contexts, are male), each composer does have a truth: his own truth; and each composer may be seen as 'dans la Vérité', provided that we are prepared to accept that the truth is not the same for each. Bach, then, is not the truth when faced with Beethoven; but doubtless he would be the truth when faced with Bach. The true moral of the music-history tale would be, not that there is no truth, but that there is no single truth, no 'Vérité Unique', applicable to all.

Satie's second article on Stravinsky begins with a very similar combination of elements. First, we have the affirmation that there is no 'Vérité en Art'. And then the generalising 'Vérité' is replaced by 'Vérité unique' — leaving open the possibility of multiple truths; a possibility confirmed by the implication that each great composer has his own truth:

> J'ai toujours dit — & je le répéterai encore très longtemps après ma mort — qu'il n'y a pas de Vérité en Art (de Vérité unique, s'entend).
> La Vérité de Chopin — ce prodigieux créateur — n'est pas celle de Mozart, ce si luxueux musicien dont l'écriture est un éblouissement impérissable. (61)

> [I have always said — & shall continue to repeat it long, long after my death — that there is no Truth in Art (no single Truth, that is).
> The Truth of Chopin — that prodigious creator — is not the Truth of Mozart, that luxurious musician whose writing dazzles unendingly.]

If each composer's truth is different, is there anything that they all have in common? Should the answer be 'no', then it might be feared that the very identity of music, its unity as a concept, would fall apart. In this article as always when discussing music he approves of, Satie sidesteps the threat, without confronting it, and almost surreptitiously restores the singularity, the unity of music, by attributing a distinguishing characteristic to all true composers; a characteristic which, by implication and association, attaches also to music itself, and becomes inseparable from all musical truths. It is timelessness, or immortality. That which unites Beethoven, Bach, Chopin, and Rameau is 'l'Immortalité'; *never* will Mozart's writing cease to dazzle; and the conclusion of the second article on Stravinsky (of which I quoted the opening above) similarly, if one reads between the lines, supposes the existence of a timeless canon of great musicians: 'Je ne sais ce que je suis, mais ce que je sais, c'est que l'homme dont je viens de vous entretenir est un des plus grands musiciens qui aient jamais existé. Que le nom de Strawinski soit acclamé!' [I know not what I am, but what I do know is this: the man about whom I have been talking to you is one of the greatest musicians who has ever existed. May the name of Stravinsky be acclaimed!] (65). So, to sum up: on the one hand, there is no unique truth in art. But on the other hand, we are, apparently, to believe that certain artists have a truth. Furthermore, this truth appears to be of a peculiar kind that renders those artists and their art truly immortal — or rather (and the distinction is not unimportant), we are to believe that Erik Satie feels sure he knows that certain artists have a truth, and that this renders them and their art truly immortal.

★   ★   ★   ★   ★

What, for Satie, are the distinctive features of Stravinsky's truth? A critic's natural instinct, I think, would be to look in Satie's article, to see what *sui generis* qualities he ascribes to Stravinsky. But the results of such an investigation are confusing. The implication that the great musician has his own personal truth is certainly accompanied by what might appear to be a description of the components of that truth:

Rien n'est livré au hasard, vous dis-je. Où a-t-il puisé sa somptueuse 'Vérité'?

Voyez en lui un logicien remarquable, sûr & énergique; car il est le seul qui ait écrit avec une aussi magnifique puissance, une aussi certaine assurance, une aussi constante volonté. (64)

[Nothing is left to chance, I tell you. Whence does he draw his sumptuous 'Truth'?

You should see in him a remarkable logician, precise and energetic; for he alone has written with such magnificent power, such unmistakeable confidence, such constant strength of will.]

Doubtless we will be able to obey Satie's injunction, and see Stravinsky thus. However, these are qualities fairly generally invoked, from the late Romantic period on, as characteristic of great artists of all kinds and periods. Would we be surprised to find Bach described as a remarkable logician? Or indeed Rameau, who, as Satie knew, applied logic to music with noteworthy persistence? And would it not have been perfectly acceptable to say that Beethoven wrote with magnificent power and constant strength of will? We will shortly see the adjective 'somptueuse', here qualifying Stravinsky's truth, applied to a Beethoven symphony (his tenth). I think, furthermore, that it would be easy enough to imagine Satie saying similar things about Picasso. In short, these brief indications are too close to the general stereotype of the Great Artist to provide a real indication of the peculiar nature of Stravinsky's own personal and distinctive 'somptueuse "Vérité"'. Has Satie, then, rather than describing Stravinsky's truth, allowed himself to define the truth of art in general? But as we know, he refuses to allow the possibility of such a definition; and he certainly never asserts that he has provided one. In fact, Satie, here as in all his writings on musicians, carefully maintains a certain vagueness, simply by omitting to say what kind of truth he is talking about. The 'scare quotes' around the word 'Vérité' in the above quotation show that he knows he has got dangerously close to the critical point where he might have to commit himself; he quickly takes avoiding action.

Satie, in other words, cannot maintain for long that there is no truth of any sort in art. Almost as soon as he banishes the old-fashioned single unique truth of art, he finds that a personal truth, unique to each artist, fills the vacuum. Unfortunately, personal truths in art have a distressing tendency to presuppose roots in a general, universal truth... to dodge this uncomfortable issue, Satie rapidly switches register. He ascribes all reflection on truth in art to the domain of criticism, which he rejects wholesale; and he confines himself to another order of truth, a merely descriptive order: 'je dois vous annoncer loyalement que je ne me livrerai à aucune critique, me contentant de vous faire une sorte de description du splendide et féerique talent qui est déployé dans cet œuvre' [I shall frankly confess to you that I will engage in no critical activity; I will merely give you a sort of description of the splendid, the enchanting talent which unfolds in these works] (63). This contrast between criticism and description, the former refused and the latter accepted by Satie, expresses another constant in his writing.

Criticism, to Satie, is a positive discourse. It is in harmony with the spirit of the scientific age so clearly formulated by Auguste Comte: 'le véritable esprit positif consiste surtout à *voir pour prévoir*, à étudier ce qui est, afin d'en conclure ce qui sera, d'après le dogme général de l'invariabilité des lois naturelles' [the true positive spirit consists above all in *seeing in order to foresee*, in studying what is, in order to conclude therefrom what will be, according to the general doctrine of the invariability of natural laws].[4] Criticism, to align itself with this dogma, seeks to establish invariable artistic laws, and to use them to prescribe what, in art, should happen next. Hence it becomes normative and prescriptive. Satie therefore rejects it energetically. Description, on the other hand, is acceptable to him because it implies no judgement, no prescription, and no reference to invariable laws. However, for that very reason, because it refuses to concern itself with invariable laws, Satie's description is of no help at all in understanding rationally why some composers are immortal, why some have a truth, while others do not. It suggests but refuses to address the question of whether truths in art are personal or universal. And this is not an inadequacy or omission in Satie's discourse. On the contrary: it is a point on which he takes a principled stand. Satie's principle is that the question of whether truths in art are personal or universal must not be addressed positively.

I think it is possible to maintain, taking the long perspective, that the only proper end of writing about music, for Satie, is to persuade us that we actually believe in personal yet immortal musical truths. This belief is irrational, and cannot be supported by critical analysis of the truths concerned. When one thinks about it, it inevitably conflicts with Satie's principle that we should not believe in a unique truth. It also conflicts, more directly, with the dominant ideological trend of his (and perhaps our) time: the scientific or positive. Satie's unique and extraordinary writing style is designed to play those conflicts off against each other. He allows science and the refusal of unique truth their positive due, he gives them victory in the field of the rational, precisely so that he can make plain the boundaries of that rational field, and suggest the existence of another, inaccessible to the positive; a second field where an irrational, unjustifiable faith in the artist's personal immortal truth can survive.

★   ★   ★   ★   ★

Irrational, unjustifiable faith, proclaimed with endlessly entertaining bile and spite, is the hallmark of the 'Eglise Métropolitaine d'Art de Jésus Conducteur' [Metropolitan Church of Art of Jesus Conductor], or EMAJC for short. Satie was the founder and sole member of this austere Christian sect, as well as its *Parcier*, which presumably means its leader. The normal register of its writings is that of the fulmination, the excommunication, the rant, always from a point of view of absolute authority, assumed to be uncontestable, in the name of the Christian Church in general. This we take as plainly ridiculous, because we know that Satie had no such authority. Should one take it as ironical, or as the expression of an extraordinary maniacal religious delusion? With Satie, there is no need to choose.

---

4   Auguste Comte, *Discours sur l'esprit positif* [1844] (Paris: Vrin, 1995), p. 74.

The key to appreciating Satie's disconcerting style, here as so often, is an understanding of the strategy that Ornella Volta, following Vladimir Jankélévitch, calls 'conformisme ironique' [ironic conformism] (268).[5] Satie imitates the discourse of the pontificator. He apes absolute, deadly seriousness. But he does so in a way that throws into relief an irrational presupposition of the pontificating discourse. The aim, indeed, is to teach us to see that irrational presupposition, to which we are normally blind. We should in this way learn to see through pontificating discourse of every kind of pontiff, from critics and teachers to priests and popes.[6] Satie's irony shows that their seriousness is based on shaky foundations, for when we think about the reasons for which Satie's proclamations are clearly ridiculous, we find that those same reasons and that same ridicule can be applied to the affirmations of all pontiffs.

The proclamations of the *Parcier* of the EMAJC ape, and mock by ironic conformism, the assumption of authority, in the first place by the esoteric cults that blossomed in the *fin de siècle*, but more widely by all churches.[7] There is in fact not one unique church, just as there is no unique truth in Art; so the claim of any church to universal authority is a perfect prey for Satie's irony.

The *Cartulaire*, which was the official organ of the EMAJC, published in June 1895 an 'Oraison pour les Bons et contre les Méchants: *athées, impies, libertins, orgueilleux, juifs déicides, hérétiques anglicans, francs-maçons simoniaques, et autres*'[Prayer for the Good and against the Evil: *atheists, the impious, libertines, the proud, deicidal Jews, heretical Anglicans, simoniacal freemasons, and others*].[8] This list of the Evil corresponds reasonably closely (allowing for the parodic mode) to the usual targets of the increasingly virulent right-wing Catholic propaganda of the time, with one exception: rather than Protestants in general, Satie here specifies Anglicans. Why? I will allow myself to suggest a biographical explanation. Satie's mother, Jean Leslie Anton, was an Anglican. So was Satie himself — for six years. His mother had him

5   Volta explains the concept more fully in 'Introduction', in Erik Satie, *Correspondance presque complète*, ed. by Ornella Volta (Paris: Fayard/IMEC, 2003), pp. 7–12 (p. 10). 'Conformisme ironique' is the title of a chapter in Vladimir Jankélévitch's book *L'Ironie* (Paris: Flammarion, 1964), pp. 119–34, in which Jankélévitch writes, commenting on Satie's *Socrate*: 'L'ironie, nature composée, s'installe dans l'erreur, non pas pour la comprendre, mais pour la perdre' [Irony, whose nature is composite, aligns itself with error, not in order to understand it, but in order to lead it to its downfall] (pp. 126–27).

6   For a definition of 'pontiff', see the quotation at the very beginning of this essay.

7   Satie was certainly inspired by the extraordinary and, to us, baffling way in which Joséphin Péladan and his Rosicrucian ilk proclaimed their occult power. Steven Moore Whiting, in *Satie the Bohemian* (Oxford: Oxford University Press, 1999), shows how Péladan's Rosicrucian sect was born and died in a milieu saturated with self-satire, where faith and hoax were never far apart. The context in which Whiting places Satie's ironic style (its first spiritual home being the 'Chat Noir' cabaret) makes it clear that to interpret the EMAJC as an ironic or satirical enterprise is entirely historically appropriate — provided one bears in mind that such satire, at the time, by no means meant straightforward rejection of the faith being satirised. The most successful such enterprise in modern times is, as far as I know, Pastafarianism, the cult of the Flying Spaghetti Monster and His Noodly Appendage.

8   Erik Satie, 'Oraison pour les Bons et contre les Méchants: *athées, impies, libertins, orgueilleux, juifs déicides, hérétiques anglicans, francs-maçons simoniaques, et autres*', *Cartulaire de l'Église Metropolitaine d'Art de Jésus Conducteur*, 2 (June 1895), 121–22 (p. 121).

baptised into the Anglican church. She died, however, in 1872; and his paternal grandparents, who had never approved of Jean Anton or of her religion and did not want a Protestant living in their house, quickly had little Eric re-baptised a Catholic. The 'Méchants', therefore, would include Satie's mother. Yet the 'Oraison' condemns her and her fellow Anglicans to burn at the stake:

> Nous frapperons Vos Ennemis et Nous les étendrons à terre. Nous tarirons la source de leur rage, nous exterminerons leurs œuvres réprouvées; nous élèverons pour eux les bûchers de la Sainte-Inquisition, et leurs corps hideux se tordront dans la douleur, pour la meilleure purification de leurs âmes. Nous vous offrirons un holocauste, Seigneur, et la fumée vous en sera agréable.[9]

> [We will strike Your Enemies and We will lay them prostrate on the ground. We will dry up the well-spring of their madness, we will exterminate their reprobate works; we will raise up for them the fires of the Holy Inquisition, and their hideous bodies will writhe in pain, for the better purification of their souls. We will offer up to you a holocaust, Lord, and its smoke will be agreeable to you.]

Should we be disturbed to find Satie stoking up for his mother the bonfires of the Inquisition? Not if we bear in mind the ironic nature of the entire EMAJC enterprise. In fact, Satie's target, here, is not his mother, but the very discourse of condemnation. As ever, he attacks it by imitating its rationale, and pushing it too far. His aim is to do this in such a way that the scepticism should attach itself not only to him personally, but also to those who speak like him.

It was this ironic assumption of the discourse of authoritative condemnation, in his role as *Parcier* of the EMAJC, that founded Satie's discourse on art. He published nothing on any artistic topic before his EMAJC period, which dates from 1893 to 1895.[10] After that, he had found his voice, and he never lost it again. The EMAJC taught him to produce a discourse which proclaimed an unfounded authority. The proclamation of unfounded authority remained, ever afterwards, the fundamental principle of Satie's writings on all forms of art. Satie writes as an unrepentantly naked emperor.

Before I go any further, I should make it clear that I am not suggesting Satie believed in neither art, nor religion. On the contrary. His scepticism is directed not at them, but at the 'pontifes' and 'pions' who would persuade us that their authority in matters of art and religion should be considered proven, and should be imposed.

Unfortunately, such people exist even among composers:

---

9   Ibid., p. 122.

10   In his *Écrits* as published by Ornella Volta, the only publications chronologically preceding the EMAJC are those which appeared in *La Lanterne japonaise* in 1888 and 1889, normally over the signature 'Virginie Lebeau'. They are comic writings, typical of the 'Chat Noir' style described by Whiting (see n. 7, above). Not a single composer is mentioned in them — except for one Erik Satie, who figures in two of the articles, as a 'rude lapin' (which one might roughly translate as 'valorous gentleman') and composer of *Gymnopédies*, the third of which, apparently, cured 'Femme Lengrenage, Journalière à Précigny-les-Balayettes' [Mistress Cogworks, Employed as a Daily at Foresign-under-Shortbrush] of a nasal polyp (113).

Parmi les musiciens, il y a les pions & les poètes. Les premiers en imposent
au public & à la critique. Je citerai comme exemples de poètes Liszt, Chopin,
Schubert, Moussorgsky; de pion, Rimsky-Korsakow. Debussy était le type
du musicien poète. On trouve dans sa suite plusieurs types de musicien pions.
(D'Indy, qui pourtant professe, n'en est pas un.)

Le métier de Mozart est léger, celui de Beethoven lourd, ce que peu de gens
peuvent comprendre; mais tous deux sont des poètes. Tout est là. (45)

[One can divide musicians into 'pions' & poets. The former hoodwink
the public & critics. Some examples of poets: Liszt, Chopin, Schubert,
Moussorgsky. Rimsky-Korsakov is an example of a 'pion'. Debussy was the
type of the poet musician. Among his followers are to be found several types of
the 'pion' musician. (D'Indy, even though he teaches, is not one.)

Mozart's musical language is light, Beethoven's is heavy (not many people
are able to understand this); but both are poets. Which is all that matters.][11]

It is indeed.

Satie here uses to define good musicians the same intermedial technique as
Berlioz, Debussy, and so many of their contemporaries: analogy with poetry. A
great musician is a poet. And to define bad musicians, he assimilates them to 'pions',
in other words to the tribe of those who think that music can be controlled. To
emphasise the point, he expresses implicit astonishment that a teacher (Vincent
d'Indy, who officiated at the Schola Cantorum, where Satie himself had been a
student) should nonetheless turn out not to be a *pion*. This is entirely in accordance
with the principles behind all the other articles which Satie published in which
he discusses composers. He never changes his mind or contradicts himself on this
point.

Satie's list of good musicians (otherwise known as poets) is exclusive. No one
ever moves from the 'bad' category to the 'good', from 'pion' to 'poète'. Living
composers, on rare occasions, do move from the 'good' to the 'bad'. This, however,
is never because Satie revises his opinion of the works he had appreciated; it is
always (or so he would have us believe) because, having been corrupted by the *pion*
mentality, certain composers lose their poetic quality, stop composing the 'good'
music of which they might have been capable, and start writing 'bad' music.[12]

11   The word *pion* is central to Satie's discourse on music. It contains two contrasting meanings.
The primary sense one might render as something like 'Surveillance Officer': it properly designates
someone (usually a student) employed in French schools, not to teach, but merely to keep order and
to discipline pupils, notably in the playground and during study periods. *Pion*, however, also means
a pawn, both on the chess-board and as someone manipulated by others. (Indeed, the *pion* in school,
while traditionally detested by pupils as a figure of authority, is also seen as someone of low status, at
the bottom of the professional hierarchy.) A *pion*, then, is someone either controlled or controlling;
and that very ambiguity focuses attention, not on what the *pion* does, but on the fact that for him,
control is what counts. Unable to find an English word that contains this dual meaning, I have kept
the French word.

12   The clearest example is Georges Auric. In April 1921, Satie wrote an introduction to a concert
of music by 'les Six' in which he names Auric, along with Poulenc and Milhaud, as representative
of the latest musical tendencies, and describes himself as their friend. Unfortunately, three years
later, Satie caught Auric (as well as Poulenc and Cocteau) hob-nobbing in Monte Carlo with Louis
Laloy, whom Satie had long detested as the most perniciously serious of music critics. Satie broke

It follows that no dead composer can ever change category. A great dead poet-composer will always be a great dead poet-composer. His greatness is, as we have seen, immortal. That is a truth with which we have to reckon.

★   ★   ★   ★   ★

Satie's articles on Stravinsky, along with his essay on Debussy and his various introductions to concerts of music by his friends, belong to a distinctive genre in his writing. In these texts, he is speaking in support of composers he liked; and he does so apparently without irony (irony, in these circumstances, being reserved for the tribe of critics). Elsewhere, however, when he is not defending his fellows, his style usually appears constantly ironical. One senses that there are many layers to the irony; but it is not initially obvious how many layers there are, or what Satie's own opinion (if any) might be. One fine example of this is his magnificent 'Éloge des critiques' [In Praise of Critics] (77–80). Another is 'Parfait Entourage' [Ideal Companions], which begins thus:

> Vivre au centre d'œuvres glorieuses de l'Art est une des plus grandes joies qui se puissent ressentir. Parmi les précieux monuments de la pensée humaine que la modestie de ma fortune m'a fait choisir pour partager ma vie, je parlerai d'un magnifique faux Rembrandt, profond et large d'exécution, si bon à presser du bout des yeux, comme un fruit gras, trop vert. (20)

> [To live surrounded by Art's glorious works is one of the greatest joys that can be felt. Amongst the precious monuments of human thought that the modesty of my means has led me to choose as my life's companions, I shall mention a magnificent false Rembrandt, profound and of sweeping execution, so delicious when squeezed with the tips of one's eyes, like some rich fruit, too green.]

Can we take seriously Satie's praise of a forgery? The peculiar analogy between the painting and a perhaps underripe yet visually attractive fruit might suggest a negative answer... but perhaps, at least before we paused to think too much about that analogy, we might have hoped that we could. After all, could it not be possible that a forger or an anonymous painter might have produced a masterpiece? In which case, might Satie not be mocking those who think that the signature and price-tag are what determine the value of a painting? But our faith in this argument wobbles as, going through the list of his apocryphal possessions, Satie turns to his favourite:

> un faux manuscrit de Beethoven — sublime symphonie apocryphe du maître — acheté pieusement par moi, il y a dix ans, je crois.
>   Des œuvres du grandiose musicien, cette 10e symphonie, encore ignorée, est une des plus somptueuses. Les proportions en sont vastes comme un palais; les idées en sont ombreuses et fraîches; les développements en sont précis et justes.
>   Il fallait que cette symphonie existât: le nombre 9 ne saurait être beethovénien. Il aimait le système décimal: 'J'ai dix doigts', expliquait-il. (20)

with Auric, Poulenc, and Cocteau, and published more than one article in which he made plain his contempt. Auric mocked Satie mercilessly in return (although, as he recounts in his autobiography *Quand j'étais là* (Paris: Grasset, 1979), pp. 21–33, he later repented). At the same time — was it a consequence, a cause, or a coincidence? — Auric's music ceased to please Satie.

[a false Beethoven manuscript — a sublime apocryphal symphony by the master — piously purchased by me, ten years ago, I believe.

Of the grandiose musician's works, this tenth symphony, which remains unknown, is one of the most sumptuous. Its proportions are as vast as those of a palace; its ideas are cool and shady; its developments are precise, judicious, exact.

This symphony had to exist; the number 9 could not be Beethovenian. He liked the decimal system: 'I have ten fingers,' he would explain.]

To find this unbelievable, ridiculous, we do not need to wait for the strange analogies and the mock justifications. We can accept that a painting well executed in Rembrandt's style might look, even to an expert, like a genuine Rembrandt. But anyone who thinks she or he has an ear for such things cannot believe that a symphony in Beethoven's late style could fool us.

In 1996, the Metropolitan Museum of Art in New York held an exhibition entitled 'Rembrandt / Not Rembrandt', showing the paintings in its considerable collection which were by Rembrandt according to some experts, and not by Rembrandt according to others. The latter, the possibly apocryphal paintings, outnumbered those Rembrandts whose attribution remained uncontested. One certainly cannot imagine anything comparable happening with the symphonies of Beethoven. The strength of our belief in the ineffably unique and utterly unmistakeable quality of Beethoven (especially late Beethoven) can be gauged by the presentation of Barry Cooper's realisation of sketches by Beethoven as part of, precisely, a tenth symphony. The universal consensus among musicologists was that no such realisation could ever really sound like Beethoven. In defending his work, Cooper maintained that it was pretty well indistinguishable analytically from Beethoven; but he accepted that it nonetheless obviously lacked a certain quality which, one can only say, escapes analysis.[13] In short, just as in Satie's day, Beethoven's *je ne sais quoi* was held to be as instantly recognisable as it was indefinable. The first of Satie's prized forgeries, then, is attributed to the most successfully imitated of painters, the second to the composer deemed most inimitable; and this enables Satie's irony to strike at the very heart of our beliefs concerning imitation.

Satie rubs our noses in the fact that we believe naively in the existence of a true, unique, inimitable, and self-identical Beethovenian voice. If we did not, why would we find Satie's appreciation of the tenth symphony so ludicrous? At the same time, by starting from the less clear-cut case of Rembrandt, he reminds us that this conviction ought to seem, if we were being rational, questionable. What, and where, exactly, is the Beethovenian truth? Is it simply to be equated with everything that Beethoven wrote? What if he had off days? Would that mean that some of his

---

13   See, for example, the frank exchange of views between Cooper and his critic Robert S. Winter in the *Journal of the Royal Musical Association*, 117/2 (1992), 324–30. 'No doubt,' writes Cooper of his realisation and completion, 'it is a distorted view of Beethoven's intentions' (p. 328). Hence, doubtless: 'A major question is whether the reconstruction actually sounds at all like Beethoven' (p. 326). To that question, Cooper does not presume to give an answer. But he does maintain that musicological analysis has generally failed to pinpoint the differences between his work and Beethoven's. 'Some critics have made the unsurprising claim that it is not as good; but their attempts to identify specific faults have been largely unsuccessful' (p. 326).

work was less true to himself than the rest? But who would have the right to judge, to say what is truly Beethovenian? Can we really afford to allow anyone to define the Beethovenian essence in a way that could be used as a serious critical (and diacritical) tool? Satie, in his usual manner (as inimitable as Beethoven's), makes us uncomfortably aware of such difficulties by ignoring them too flagrantly. Not everyone, he admits, may find the apocryphal Tenth as obviously impressive as Beethoven's other symphonies. But he refuses to take this as proof that the Tenth does not contain the true Beethovenian essence.

> Venus pour absorber filialement ce chef-d'œuvre, de leurs oreilles méditatives et recueillies, quelques-uns, sans raison, crurent à une conception inférieure de Beethoven, et le dirent. Ils allèrent plus loin même.
> Beethoven ne peut être inférieur à lui-même, dans aucun cas. Sa technique et sa forme restent augurales, même dans l'infime. Le rudimentaire ne lui est applicable. Il ne s'intimide pas du contrefait imputé à sa personne artistique. (20)

> [Of those who came filially to absorb this masterpiece, through their meditative and contemplative ears, some, without justification, thought it an inferior conception of Beethoven, and said so. They went still further.
> Beethoven cannot be inferior to himself, in any circumstances. His technique and his form remain augural, even at the most minute scale. The rudimentary cannot apply to him. He is not to be intimidated by the counterfeit imputed to his artistic person.]

This argument is so utterly irrational on the surface that it would be otiose for me to point out how. And yet if we are brave enough to allow ourselves to think about it as another exercise in ironic conformism, we might begin to suspect that it is no more irrational than the general supposition that Beethoven's style is unmistakeable. Is it actually possible to determine, on internal musical grounds, with positive scientific certitude, which music is by Beethoven, and which is not? If it were, would that not mean we had found the Beethovenian recipe, and could therefore produce more Beethovenian music? In which case, we would no longer be able to determine, on internal musical grounds, which music is actually by Ludwig van Beethoven himself... or to put it another way: either the distinguishing features of Beethoven's unique voice are susceptible of positive analysis, in which case they can be reproduced, and his voice ceases to be unique; or they are not susceptible of positive analysis, in which case it is impossible to demonstrate scientifically that an apocryphal work is not worth a work that is truly by him.

There is no way out of this double bind, and Satie takes pleasure, with ironic conformism, in tying his own work up in this knot:

> Tout le monde vous dira que je ne suis pas un musicien. C'est juste.
> Dès le début de ma carrière, je me suis, de suite, classé parmi les phonométrographes. Mes travaux sont de la pure phonométrique. Que l'on prenne le 'Fils des Etoiles' ou les 'Morceaux en forme de poire', 'En habit de Cheval' ou les 'Sarabandes', on perçoit qu'aucune idée musicale n'a présidé à la création de ces œuvres. C'est la pensée scientifique qui domine. [...]
> Que n'ai-je pesé ou mesuré? Tout de Beethoven, tout de Verdi, etc. C'est très curieux. (19)

[Everyone will tell you that I am not a musician. This is correct.

Since the beginning of my career, I have, immediately, classified myself as among the phonometrographs. My works are pure phonometrics. Take the 'Son of the Stars' or the 'Pieces in the Shape of a Pear', 'In Horse Costume', or my 'Sarabands', you will see that no musical idea presided over the creation of these pieces. It is, rather, scientific thought which predominates. [...]

What have I not weighed or measured? Everything by Beethoven, everything by Verdi, etc. It is most curious.]

The ironic conformism, in this passage, consists in the affirmation that music can be measured; in other words, that it is accessible to positive reason. The phonometrograph measures sound scientifically. Now, if music were a science, whose truths could be expressed in terms of generally valid laws, as can all the truths of science, then such measurement, properly carried out and followed by analysis, should indeed surely allow us to make music, having ascertained the laws of music. But in fact, music is not a science. It is an art, and therefore, it has no laws that can be formulated. Harmony, as Rameau said, can be measured and analysed, learned and applied in a scientific manner; but harmony, as Rameau also said, is not all there is to music. Rigorously scientific music cannot exist, because science requires us to believe that all phenomena are determined by rules, by natural laws, whereas art demands always the new, the individual, which can never be reduced to the functioning of rules. Music cannot be reduced to science; it lives in opposition to scientific values.

★　★　★　★　★

The painter Georges Braque was the most faithful companion of Satie's last years. Braque visited Satie regularly, including when he was in hospital, and they would converse for hours. They appreciated each other's work. Braque illustrated the first edition of Satie's *Le Piège de Méduse* [Medusa's Trap] (the only literary work by Satie to appear in book form in his lifetime) with three remarkable woodcuts, and there would be plenty to say about the many other works by Satie that Braque illustrated, or represented in his own paintings.

Nothing has come down to us of what they said to each other, or of the ideas that Satie might have nurtured in or suggested to his younger friend. This is not surprising. Neither of them was generally inclined to share his conversations, and Braque was notoriously sparing with his words. We have, then, no evidence of direct influence. However, Braque's ideas concerning the relationship between art, truth, and positive or scientific forms of reasoning are, at the very least, strikingly compatible with those of Satie. Both Satie and Braque tell us that art is the domain in which there is no single, definable, verifiable truth. For both of them, too, art is in permanent combat with an enemy discourse, a non-artistic, socially dominant model of human thought in which a positive, serious, rational model of truth-telling inevitably holds sway.

Their style, certainly, is different. Braque's calm and dense formulations are more like Mallarmé's critical prose than Satie's absurd irony. But their sense of the fundamental incompatibility between art and science is the same.

Science, for Braque, has as a core value the possibility of exact repetition, the logic of the precise copy: 'Le fait scientifique, pour moi, est caractérisé par le pouvoir acquis de répétition. Il n'y a vraiment science que lorsque le pouvoir de répétition à l'infini est acquis' [The scientific fact, for me, is characterised by the acquired power of repetition. There is really no science except where the power of infinite repetition has been acquired].[14] In art, on the contrary, exact repetition signifies the absence of value. No true work of art is the copy of anything — not even of an idea in the artist's head:

> Dans le tableau, ce qui compte, c'est l'imprévu. C'est lui qui reste. Si je pouvais concevoir un tableau mentalement, je ne me donnerais jamais la peine de l'exécuter. Certains artistes exécutent leurs conceptions mentales. Quand ils peignent, c'est absolument comme s'ils faisaient une copie. Aussi l'esprit est-il absent du tableau. Le peintre a imité son idée.[15]

> [In the painting, it is the unforeseen that counts. That is what remains. If I could conceive of a painting in my head, I would never bother to paint it. Some artists paint the ideas in their heads. When they paint, it is exactly as if they were making a copy. As a result, the spirit is absent from their painting. The painter has imitated his idea.]

> Avant de se passer dans l'œil, tout se passe dans ma tête. Tout d'abord l'idée, puis l'organisation du tableau, le tableau qui doit affirmer, préciser ses intentions. Il me faut lutter à la fois contre l'idée qui s'est implantée et le tableau qui défend sa propre existence, son indépendance bientôt. S'il devient la copie d'une pensée, c'est fichu.[16]

> [Before it happens in the eye, everything happens in my head. First comes the idea, then the organisation of the painting, the painting which has to affirm and set out its intentions. As for me, I have to fight at the same time against the idea which has implanted itself, and against the painting which is defending its own existence, and soon its independence. If it becomes the copy of a thought, it is done for.]

The painter begins, certainly, with a thought, an idea in his head. But if the painting is a mere copy of that idea, then it is not worthy of consideration as a painting. The spirit is absent from it. For the spirit can never be copied, nor can it be a copy. Art refuses the fundamental scientific principle of reproducibility. This echoes the logic we have seen at work in Satie's celebration of the apocryphal. If a Beethoven symphony is not the copy of an idea in Beethoven's head, or indeed of anything else we can identify, then its internal workings can offer us no scientific, objective means of certifying its authenticity. Conversely, we have no objective means of denying the internal, intrinsic value of an apocryphal work.

This causes an obvious problem for the artist working in a capitalist society. The value of his work, the price he can charge, depends entirely on its authenticity. If

---

14 Georges Charbonnier, *Monologue du peintre: entretiens avec Braque* [and others] (Neuilly-sur-Seine: Durier, 1980), p. 20.
15 Ibid., pp. 26–27.
16 André Verdet, *Entretiens, notes et écrits sur la peinture: Braque, Léger, Matisse, Picasso* (Paris: Galilée, 1978), p. 43.

this cannot be proven, what is to prevent a forger from making endless Braque paintings, and legitimately selling them as such, thus flooding the market and bringing down the price? But no: we cannot believe this could happen. And the reason is not that it is possible to determine the value of a painting by Braque by objective analysis of the quality of the painting itself. It is that we all accept, whether we are willing to admit it or not, the principle according to which the artist's genius passes into the work in ways we cannot analyse. Therefore, the crucial point is whether or not we believe that Georges Braque actually, physically, himself painted the painting. That belief is, for us, our primary guarantee that his spirit is within it; and that, generally, for the art market, suffices. If we believe a painting is by Rembrandt, it does not matter whether it really is by him or not. The price is determined by our faith.

In the art market, then, as according to Satie and Braque, there is a limit to the reach of science in the evaluation of art. That limit had been recognised, more than a decade before Braque's birth, by one of the greatest scientists of the age. And the recognition had not gone unnoticed.

★   ★   ★   ★   ★

We have seen how Erik Satie denies there is any single Truth in Art, by maintaining that different composers have different Truths. In this, he was swimming with a current which had been lent force half a century earlier by the great German physicist Hermann Helmholtz, the father of the science of acoustics. Helmholtz was always careful to distinguish between those aspects of the material of music which science could analyse, and those which escaped science, because they are not based on invariable laws. His ideas became popular in France in 1868, with the publication, in French translation, of his *Théorie physiologique de la musique*. Helmholtz's book must have fallen quite rapidly into the hands of a certain young unpublished but aspiring poet by the name of Isidore Ducasse, who was to become famous long after his death under his chosen nom de plume: the comte de Lautréamont.

In 1869, only a year after Helmholtz's book appeared in French, Lautréamont had already finished writing the work which was to bring him posthumous fame: *Les Chants de Maldoror*. In the last of the six *chants* (songs, or cantos) which compose the work, a quotation from Helmholtz occupies a vital place. As usual with Lautréamont, the source is not given. But unusually, he does place the quotation in inverted commas:

> Je jette un long regard de satisfaction sur la dualité qui me compose... et je me trouve beau! Beau comme le vice de conformation congénital des organes sexuels de l'homme, consistant dans la brièveté relative du canal de l'urètre et la division ou l'absence de sa paroi inférieure, de telle sorte que ce canal s'ouvre à une distance variable du gland et au-dessous du pénis; ou encore, comme la caroncule charnue, de forme conique, sillonnée par des rides transversales assez profondes, qui s'élève sur la base du bec supérieur du dindon; ou plutôt, comme la vérité qui suit: 'Le système des gammes, des modes et de leur enchaînement harmonique ne repose pas sur des lois naturelles invariables, mais il est, au contraire, la conséquence de principes esthétiques qui ont varié avec

le développement progressif de l'humanité, et qui varieront encore;' et surtout, comme une corvette cuirassée à tourelles![17]

[I gaze, long and with satisfaction, upon the duality that composes me... and I find myself beautiful! Beautiful as the congenital defect of the male sexual organs consisting of the relative shortness of the urethral canal and the division or absence of its lower wall, with the result that the canal's opening, at a variable distance from the glans, is on the underside of the penis; or again, as the fleshy wattle, conical in form, furrowed by fairly deep transversal wrinkles, which rises from the base of the upper beak of the male turkey; or rather, as the following truth: 'The system of scales, of modes, and of their harmonic relations does not rest on invariable natural laws, but is, on the contrary, the result of aesthetic principles which have varied in the past and will continue to vary with the progressive development of humanity;' and above all, as an armoured corvette with turrets!]

The harmonic system that underpins what we now call the Common Era of Western music rests on no invariable natural laws... This principle, set out by Helmholtz and relayed by Lautréamont, could be called the doctrine of the relativity of aesthetic principles. Helmholtz sets out clearly how this doctrine poses a limit to the reach of science, when he states that the analysis of musical style is 'pas une question qui rentre dans les attributions de la science' [a question which is not within the remit of science].[18] Style varies, and must vary; but science only concerns itself with invariable laws. Music makes use of such laws, as it makes use of harmony, which can be analysed scientifically; but the way in which it uses them escapes analysis. It uses laws; it is not governed by laws. Aesthetic principles change, and it is these principles, not harmonic theory (or any other scientific theory), which determine whether or not a given work deserves the name of music.

Helmholtz deduced from the doctrine of the relativity of aesthetic principles that there is no fixed link between theories of harmony and musical value. In this, he was prophetic; for the time would shortly come when music, ably assisted by Satie as well as by Debussy, Schoenberg, and Stravinsky, would declare its independence from 'le système des gammes, des modes et de leur enchaînement harmonique'. That independence would, of course, leave intact the question of where on earth we might look to find a coherent value uniting all the various styles we call musical.

One of the commonest answers to that question was, and had long been, offered by the word 'beauty'. After all, had Keats not told us in 1819, in 'Ode on a Grecian Urn', that 'Beauty is truth, truth beauty'? But that answer was never without problems. Is beauty necessarily truthful? Is the truth necessarily beautiful? To these questions, as to the question of whether there is Truth in Art, the only useful kind of answer is one that shows us why they are so intractable. What we need is a guide to the labyrinth in which they threaten to lose us. Lautréamont is the best such guide I have found.

17   Isidore Ducasse, comte de Lautréamont, *Les Chants de Maldoror, Poésies I et II* (Paris: Flammarion, 1990), p. 300.
18   Hermann von Helmholtz, *Théorie physiologique de la musique fondée sur l'étude des sensations auditives*, trans. by M. G. Guéroult (Paris: Masson, 1868), p. 307.

'Je me trouve beau', he writes, in the passage where he cites Helmholtz. Beautiful as... normally, when we say of a person that she or he is *beautiful as* something, we are careful to choose the something, the term of comparison, from the stock of things that are generally recognised as beautiful in our culture. Lautréamont does the opposite. Is he being ironic? Or is he mocking our taste? On one level, what he is doing, in a manner that foreshadows Satie's ironic conformism, is taking to its logical extreme the doctrine of the relativity of aesthetic principles, which he had earlier asserted in one of its most traditional forms by citing the proverb that 'tous les goûts sont dans la nature' [all tastes may be found in nature].[19] Certainly, his tastes differ from ours, he says; but that does not prove that his are bad. For nothing in nature, nothing in science, nothing in any invariable law, can determine the beautiful; therefore, nothing in nature certifies which tastes are good and which are bad. That is the truth which he conscripts Helmholtz to certify. Natural laws are invariable, and may be set out by science. But aesthetic principles are variable, and science cannot evaluate them. There is no overlap between the aesthetic and the reach of scientific truth.

Certainly, the variability of aesthetic principles is generally admitted in the twenty-first century. However, our point of view, which has been decisively inflected by the rise of cultural studies, is not at all that of the age of Helmholtz, Lautréamont, Satie, and Braque. We believe that each community (or perhaps each society, or at worst each individual) has its own aesthetic principles, which are open to analysis from the perspective of cultural history. Aesthetic principles thus belong, according to the generally accepted and institutionalised categorisation of kinds of knowledge and research in our education system, to the domain of the human sciences, rather than the hard sciences. We do not think they can be investigated in the same way as the laws of physics or acoustics. Rather, we think they can and should be treated in the same way as other cultural phenomena, for example the linguistic or the sociological. But this would have been inadmissible for the nineteenth century, for a reason which is easy enough to set out. The nineteenth century maintained the principle according to which, behind the undeniable diversity of aesthetic principles, there lurked a single universal beauty. As Flaubert famously put it: 'il n'y a *qu'un Beau*' [the beautiful is *one*].[20] This unity, this singleness of beauty is what guaranteed the unity, the singleness, indeed the very existence of art as a category. For Flaubert, as for Mallarmé, Baudelaire, Berlioz, Debussy, Manet, Cézanne, Satie, and I am sure Helmholtz too, each work of art must fulfil two conditions. It must be unique, different from everything that has gone before, original, and thus each time the proof of the infinite variability of art. But *at the same time*, it must constitute the irrefutable proof, by the beauty within it, that art exists as a single, eternally invariable category.

Beauty thus operates in art according to the same strange logic as truth. As Satie taught us at the beginning of this essay, there is no Truth in Art. And yet,

19 Lautréamont, *Les Chants de Maldoror*, p. 221.
20 Gustave Flaubert, *Extraits de la correspondance ou Préface à la vie d'écrivain*, ed. by Geneviève Bollème (Paris: Seuil, 1963), p. 146.

each artist has his own individual truth. What is the relationship between those individual truths? We are obliged to suppose there is one, even though we have no direct, scientific, positive access to it. Rationally speaking, there is no truth in art; nonetheless, at a deeper level in which we demonstrably believe even though we cannot support it through objective analysis of artistic works, all the truths in art meet as one, creating the only meaning that the word 'art' can have. Similarly: is every work of art beautiful? Absolutely not. There is no definition of 'beautiful' that applies to all works of art. If the opposite of 'beautiful' is 'ugly' or 'revolting', well, there are plenty of works of art that may well appear to us both ugly and revolting, including many parts of *Les Chants de Maldoror* itself. And yet... what if each artist has his or her own beauty? And what if, at a deeper level in which we demonstrably believe even though we cannot support it through objective analysis of artistic works, all these beauties, unrelated on the surface, actually in art meet as one, giving the word 'beauty', as well as the word 'art', the only coherence they can have?

It has often been said that *Les Chants de Maldoror* is the epic of doubt. Lautréamont attacks all our beliefs and principles, religious, moral, and aesthetic, and leaves nothing intact. However, there are two fundamental concepts, two principles which he never attacks, which remain intact from the beginning to the end of the work. The first is the right of science to work within its own domain, as an objective study of the natural world. Our hero Maldoror, and the narrator of the work (whose identity may or may not be separate from that of Maldoror), adore science. They adore it particularly when it describes natural phenomena that challenge our normative sense of what should be morally or aesthetically admissible. That, after all, in a sense, is what Helmholtz does. It is also the effect of the description, in the tone of a medical textbook, of the 'vice de conformation congénital des organes sexuels de l'homme', in the passage quoted above. For Maldoror, science is an invaluable witness for the prosecution as he seeks to condemn that cowardly conformism that we generally exhibit in our artistic tastes. Maldoror attacks God and humans mercilessly, but he never attacks or mocks science. When, in *Les Chants de Maldoror*, scientific texts are quoted, explicitly or implicitly, those quotations respect the meaning of the source. They do not deform the sense of the original. This is the exact opposite of what always happens when texts concerned with religion, philosophy, or literature are quoted by Lautréamont: he systematically deforms his sources in those fields, whereas scientific arguments are faithfully transmitted.

The second principle that is constantly maintained in *Les Chants de Maldoror* concerns literature. It is that literature does exist, as a single coherent category. As Mallarmé put it: 'oui [...] la littérature existe' [yes [...] literature exists].[21] Yes, as we have seen, Lautréamont says (and it would be impossible to disagree with him!) that his literature is different from other people's literature. But is that not the case for every literature worthy of the name? Uniqueness, originality, and difference are fundamental values in art, as they are not in science. Every literature is by definition

21   Stéphane Mallarmé, 'La Musique et les Lettres', in *Œuvres complètes*, II, 53–77 (p. 66).

different. That very difference thus becomes a universal literary attribute. It creates and reinforces, rather than undermining, the bond between all works of literature, holding them together within a single category. Lautréamont never hints at any doubts, either concerning the continuity of its existence, or concerning the place of his own work within the category. There is, as ever, a certain tension between the variability of literary phenomena, and the invariability of literature as such; but that tension is not a threat.

At the beginning of the fifth *Chant*, Lautréamont addresses his reader directly:

> Ne fais pas attention à la manière bizarre dont je chante chacune de ces strophes. Mais, sois persuadé que les accents fondamentaux de la poésie n'en conservent pas moins leur intrinsèque droit sur mon intelligence. Ne généralisons pas des faits exceptionnels, je ne demande pas mieux: cependant mon caractère est dans l'ordre des choses possibles. Sans doute, entre les deux termes extrêmes de ta littérature, telle que tu l'entends, et de la mienne, il en est une infinité d'intermédiaires, et il serait facile de multiplier les divisions; mais, il n'y aurait nulle utilité, et il y aurait le danger de donner quelque chose d'étroit et de faux à une conception éminemment philosophique, qui cesse d'être rationnelle, dès qu'elle n'est plus comprise comme elle a été imaginée, c'est-à-dire avec ampleur.[22]

> [Do not direct your attention to the bizarre manner in which I sing each of these stanzas. But, be persuaded that the fundamental accents of poetry conserve no less their intrinsic rights over my intelligence. I fully agree that we should not create generalisations out of exceptional events; nonetheless my character is of the order of the possible. Certainly, between the two extremes of your literature, as you understand it, and mine, there exists an infinite number of intermediate positions, and it would be easy to think up endless divisions; but, there would be no point, and to do so would be to run the danger of giving a false and narrow aspect to an eminently philosophical conception, which ceases to be rational, as soon as it is not understood as it was originally imagined, that is, broadly.]

Just as Satie allows different composers to have different truths, so Lautréamont here allows that his literature is not the same as literature as his reader understands it. Rationally, then, there must be room for several different literatures to exist. And yet at the same time, just as all true composers are poets for Satie, so for Lautréamont there is a hidden unity in literature, which he defines through the word *poésie*. There is one single clearly universal *poésie*, whose 'accents fondamentaux', we are to believe, continue to exercise their rights over Lautréamont's intelligence. Yes, he tells us, we can perfectly well distinguish between innumerable different literatures; but he encourages us not to, in the name of a higher reason, a higher philosophy, a philosophical conception that we must receive, not as the result simply of reasoning, but as *imagined*, broadly — 'imaginée [...] avec ampleur'.

Once again, then, we find ourselves witnessing that curious stand-off between the principle that there is only one art, only one truth, only one beauty; and the observation that what the eye of reason or of science sees is always a multiplicity of

---

22   Lautréamont, *Les Chants de Maldoror*, p. 250.

arts, beauties, and truths. Any attempt to formulate in rational or scholastic terms the universal characteristics of art is a mistake. The single unifying timeless truth of art cannot be established by any school, or indeed by any artists. As Satie put it:

> L'école a un but gymnastique, sans plus; la composition a un but esthétique, où le goût seul joue un rôle.
>
> Ne confondons pas. La connaissance de la grammaire n'implique pas la connaissance des lettres; elle peut servir ou être tenue à l'écart par la volonté de l'écrivain et sous sa responsabilité. La grammaire musicale n'est pas autre chose qu'une grammaire. [...]
>
> Qui a établi les vérités régissant l'Art? Qui?
>
> Les Maîtres? Ils n'en avaient pas le droit & il est malhonnête de leur accorder cette puissance. Tous ont eu à se plaindre des histoires de métier. Voyez Rodin, Manet, Debussy, etc. Les Maîtres ne sont pas pris dans la gendarmerie, pas plus que chez les pions ou autres magistrats. (48–49)

> [Schools have a gymnastic purpose, no more; composition has an aesthetic purpose, in which taste alone has a role to play.
>
> Let us not confuse categories. One can understand grammar without understanding literature. A knowledge of grammar can be used or set aside according to the will of the writer and under his responsibility. The grammar of music is only a grammar. [...]
>
> Who established the truths governing Art? Who?
>
> The Masters? They had no right to do so and it is dishonest to attribute this power to them. All suffered from quibbles connected to their craft. Examples: Rodin, Manet, Debussy, etc. The Masters were not recruited from among the ranks of policemen, nor of *pions* or other agents of law enforcement.]

What is the answer to Satie's question? Who established the truths governing art? There is, in fact, no answer. All Satie can do is to tell us who we should not listen to: anyone who tells us that any specific individuals, be they the greatest artists of their time, could have established any such truths. No one has had or will have that power. Anyone who claims to have it belongs to the despised category of the *pion*: the man who seeks to enforce school rules.

In accordance with exactly the same logic, we find that in *Les Chants de Maldoror*, a work in which hatred and loathing often seem the dominant mood, perhaps the most powerful and unmitigated hatred of all is reserved for teachers:

> Quand un élève interne, dans un lycée, est gouverné, pendant des années, qui sont des siècles, du matin jusqu'au soir et du soir jusqu'au lendemain, par un paria de la civilisation, qui a constamment les yeux sur lui, il sent les flots tumultueux d'une haine vivace, monter, comme une épaisse fumée, à son cerveau, qui lui paraît près d'éclater. Depuis le moment où on l'a jeté dans la prison, jusqu'à celui, qui s'approche, où il en sortira, une fièvre intense lui jaunit la face, rapproche ses sourcils, et lui creuse les yeux.[23]

> [When a boarder, in a grammar school, is governed, for years on end, which are centuries, from morning to night and from night to the morrow, by a pariah of civilisation, whose eyes are constantly upon him, he feels the raging torrents of an ever-gnawing hatred, rise, like a thick smoke, to his brain, which he feels is

---

23   Ibid., pp. 125–26.

FIG. 4.1. Vincent van Gogh, *Shoes* (1886). With kind permission of the Van Gogh Museum, Amsterdam (Van Gogh Foundation) <https://vangoghmuseum.nl/en/collection/s0011V1962> [accessed 22 November 2021]

about to explode. From the moment when he was cast into this prison, to the moment, which approaches, when he will be released from it, an intense fever yellows his face, pulls together his eyebrows, and hollows his eyes.]

★   ★   ★   ★   ★

On the subject of Truth in Art, Jacques Derrida had much to say; and if one looks carefully, one will see, I think, that whenever he reflects on that topic, questions of the value (or perhaps rather the problematic status) of institutionalised pedagogy are never far away.

Derrida never analysed the writings of Erik Satie, which, as far as I can tell, were unknown to him (as were the writings of composers generally), or indeed those of Georges Braque, or of Lautréamont, whom he admired greatly, but always from a safe distance, for which one cannot blame him. Since he also tended to avoid writing anything which would require him to confront head-on the contentious notion that a category called Art exists which transcends media, he did not speculate directly on the question of Truth in the Arts in general. Nonetheless, he did write ground-breaking essays on truth in literature, and on truth in painting.[24] If one puts the two together, one can see clearly enough, through what they have in common, what truth in art might have meant to him. It comforts my intermedial mindset that he found much the same dynamic in both painting and literature; for to me, that is the dynamic that underpins all the arts, and glues them together.

Is there truth in painting? A one-size-fits-all truth? Derrida's answer is embodied in a pun. The last part of his book *La Vérité en peinture* [The Truth in Painting] is entitled 'Restitutions de la vérité en pointure'. The 'pointure' in question is most obviously a reference to shoe size. Is Derrida suggesting that the truth of art can only be given back to us by assessing the size of a pair of shoes? Perhaps, indeed, he is. Perhaps Satie's phonometrography is paralleled by Derrida's careful analysis, over a hundred pages, of whether it matters whose foot a shoe might fit.

Derrida discusses a painting by Van Gogh in which one sees a pair of shoes, and the pedagogical analysis of that painting by the art historian Meyer Schapiro. Schapiro tells us that the shoes are a pair of men's town shoes; specifically, those of the painter himself, which he has, says Schapiro, represented in the painting. Schapiro also tells us that Martin Heidegger, who had previously written about the same painting, had erroneously affirmed that they were peasant shoes. Who is telling the truth about the painting? Is it Heidegger, or Schapiro? Derrida invites us to be sceptical about Schapiro's approach. He invites us to look, with him, closely at the shoes. Nothing he finds supports Schapiro's interpretation. It is by no means obvious that they are, as Schapiro says, town shoes. It is even less obvious that they are men's shoes. They could at least as well belong to a woman (or indeed a child). Nor are they obviously even a pair of shoes. They look suspiciously like two left shoes. Nor, again, do we have any firm evidence concerning the shoes that Van

---

24   Derrida wrote relatively little about the art of music. However, he certainly thought it had a special relationship with the truth. See Chapter 5 in this volume.

Gogh actually wore. We do, on the other hand, have plenty of evidence that he liked to paint things (including shoes) that belonged to other people. All of which adds up to a pretty convincing attack on the self-confidence of Schapiro's claim.

But, one might ask, why bother spending so many pages on this attack? Of what interest is it that Schapiro might be wrong to tell us that these are definitely Van Gogh's shoes? The answer is that for Derrida, Schapiro's approach is emblematic of a certain approach to the truth, that of the traditional pedagogical critic;[25] an approach that, for Derrida, amounts to looking for the wrong kind of truth in art.

> Schapiro [...] prétend détenir la vérité des chaussures (du tableau) de Vincent (Van Gogh). Et comme il doit la vérité, il la restitue. Il identifie (en tous les sens de ce mot) la peinture et les chaussures, leur assigne leurs points ou leur pointure propre, nomme l'œuvre et attribue le sujet de l'œuvre (les chaussures) au sujet de l'œuvre, soit à son sujet véritable, le peintre, Van Gogh.

> [Schapiro [...] claims to hold the truth of the shoes (of the picture) of Vincent (Van Gogh). And as he owes the truth, he restitutes it. He identifies (in all senses of this word) the painting and the shoes, assigns them their points or their proper size [*pointure*], names the work and attributes the subject of the work (the shoes) to the subject of the work, that is, to its true subject, the painter, Van Gogh.][26]

The pedagogue who claims to possess the truth about the subject of the painting must believe in the existence of that subject, before the existence of the painting itself. Schapiro tells us the shoes were there, before Van Gogh came along to represent them in his work. He is not so naive as to think that every painting must represent such a real external object. Nonetheless, there is, for Schapiro, a necessarily pre-existing subject of every painting, which is the painter himself. Van Gogh must have been there before his painting, and he paints, in a sense, himself as subject. Hence Schapiro's preference for believing that the shoes are his shoes; this would make it easier to see him, or at least his shadow, in the painting. Derrida thus connects Schapiro to the pre-structuralist school of 'l'homme et l'œuvre' [the man and the work], that critical approach which looks always through the work to the author, presupposing that the author exists as of right before and beyond the work. For Derrida himself, there is no such clear direction of travel, for the truth of the artwork. He defends Heidegger against Schapiro, not because he agrees unreservedly with Heidegger (he does not), but because at least Heidegger knows and allows that the truth of the artwork is not the truth of a representation, of the subject painted or of the artist. According to Heidegger (according to Derrida), the work:

> n'a pas 'servi' de *Veranschaulichung* ou de *Darstellung*, il [Heidegger] précise: 'C'est bien plus l'être-produit du produit qui arrive, proprement (*eigens*) et seulement par l'œuvre, à son paraître.' Ce paraître de l'être-produit n'aurait pas

---

25   Jacques Derrida: 'Tout ça est classique, affaire de classe, de pédagogie aussie et de classicité' [All that is classical, class-business, the business of pedagogy and classicity] (*La Vérité en peinture* (Paris: Flammarion, 1978), p. 335; *The Truth in Painting* trans. by Geoffrey Bennington and Ian McLeod (Chicago: University of Chicago Press, 1987) p. 293).

26   Ibid., pp. 313; 274–75.

lieu dans un ailleurs que l'œuvre d'art pourrait, en y renvoyant, illustrer. Il a lieu proprement (et seulement) en elle. Dans sa vérité même.

[did not 'serve' as *Veranschaulichung* or *Darstellung*, and he [Heidegger] goes on to specify: 'Much more is it the being-product of the product which arrives, properly (*eigens*) and only through the work, at its appearing.' This appearing of the being-product does not, according to Heidegger, take place in an elsewhere which the work of art could illustrate by referring to it. It takes place properly (and only) in the work. In its very truth.][27]

These sentences are not at all easy to read. Heidegger (even as quoted and explicated by Derrida) is much more difficult to follow than Schapiro. This is not incidental. Schapiro's pedagogical approach suits our everyday positive mindset. He tells us what the shoes are, whose they were, and why they were painted. The shoes take their legitimate place, for him, in an elsewhere, which we might call real life. The work of art illustrates that elsewhere, it refers to it, it reproduces it. To appreciate this logic, we do not need to worry about the status of truth, any more than I would have to worry if I looked at a photograph of a pair of shoes and tried to work out to which of my sons they belonged. Heidegger's concept of truth in art, and even more so Derrida's, is, like Satie's, more difficult. It creates difficulties in expression; it always leads to paradoxical use of vocabulary, and to the use of terms whose sense refuses to settle. Let us not be falsely optimistic: for that reason, the truth about the truth in art has been little understood, and will continue to be little understood. It demands intellectual courage and intrepidity from anyone who would pursue it. But let us try to display that courage, and to figure out what might be happening in those sentences where Derrida tries to tell us the truth about what Heidegger says about the truth in art.

Let us begin our attempt at figuring with the penultimate sentence, by replacing all its pronouns by their antecedents. This gives us: 'Le paraître de l'être-produit a lieu proprement (et seulement) en l'œuvre d'art' [The appearing of the being-product takes place properly (and only) in the work of art]. Which, at least, gives us nothing more nor less than a definition of the unique quality of the work of art. The process here defined, the 'appearance of the being-product', does not happen (at least, it does not happen 'proprement', cleanly or properly), anywhere else. What, then, does happen elsewhere, outside art, in science perhaps, or in everyday life? The answer is that outside art, we see the thing, the product itself, and not the process of its appearance as such. That seeing of the thing itself can be repeated and shared. Its subject does not escape us. I can look at a photograph not considered as a work of art and say: those are my second son's shoes. I can share this truth with you, you can repeat it, and it will lose nothing for being repeated. Indeed, I might have taken the photograph in order to identify his shoes, so that you would know which ones were his (the tatty black lace-ups). But the truth in art, in a painting considered as art (for like photographs, paintings can be considered either as artworks, or as representations, and there is no positive way to establish the truth about where the borderline is), is different. If such a truth can be held to exist. After all, this essay

27   Ibid., pp. 337; 295.

began from Satie's affirmation that there is no Truth in Art, and perhaps we find here another reason to accept there is none.

The most traditional opposition of all in the study of works of literature and painting is between appearance and reality. Heidegger is here saying, ventriloquised by Derrida, that the truth about the artwork is that it shows us not reality, but appearing, the process of appearing itself. There would, then, be no truth in art; only appearance. Worse: this appearing happens, not in the world of things, as when a mole emerges from its hole, and then vanishes again, leaving us certain that the creature still exists, though now below ground; it happens only in the work, only within the work, as an internal and not an external truth. If such a thing can be called a truth at all.

Thus Derrida ties us in the same knot as Satie; and at a central point in his argument, the word 'truth' is excluded from the domain of art. Schapiro is wrong to think he can tell us the truth about the painting, just as the 'pion' or 'pontife' is wrong to claim to be able to situate truth in music. The reason, in both cases, is the same. Truth, we think, is a relationship (whether of adequation or of revelation) between something said or shown, and something that existed before the saying or showing. But the work of art, by its very definition, does not derive its value from any demonstrable link to anything that preceded it. The truth of Bach is not the truth of Chopin. The painter does not imitate his idea. Maldoror (or Lautréamont) can be as beautiful as... something that we had never known was beautiful; and the value of Van Gogh's painting is unrelated to the identity of the shoes he painted. Rather, the art of the artwork is in a becoming, an appearing, an unfolding, a process, which never links back to anything that was stably there before. What happens, then, if we apply the word 'truth' to that process? Should we allow ourselves to bring back the word, to signify something distinct? Or should we let it go?

The fact is that we cannot prevent its return. We cannot help expressing our appreciation of that process in terms of its truth. As Derrida puts it, explaining the condition on which he would find Heidegger's approach preferable to Schapiro's: 'C'est la vérité de l'être-produit comme tel qui porte' [It is the truth of the being-product as such which carries weight].[28]

The truth keeps appearing in the artwork, even though there is no Truth in Art. The appearing of the being-product (if I may allow myself to re-organise Derrida's sentences) takes place *in* the artwork *in* its truth. This *in* marks an appartenance, a limit within which another kind of truth finds its place, for Derrida as for Satie. In art, the unique truth keeps on not appearing. There is no space for it. But for each artist or composer, or perhaps for each work, or perhaps every time one of us experiences an artwork and sees what appears, we see the truth of that appearance. There will never be a means for us to say where that truth is stationed, whether it is within the mind of its creator, within the work, or within the relationship between us and the work. It cannot, in fact, be any one of those things. It appears between them — and between all of them and our concept of art in general.

28   Ibid., pp. 371; 325.

Up to that point, I will be so bold as to say that I think Satie, Derrida, Lautréamont, and Braque could all have agreed. Where Derrida parts company with them is in the way he allows himself to use the word *vérité*, when he speaks in his own name.

We have seen how Satie allows the word *vérité* to appear with meanings that appear logically incompatible. Lautréamont, as ever, takes this to the extreme. He is quite happy to use the word to refer to an incontrovertible, clear, scientific, invariable set of laws, manifested in the physical universe and reflecting an immutable divine order, most clearly in mathematics:

> Vous, ô mathématiques concises, par l'enchaînement rigoureux de vos propositions tenaces et la constance de vos lois de fer, vous faites luire, aux yeux éblouis, un reflet puissant de cette vérité suprême dont on remarque l'empreinte dans l'ordre de l'univers.[29]

> [You, o concise mathematics, by the rigorous concatenation of your tenacious propositions and the constancy of your iron laws, you make shine, before our dazzled eyes, a mighty reflection of that supreme truth of which we see the imprint in the order of the universe.]

But he is equally happy to use the word to refer to something that remains forever out of our reach, because it does not actually exist in any place:

> Oh! si au lieu d'être un enfer, l'univers n'avait été qu'un céleste anus immense, regardez le geste que je fais du côté de mon bas-ventre: oui, j'aurais enfoncé ma verge, à travers son sphyncter sanglant, fracassant, par mes mouvements impétueux, les propres parois de son bassin! Le malheur n'aurait pas alors soufflé, sur mes yeux aveuglés, des dunes entières de sable mouvant; j'aurais découvert l'endroit souterrain où gît la vérité endormie, et les fleuves de mon sperme visqueux auraient trouvé de la sorte un océan où se précipiter![30]

> [Oh! if instead of being a hell, the universe had been nothing but an immense celestial anus, see the gesture that I am making in the region of my groin: yes, I would have thrust my virile member, through its bloody sphincter, smashing, by my impetuous movements, the very walls of its pelvis! Misery and pain would then not have blown, onto my blinded eyes, entire dunes of shifting sand; I would have discovered the underground place where lies sleeping the truth, and the rivers of my viscous sperm would thus have found an ocean into which to cast themselves!]

The universe is not an immense celestial anus, we cannot bugger it, and therefore we cannot get to the truth. We might be quite comfortable, if we are used to reading poetry, with this sense that the truth is forever beyond us, and the universe gives us no means to access it. But how does that meaning of the word *vérité* sit with the 'vérité suprême' that mathematics reveals to us, reflected serenely in the order of the visible universe? Once again, what we see here is that the word 'truth' does not correspond to any single truth.

Derrida, however, began his writing academic life as a philosopher, and although his writing became steadily more poetic, he never, I think, entirely lost

29   Lautréamont, *Les Chants de Maldoror*, pp. 162–63.
30   Ibid., p. 265.

the philosopher's sense that the discrete terms one uses ought to correspond to discrete concepts. His sensitivity to the true diversity of the notion of truth in art is exemplary; but he cannot quite bring himself to use the word, in his own voice, with the full range of meanings it comes to have when Satie, Lautréamont, or Mallarmé use it. In *La Vérité en peinture*, his strategy, when he wants to present the truth in art, is to quote other people using the word in its artistic sense. In the passages I have quoted above, it is to Heidegger that he turns. Towards the end of 'Restitutions de la vérité en pointure', it is to Antonin Artaud.

Artaud, Derrida tells us, protests against the idea that there might be ghosts in the paintings of Van Gogh. Every ghost, says Artaud, is the ghost of something. But a painting by Van Gogh is not the ghost of anything. It is not the trace, shade, or remainder of anything that existed before it. That is the truth of the painting: it reflects no subject and no object: 'Artaud [...] proteste au nom d'une certaine vérité, sans sujet, sans objet, accordée à une musique qui revient souvent dans son texte (malgré sa "préférence", à cause d'elle, Van Gogh serait "un formidable musicien")' [Artaud [...] protests in the name of a certain truth, without subject, without object, tuned to a music which recurs often in his text (despite his 'preference', because of it, Van Gogh is a 'formidable musician' according to Artaud)].[31] What was Van Gogh's 'preference', in spite of which Artaud considers him a formidable musician? It is expressed in a quotation from a letter which Derrida had placed at the head of 'Restitutions de la vérité en pointure': ' "Mais elle m'est si chère, la vérité, le *chercher à faire vrai* aussi, enfin je crois, je crois que je préfère encore être cordonnier à être musicien avec les couleurs" ' ['But the truth is so dear to me, and so is the *seeking to make true*, that indeed I believe, I believe I would still rather be a cobbler than a musician with colours'].[32] Yet again, the word seems to tie us in knots. Artaud, 'in the name of a certain truth', sees in Van Gogh a 'formidable musician'. Van Gogh himself, in the name of the same truth (or is it a different one?), seems to think that being a musician would be less true to his values than being a cobbler. Should the painter, to be true to himself, be a musician, or not? As ever, one can only cope with this question by taking into account the variety of the kinds of truth it calls upon. We shall return to the question of the intermedial truth of art, after a detour through literature.

★   ★   ★   ★   ★

Half a dozen years before his study of the truth in painting, Derrida had written a long essay concerning the truth in literature. It was 'La Double Séance' [The Double Seance], published in *La Dissémination*. At the beginning of this text, Derrida defined thus his ambition:

> Cette double séance dont je n'aurai jamais l'innocence militante d'annoncer qu'elle est concernée par la question *qu'est-ce que la littérature*, trouvera son coin ENTRE la littérature et la vérité, entre la littérature et ce qu'il *faut* répondre à la question *qu'est-ce que*?[33]

31   Derrida, *La Vérité en peinture*, pp. 435; 381.
32   Ibid., pp. 291; 254.
33   Jacques Derrida, 'La Double Séance', in *La Dissémination* (Paris: Seuil, 1972), pp. 201–317

[This double seance of which I will never have the militant innocence to announce that it is concerned by the question *what is literature*, finds its corner BETWEEN literature and truth, between literature and what one *must* answer to the question *what is?*]

BETWEEN literature and truth... what lies between them? One cannot begin to determine that, surely, without attributing, as a working hypothesis, a sense to each of those two slippery words. Literature will come later, as it usually does. Here, what Derrida gives us, in the fold of his typically appositional syntax, is his own definition of the truth. Truth is, or at least is, here, syntactically equivalent to, 'ce qu'il *faut* répondre à la question *qu'est-ce que?*'.

We might call that a philosophical definition of the truth. It is certainly not the truth that Satie finds in Chopin or Bach, nor the truth that Lautréamont imagines beyond the non-existent anal sphincter of the universe. There is no obligatory response to the question posed by those truths. They are quite happy to receive no answer, and indeed they usually do not. At all levels, art is a constant invention. The artwork poses a question to which there never even appears to be a stable answer. Therefore, if one takes Derrida's definition of the truth, there is no truth in art; and he would be absolutely right to look, not for truth in literature, but for something between literature and truth.

Derrida, in 'La Double Séance', remains faithful to this philosophical definition of the truth, which excludes it from art. In the essay, therefore, there is no Truth in Art. We see this most clearly when Derrida extracts from what Plato has to say about the book the following Platonic principle: '*La vérité du livre est décidable*' [*The truth of the book is decidable*].[34] He sets out to show that Plato's principle cannot apply to literature as Mallarmé understands and creates it. The Mallarmean text contains no decidable truth. As ever, the artwork's ability to evade the decidable truth has to do with the strange way it relates to the dynamics of repetition, of the copy: 'Un discours sur le rapport entre littérature et vérité bute toujours sur la possibilité énigmatique de la répétition, dans le cadre du *portrait*' [Any discourse on the relationship between literature and truth will always be tripped up by the enigmatic problem of repetition, framed by the *portrait*].[35] The truth, as Derrida sees it here, can only operate where we can believe in the value of reproducing something that was previously present. The truth is a repetition, a representation. Art is not. Therefore, the operation of art is not the operation of truth. It is something else: 'L'opération qui n'appartient plus au système de la vérité ne manifeste, ne produit, ne dévoile aucune présence; elle ne constitue pas davantage une conformité de ressemblance ou d'adéquation entre une présence et une représentation' [The operation which no longer belongs to the system of truth does not make manifest, does not produce, does not unveil any presence; no more does it constitute a conformity of similarity or adequation between a presence and a representation].[36]

(p. 203). The innocent militant to whom Derrida alludes is Sartre, the question 'qu'est-ce que la littérature?' being the title of a famous book by Sartre published in 1948.
34   Ibid., p. 210.
35   Ibid., p. 214.
36   Ibid., p. 236.

The operation of literature reveals no presence and represents nothing previously present; therefore, truth does not govern it. Once again, we find no truth in art.

This splendidly clear statement comes on p. 236 of the book *La Dissémination*. The essay 'La Double Séance' occupies pp. 201–317 of that book. We are therefore here less than a third of the way through the essay. Up to this point, as we might have expected since he had told us from the beginning that his text would find its corner between literature and truth, we have frequently encountered the word *vérité*. Curiously, however, after p. 236 the word *vérité* slips away. In the last fifteen pages of the essay, it is totally absent. Why? My answer would be: after having shown that there is no truth in art according to the philosophical sense of the word 'truth', Derrida goes on to ask the question: well then, if there is no truth in literature, what is there? What is the operation that does not belong to the system of truth? In answering this question, Derrida does not resuscitate the word *vérité*, giving it a new sense unknown to philosophy. Instead, he abandons it to its philosophical fate, and moves on to new terms and conditions.

In *La Vérité en peinture*, as we saw, the word *vérité* is used both in the philosophical sense, and in the other sense, the sense in which it returns, the ghost of its former philosophical self, in art. But Derrida is careful never to use it in the latter sense when he speaks in his own voice. Instead, he recruits other writers — notably Artaud and Cézanne — to use the word for him; as if, being a trained philosopher, he could not quite bring himself to use the master word of philosophy in a sense which contradicts the senses it has always had in philosophy. Mallarmé, on the other hand, like Satie and Lautréamont, had no such scruples.

★   ★   ★   ★   ★

Mallarmé, as do we all, accepted that the operations of science, like those of social life, of pedagogy, and of religion, depend on the existence and revelation of endless truths. Indeed, he quite frequently uses the word *vérité* when he is discussing the social and political context within which art has to evolve. But the one true truth is not, for him, of that order. It is not the truth that Derrida ascribes to Plato, or Satie to critics, *pions* and pontiffs, or Lautréamont to mathematics. It is single, and singular. It is always related to the experience of art. And it is never the representation of anything. Here is a first example of how this singular truth emerges, for Mallarmé:

> Le vers va s'émouvoir de quelque balancement, terrible et suave, comme l'orchestre, aile tendue; mais avec des serres enracinées à vous. Là-bas, où que ce soit, nier l'indicible, qui ment.
>
> Un humble, mon semblable, dont le verbe occupe les lèvres, peut, selon ce moyen médiocre, pas! si consent à se joindre, en accompagnement, un écho inentendu, communiquer, dans le vocabulaire, à toute pompe et à toute lumière; car, pour chaque, sied que la vérité se révèle, comme elle est, magnifique.[37]

---

37   Mallarmé, 'La Musique et les Lettres', in *Œuvres complètes*, II, 73.

[Verse will be moved by some rocking motion, terrible and sweet, like the orchestra, wing outstretched; but its claws rooted in you. There, wherever it may be, to deny the unsayable, which lies.

A humble man, my fellow being, whose Word occupies lips, can, using this means, mediocre, no! if, as an accompaniment, an unheard echo consents to join, communicate, in the vocabulary, to all pomp and to all light; for, to each of us, it is fitting that the truth reveal itself, as it is, magnificent.]

Here we have, in 'La Musique et les Lettres', a truth which is magnificent, not a lie told by pontiffs; and the condition of its magnificence is an echo that cannot be heard. In 'L'Action restreinte', at the end of a passage which has always been read as a description of the poet's ideal, we find a second such truth:

L'écrivain, de ses maux, dragons qu'il a choyés, ou d'une allégresse, doit s'instituer, au texte, le spirituel histrion.

Plancher, lustre, obnubilation des tissus et liquéfaction de miroirs, en l'ordre réel, jusqu'aux bonds excessifs de notre forme gazée autour d'un arrêt, sur pied, de la virile stature, un Lieu se présente, scène, majoration devant tous du spectacle de Soi; là, en raison des intermédiaires de la lumière, de la chair et des rires le sacrifice qu'y fait, relativement à sa personnalité, l'inspirateur, aboutit complet ou c'est, dans une résurrection étrangère, fini de celui-ci: de qui le verbe répercuté et vain désormais s'exhale par la chimère orchestrale.

Une salle, il se célèbre, anonyme, dans le héros.

Tout, comme fonctionnement de fêtes : un peuple témoigne de sa transfiguration en vérité.[38]

[The writer, of his woes, dragons that he has cherished, or of a moment of joy, must institute himself, in the text, as the spiritual histrion.

Boards, chandelier, obnubilation of fabrics and liquefaction of mirrors, in the order of the real, leading to the excessive leaps of our veiled form around a point of rest, of the virile stature, a Place presents itself, as stage, magnification before all of the spectacle of Oneself; there, correlative with the intermediaries of light, flesh, and of laughter the sacrifice that is here made, concerning his personality, by the one who inspires, reaches complete resolution or it is, in a resurrection elsewhere, the end of him: of him whose Word echoed and henceforth vain is exhaled by the chimaera of the orchestra.

A theatrical space, he celebrates himself, anonymous, in the hero.

The whole, as an operation of festivals: a people bears witness to its own transformation into truth.]

Like the Truth of Chopin, Mozart, Beethoven, or Bach according to Satie, like the truth of Van Gogh according to Artaud, Mallarmé's truth only comes into existence through an artistic context. Furthermore, that artistic context is transmedial. For the poet as for the painter, music has to come into play. That is how the truth, escaping the medium of expression, can find its place beyond the reach of presence. The universe does not need to be a celestial anus if we can have faith

---

38   Stéphane Mallarmé, 'L'Action restreinte', in *Œuvres complètes*, II, 214–18 (pp. 215–16).

in a transmedial artistic truth that exists beyond the reach of our words as of our gestures. It cannot be seen, it cannot be quoted, it cannot be reproduced, it cannot be imitated or demonstrated, above all it cannot be discovered. In art, but only within the experience of art, it reveals itself, and transfigures us.

★   ★   ★   ★   ★

Time to sum up. The word *vérité* has, for the authors I have been citing, two different senses. One I have allowed myself to call 'philosophical'. It is in this sense that pedagogues of all stripes use it. Derrida uses it, too, when he writes in his own name, though his aim is always to bring us to see its limits. This is the truth accessible to positive reason, the truth that can lead us to the invariable laws of science, the truth that can be discovered, then repeated. The other sense of the word *vérité* is the one given to it (as Derrida shows) by Mallarmé or Artaud in the artistic context: it emerges in the artistic experience, to which no analysis can have access. Satie and Lautréamont use the word in both senses, revelling in the irony this duplicity permits and the confusion it creates, mocking our stupidity in trying to believe the word can have a single meaning.

Why, indeed, do we persist in this stupidity? Come to think of it, would it not be more sensible to find a second word for the second sense? Why does even Derrida, with all the subtlety of his analysis, propose no such second word? Why persist in calling 'truth' something that so plainly, in so many ways, refuses to behave as we expect the truth to behave? The only answer I have available is an indirect and incomplete one. It may well seem obscure. Still, I shall not worry too much about that. In the operation of art, clarity cannot be the overriding criterion by which we judge an explanation. Schapiro is clearer than Heidegger, because he understands less. Critical clarity can only be achieved if one is willing to swallow the small-minded truth of the pontiffs or *pions* whom Satie so execrated.

I will not try to tell you, any more than Derrida does, what the truth in art is. But I will tell you how it hides, and one of the conditions for us to sense its presence. The truth in art reaches us as if it were the appearance, within the material of one art, of something whose proper place would have been in the physical medium of another art.

The truth in art may be an echo, in poetry, of the dance. It may be the shadow of a visual image in music. It could be the reminiscence of a word in painting. Perhaps it is the ghostly presence of a novel in a film, or of a legend in an opera. Nothing is really imitated, nothing is received as simply copied in art; and this is precisely because in the medium of the artwork, in the means of expression proper to each art, we perceive something which should only be able to exist in the medium of a different art. That something is not in itself the truth. But the mode of its appearance is the condition of the truth in art. Its necessary original absence is the guarantee of the originality of the appearance of the truth, each time.

Our perception of it can never be stable. We can never reach it, since it is never there. Nonetheless, we find ourselves drawn always towards it by the heroism of the artist who risks and inevitably loses her or his proper voice, since she or he causes something to appear which cannot be made to appear in the medium being used to create the artwork.

Otherwise put: the truth in art depends on the union of two forces. The creator must accept to be sacrificed, lost in the inhuman illogicality of the artistic enterprise, which is that of making a non-representation appear. And the audience must be open to joining in that sacrifice. We must let ourselves become, rationally speaking, stupid. We have to allow ourselves, we who do not believe in ghosts, to perceive the phantom of what never lived, the echo of something that never made a sound, from beyond what can possibly be there before us, there in the work as it is accessible to our senses and to our common sense.

Let us conclude by observing this operation in some of the quotations we have already examined. Once one has learned what to look for, one can always find that echo from the material of another art which is the condition of the revelation of truth in art. No need, I think, to go over again how Mallarmé provides this echo; the reference to the orchestra is clear enough. Satie, who does not like to make things easy for his reader, plays his cards closer to his chest. Nonetheless, the clues are there. For example:

> J'ai toujours dit — & je le répéterai encore très longtemps après ma mort — qu'il n'y a pas de Vérité en Art (de Vérité unique, s'entend).
> La Vérité de Chopin — ce prodigieux créateur — n'est pas celle de Mozart, ce si luxueux musicien dont l'écriture est un éblouissement impérissable [...]. (61)

> [I have always said — & shall continue to repeat it long, long after my death — that there is no Truth in Art (no single Truth, that is).
> The Truth of Chopin — that prodigious creator — is not the Truth of Mozart, that luxurious musician whose writing dazzles unendingly [...].]

Satie is here talking about Mozart as a musician. He praises him by referring to his writing, his 'écriture'... is that a reference to the material of another art? After all, a musician does write. And yet in any definition of music, of the material proper to music, it is sound that is evoked, not writing. Satie then doubles the effect. Just as music is normally heard as sound, not read as writing, so writing is usually read, and not received for its visual effect. But Satie says that Mozart's writing dazzles us. Can writing dazzle? Certainly, this is not a strikingly strange metaphor. We are used to such things. The intermedial twist is subtle. But it is all the more effective in taking us away from seeing the truth in music solely in terms of what happens in its primary material, which is sound. The truth in that art is not in its medium.

Lautréamont presents literature as poetry in the most traditional way, by saying that he sings his poetry. Artaud is given by Derrida the task of similarly presenting Van Gogh as a musician. As for Van Gogh himself, he doubles the effect, as Satie did. He accepts, it seems, that he is a musician — a musician with colours. However, in search of the truth, he believes he would prefer to be a cobbler... why? I would say: because in his day, the analogy between painting and music had become current, and the idea had been mooted that the two arts might use similar means. But the cobbler works with nails and leather; now that is a fundamentally different medium.

And different it must remain. We know, if we understand the way the truth works in art, that Van Gogh is not telling us he is going to become a cobbler (of course, he never did). Rather, he is telling us how he imagines himself: as someone whose truth is elsewhere, in a medium inaccessible to the craft he exercises.

A sentence from a letter by Cézanne catches Derrida's attention, so much so that he uses it as an epigraph both at the beginning of *La Vérité en peinture*, and at the opening of 'Restitutions de la vérité en pointure': 'Je vous dois la vérité en peinture, et je vous la dirai' [I owe you the truth in painting, and I will tell it to you].[39] Cézanne owes us the truth in painting. But he knows he cannot give us that truth in the medium of painting, which is paint. He will have to say it. Nor will he say it in words; he is no more a poet than Lautréamont is a singer. He will, we realise, say it in painting, where it cannot be said. He will never have told us the truth in words. Nor will he have painted the truth in painting. Has he, then, been deceiving us? Yes, he has, if what we look for in his words is the truth of art in words, or if we look in his paintings for the truth of art in paint. No, there is no deception, if his words evoke for you his paintings, or if you hear in his paintings the echo of his own true voice.

39   Derrida, *La Vérité en peinture*, pp. 6, 291.

PART III

❖

On the Life of the Soul,
and Immortality

The word 'soul' bothers us. It is untimely and unfashionable. We do not like to use it. It crops up more often than we like in poetry and poetic writing. It is a word that means little to most of us, in the twenty-first century. We swerve as we read it, hoping, as we get beyond it, that it might have meant little more than 'mind' or 'spirit' or 'heart', or that it is a relict of old Christian doctrine. But that is not how it has kept art alive, for the past two centuries.

We will see, in these essays, Edgar Allan Poe, Charles Darwin, Charles Baudelaire, Tristan Tzara, and Jacques Derrida all placing it at the heart of their reflections on art. As they do so, the soul ceases to belong (as perhaps it used to in religion) to God and to humanity. They ask us to share it with animals and with vegetable matter, with wooden posts, with birds, and with boats. That willingness to share the soul is the price of art. From Poe's time to Derrida's at least, poetic writers have known this. However, those whom Derrida calls 'philosophers', those whose mode of thinking Darwin considers scientific, refuse to know it. They either deny the soul exists, or they refuse it to the non-human. They will not share it and share in it; and for that reason they cannot know poetry.

Derrida finds the soul in a violin's soundpost. Poe hears it issue from a raven's beak. Darwin sensed it, when young, in the rainforests of Brazil. But then he lost the ability to see it, as if it were a colour to which he had become blind; and he lost, at the same time, his ability to read poetry or enjoy music. The capacity to appreciate art depends on our willingness to enter the time of the soul, which is not that of philosophy, of science, of reason, or indeed of life and death. Not that the soul is without time. It contains movements or rhythms which we can only imagine as working in time. Rationally speaking, it has not always existed, and it will not live for ever. But it is nonetheless immortal, because what we call 'death' does not enter into it.

The time of the soul is the time of art. The three essays in this part aim to show how art and soul explain and create each other. The first of the three, originally published in *The Edinburgh Companion to Literature and Music*, traces how the soul and its music become the equals of death in the writing of Derrida, Barthes, and Paul de Man. The third began life (in French) as a lecture given in London at the 2018 postgraduate conference of the Society for French Studies, whose theme was repetition. It celebrates the soul's defiance of the age of mechanical reproducibility, in Poe's writing as in Tristan Tzara's (whose use of the word *âme* might surprise many who think they know that Dada had no time for such metaphysical notions). The central essay of the three, a direct address to Charles Darwin (originally given at a postgraduate Word and Music study day in Liège, organised by Giulia Mascoli), is different. In it, I do not aim simply to explain Darwin's thought. Rather, I am foolhardy enough to tell Darwin that he failed to follow through the logic of his deepest conviction, which was that the lower animals share a sense of beauty with us. That failure led him to become, distressingly, blind to the beauty of art.

Darwin tells us explicitly that between humans and animals, there is no absolute difference, only a series of gradations. Does this mean we should allow ourselves to find poetry in animals? He never quite managed to say that we should. It is a step which he could not bring himself to take. Yet his writing seems to goad us to take it. If we are bold enough to take that step for him, we discover answers to questions that remained mysteries to him. We find ourselves able to appreciate Darwin himself as a poetic writer; and it becomes possible to suspect that science itself is rooted in poetry, in the time of the soul.

CHAPTER 5

❖

Derrida, de Man, Barthes, and Music as the Soul of Writing

What is music? Conventional critical wisdom is that we have no generally valid answer to this question. But why do we have no answer? The obvious reason would be this: music has no stable identity, and therefore there is no point asking in general terms what it is. Music is only what we choose to call by that name, and that varies according to cultural context.

However, a very different reason for our inability to define music emerges from French critical theory. It is a reason that has deep roots in European cultural traditions stretching back centuries. It is simply this: music tells us a kind of truth which verbal language cannot convey. Certainly, we cannot define it in words. But that is not because it has no stable identity. It is because language has its limitations. Those who (like critics generally) refuse to believe in any kind of truth that cannot be put into words will therefore not be able to see what music is. Or at least, they will not be able to allow themselves to admit they know what music is. But when they love, they know what music is, whether they admit it or not; especially, when they have loved and lost.

On 18 January 1984, Jacques Derrida, then doubtless the world's most famous living literary theorist, spoke at Yale University in homage to his friend and colleague Paul de Man, who had died less than a month earlier.

Derrida's audience was largely anglophone. He began by excusing himself for speaking in French, his language, which was the one in which he had always conversed with Paul de Man. He had not the heart, he said, to translate it. In any case, he suggested, it hardly mattered if some of those present could not understand his French. What counted, at such a time, was not really what one might say; it was for those present to feel together, 'with voice and with music'.[1]

What music? How could Jacques Derrida, who was no musician, make music bringing together his friends in mourning? And why would they need music? Was

---

[1]   See *The Lesson of Paul de Man*, ed. by Peter Brooks, Shoshana Felman, and J. Hillis Miller (= *Yale French Studies*, 69 (1985)), 323–26 (p. 323). Derrida's tribute (untitled) is given in French on pp. 13–16, and in English (translation by Kevin Newmark) on pp. 323–26. All references in brackets in this essay are to that publication. The translation, according to a note in the journal, had 'the approval of the author' (p. 326).

not his Yale audience composed of men and women of words, rather than of music? The answer to these questions is offered through a word that emblematically, here, resists translation: *âme*. With it, Derrida gives us to understand why the words that bring us together are only to be understood as music.

Those present at Yale on that day had, said Derrida, 'as one says in French, "la mort dans l'âme", death in the soul' (p. 323). And what, precisely, in this context, might the soul be, for the great theorist who taught the literary world how to be wary of such metaphysical concepts? He gives the answer in the last paragraph of the essay. The soul he has in mind is a little piece of wood keeping two other pieces of wood apart, and enabling the communication of music. The soul has death in it because it is itself, whatever else it might be, a thing.

He recounts how, after a jazz concert in Chicago to which de Man had taken him and his son Pierre, he had listened to the two of them talking about musical instruments, and had discovered that the word *âme* means not only 'soul', but 'soundpost', in stringed instruments such as violins or basses:

> I learned that the 'soul' is the name one gives in French to the small and fragile piece of wood — always very exposed, very vulnerable — that is placed within the body of these instruments to support the bridge and assure the resonant communication of the two sounding boards. I didn't know why at that moment I was so strangely moved and unsettled in some dim recess by the conversation I was listening to: no doubt it was due to the word 'soul' which always speaks to us at the same time of life and of death. (326)

'I didn't know why': this expression (more commonly, in the present tense, 'je ne sais pas pourquoi') is frequent in Derrida's writing, and always a vital invitation to the reader to ask, precisely, why, why Jacques Derrida did not know. Why was he moved in a manner beyond his understanding at the time? It is a matter of life and death. The soul, here, is a material, physical thing, an object. It allows (though it does not itself create) the emergence of music, the communication of music, from one sounding board to another. Derrida has already told us that 'only music today seems to me bearable, consonant, able to give some measure of what unites us in the same thought' (p. 325). He is speaking, not making music, but speaking is unbearable: what we need is music. Where can it come from? Only from a thing, a thing within an instrument; its soul is a thing, an unseen, vulnerable thing. Words might give the false impression that they come from a person, from the soul within a person, a soul (or, indeed, a heart) so immaterial that we imagine it might, after all, not be a thing. But music materialises the incomprehensible unity of the thing and the soul. And that materialisation is what, in the face of death, we need.

Derrida did not know why he was so moved by that identification, created within his own language, between the small piece of wood and the soul. It is, indeed, what we cannot know. How can a soul be a thing? We cannot understand; but in music, we hear that it is. The genius of the great francophone theorists of the late twentieth century, including Derrida, de Man, and Barthes, is that they allow us to see and think about this fact, which we cannot understand. Indeed, what they give us, if we know how to read, is the gift of music in writing; not writing as an explanation of music (that is not possible), but an actualisation in words of the ultimately incomprehensible way that music works, bringing us together in the face of death, because it is at once a thing, and possessed of (or by) a soul.

Let us remember that Jacques Derrida was moved, in ways he was unable to understand, by the soul of the stringed instrument only because his son and his friend were speaking French. It would not have worked in English. That power of music to unite us all — whatever language we speak — is explained to us through something that conspicuously fails to transcend languages. Or does it? It is true that English cannot bring together for us, as French does, the soundpost and the soul. But every language offers, through its ambiguities, its coincidences of sound and of pattern, through the happenstance of etymology and fortuitous analogies of rhythm, opportunities to make connections between things and souls, between the real world of discrete objects and an ideal musical togetherness. Perhaps that is what we should call poetry: words taking advantage of those opportunities within a language, in order to give us an obscure understanding of what music does, bringing us together in the face of death. If we did not have music, would this be possible? Would we have poetry?

Less than three years earlier, Derrida had published another text on the death of a friend and colleague: 'Les Morts de Roland Barthes' [The Deaths of Roland Barthes]. Again, it evokes music from the beginning; again, music appears as a force for bringing together, for uniting; and again, Derrida gives us to understand this force through a play on words that only works in French. The play, here, is with the verb *accorder*, which can mean 'to tune' (as when the various instruments in an orchestra tune themselves to the same pitch), or 'to make agree', including in the grammatical sense (as when nouns, verbs, adjectives, and articles are made to agree in number). In fact, the untranslatable plays on words had begun within the very title. 'Les Morts de Roland Barthes' might mean the several deaths that Barthes died, or the many dead people that Barthes had mourned (*morts* meaning either 'deaths' or 'dead people'). Both senses are taken up in the essay; and music brings both together, makes them agree, tunes them to each other. Each death, for Derrida, is unique, and each is the end of the world; that became the repeated refrain of the publications of the last two decades of his life. But in music, that uniqueness of each death becomes something we can share. Every unique death can be tuned to every other. Words cannot embody that tuning, because each language is itself unique; as Mallarmé had said a century earlier, the multiplicity of languages prevents any one of them from being materially the truth.[2] But thanks to music, thanks to what words (in any language) can say about music, they can evoke the mechanism of that tuning, and give us, if not to understand it, at least to feel that there is a unique direction of ideal incomprehension towards which it is worth directing our ears: incomprehension of the fact that a thing cannot be a soul.

When words do this, when they evoke the incomprehensible way that music tunes life with death, they cease to operate with scientific or philosophical rigour. From the standpoint of science, a soundpost is not the same thing as a soul; a metaphor and an accident of language may bring them together, but objective

2   Stéphane Mallarmé, 'Crise de vers', in *Œuvres complètes*, II, 204–13 (p. 208).

truth, philosophical conceptuality, separates them. Derrida, however, finds the value of Barthes's writing in a kind of operation that works precisely within those very accidents of language, within the material of the language, using the language as an instrument or thing, through which concepts are composed. Nor is Barthes content to use the French language as he finds it. He makes of it an instrument that only he can use, creating idiolectal terms and oppositions, and composing between them, as no one else could.[3] In the manner of this composition, says Derrida, we can hear a certain music:

> His *manner*, the way in which he displays, plays with, and interprets the pair *studium/punctum* [...] in all of this we will later hear the music [...]. The conceptual rigour of an artifact remains supple and playful here, and it lasts the time of a book; it will be useful to others but it suits perfectly only the one who signs it, like an instrument that can't be lent to anyone, like the history of an instrument. For above all, and in the first place, this apparent opposition (*studium/punctum*) does not forbid but, on the contrary, facilitates a certain *composition* between the two concepts.[4]

Is that composition musical? It might seem not. It is words that are here played on, not sounds. The sense, in words, of composition, is also: negotiation and compromise; it is arrangement, too, bringing together of elements; and of course, it is bound by the limits of the language, not quite the same in English as in French. But music, too, as we receive it, can only be negotiation and compromise, arrangement, bringing together of elements, and not quite the same to French ears as to anglophone ones; hence, in every sense, 'the composition is also the music. One could open a long chapter here on Barthes as musician'.[5]

Barthes, like Paul de Man but unlike Derrida, was a musician himself in the sense that he made music. He played the piano (and, in his younger days, sang). Much of his writing on music works with the physical experience of making music, and with a kind of sensuous listening that finds music in the body of the performer, in the grain of the voice and the fingers of the pianist (or harpsichordist), rather than in any message to be conveyed. Music, to Barthes as to Derrida, is a kind of language that is inseparable from materiality. Just as the soul of the violin is to be located in a piece of wood, so the life of a song is in the physical body of its singer. Of course we are always free, rationally free, to say that this is nonsense. We might say that a violin has a soundpost, but it does not have a soul, and if it appears to do so, that is because the music it plays comes from the heart of the player. Similarly, a song does not have a life, and if it appears to us to do so, that is not merely an effect of its resonance in the singer's body; the singer must put his or her heart into it. But what is that heart? What kind of thing is it? Where will we find it, if we look for it? Is it a physical thing, part of the musician's body after all? As we seek it out, can we

3   Derrida is discussing the opposition between the terms *studium* and *punctum* that Barthes builds up in *Camera Lucida*. What Barthes means by this opposition need not concern us here; my point concerns the way the opposition operates.

4   Jacques Derrida, 'The Deaths of Roland Barthes', in *The Work of Mourning*, ed. by Pascale-Anne Brault and Michael Naas (Chicago: University of Chicago Press, 2001), pp. 34–67 (pp. 40–41).

5   Ibid., p. 42.

do any better than to reproduce that movement of emotion and incomprehension which Pierre Derrida and Paul de Man inspired in Jacques Derrida when they told him what they knew about the soul of instruments? I think that for Barthes as for Derrida, between the soul, life, the heart, and the thing, there is always composition: negotiation, compromise, arrangement, a stand-off always to be reframed, a work of music always to be written. And for both of them, that work, that composition, set to work in language by music, is that which allows words to become the very opposite of a mere expression of things: the language of love, especially of love for those who cannot be with us.

Barthes's last book *Camera Lucida* (1980) is, in one sense, a book about the nature of the photograph, as an incontrovertible reproduction of reality. If that were all it was, it might now seem, in the era of digital photography, outdated. It is not at all outdated. It remains as poignant and as thought-provoking as ever, because its underlying theme is far more generally the relationship between death and representation in art; and more particularly, because Barthes's musings on this theme are inexorably intertwined with his reflections on his own reactions to the recent death of his mother. Famously, he writes at some length about a photograph of her in a winter garden which is not itself reproduced in the book. That photograph's absence, the absence of the reproduction of the representation of his mother, is balanced by the presence of references to music as he evokes that photograph. In 'The Deaths of Roland Barthes', Derrida quotes two particularly moving sentences from *Camera Lucida* in which music is invoked to express the nature of what passed between mother and son: 'the Winter Garden Photograph was for me like the last music Schumann wrote before collapsing, that first *Gesang der Frühe* that accords with both my mother's being and my grief at her death'.[6]

What could be stranger, nearer to the collapse of reason which seemed to threaten Schumann as he wrote this short and lovely piece, than to bring together, to tune together, to create an agreement between, the being of his mother, and his grief at her death? Surely there was a world of difference between her being, what she actually was in life, and his grief? But that world of difference, the difference between those we love and our grief at their loss, is, precisely, where music arises. Music does not collapse the difference. The grief and the being do not, in fact, accord with each other. Rather, it is music that accords with both. It is like a soundpost, a thing, between them, keeping them apart with its soul, but creating as it does so the space for their union, their togetherness: the space of the soul. At the same time, it creates the space for a language that, by speaking of or as music, can voice that togetherness. This language which depends on a sense of music for its very existence is the only proper language of love.

The musical language of love has an enemy brother, an eternal antagonist: the language of signification, which is also the language of expression, of representation, of science, and of philosophy. That language of signification is not the one in which Barthes and his mother lived together:

In a sense I never 'spoke' to her, never 'discoursed' in her presence, for her; we

6   Ibid., p. 43.

supposed, without saying anything of the kind to each other, that the frivolous insignificance of language, the suspension of images, must be the very space of love, its music.[7]

The suspension of images, the insignificance of language: every reader of Barthes's writing on literature will recognise in this description the condition, for him, of the literary experience. Like Derrida, like de Man, like Mallarmé nearly a century earlier, Barthes perceived literature always in unstable opposition to a non-literary approach to language. The non-literary sees in words only what they signify, represent, or express. But expression, for Barthes, is the antithesis of literature, as it is of music. His musical bête noire was singers who failed to appreciate this. He detested the art of Dietrich Fischer-Dieskau because it was 'inordinately expressive [...] dramatic, *sentimentally clear*, borne by a voice lacking in any "grain"'.[8] Fischer-Dieskau pandered to a popular taste that accepted music and art only on condition that 'they be clear, that they "translate" an emotion and represent a signified (the "meaning" of a poem)'.[9] What Barthes wanted from a singer was not an expression: it was a voice with a grain, which speaks to us of that material thing, the body, from which, like love, it issues.

Derrida had said at the beginning of his homage to de Man that it was 'with voice and with music' (323) that those present could be together in a common thought; with voice, not with the meaning of words which, like the soul, he could not bear to translate. In the same way, the words that brought together Barthes and his mother could be words of love because their task was not to signify or to express anything; it was to bear the unique grain of a voice. What Roland Barthes knew as music was not only the space of his love and of his togetherness with his mother, but also the condition of the language of that love. Would you be kind enough not to understand, not to know why, if I were to hear in that music the origin of poetry?

7   Ibid.
8   Roland Barthes, 'The Grain of the Voice', in *Image, Music, Text*, ed. and trans. by Stephen Heath (London: Fontana, 1977), pp. 179–89 (pp. 183–85).
9   Ibid., p. 185.

CHAPTER 6

❖

The Beauty of
Charles Darwin's Soul

for Heidi, musician and evolutionary biologist

Mr Darwin.

Your beautifully written autobiography contains the greatest of all challenges to those of us who love music and poetry, and also share the scientific principles that underpin your theory of evolution. For it seems to tell us something we dread to hear: that one can believe in science, or in art, but not in both.

You tell us that as you developed your theory of evolution, and became convinced by it yourself, you ceased, at the same time, to appreciate the arts. You had loved them when you were young, with a passion that we share. But you lost that love. As your thinking became rigorously scientific, it killed off your ability to enjoy art.

As a professor of word and music studies who greatly admires your thought and aspires to share your intellectual values, I was saddened by this, and worried by the possible moral of your autobiographical tale: that a true acceptance of Darwinian principles, just as it indubitably leads to a loss of faith in the creationist Christianity with which you grew up, leads also to a loss of faith in music and poetry. I wondered if there was a way to avoid that moral. I decided to look for a way of understanding your loss of faith in art that would allow one to find a new place for music and poetry, while still accepting your scientific understanding of how our species evolved.

I began from a comparison between what you wrote in 1876 in your Autobiography, and the way in which music and poetry had appeared in *The Expression of the Emotions in Man and Animals*, which you had published only a few years earlier, in 1872. Here is how you describe yourself, in your Autobiography, as a student in Cambridge when you were about twenty:

> I also got into a musical set, I believe by means of my warm-hearted friend Herbert, who took a high wrangler's degree. From associating with these men and hearing them play, I acquired a strong taste for music, and used very often to time my walks so as to hear on week days the anthem in King's College Chapel. This gave me intense pleasure, so that my backbone would sometimes shiver. I am sure that there was no affectation or mere imitation in this taste, for I used generally to go by myself to King's College, and I sometimes hired the chorister boys to sing in my rooms.[1]

[1] *The Autobiography of Charles Darwin*, ed. by Nora Barlow (New York & London: W. W. Norton, 1993), p. 61.

Three decades later, however, you had lost that strong taste for music:

> I have said that in one respect my mind has changed during the last twenty or thirty years. Up to the age of thirty, or beyond it, poetry of many kinds, such as the works of Milton, Gray, Byron, Wordsworth, Coleridge, and Shelley, gave me great pleasure, and even as a schoolboy I took intense delight in Shakespeare, especially in the historical plays. I have also said that formerly pictures gave me considerable, and music very great delight. But now for many years I cannot endure to read a line of poetry: I have tried lately to read Shakespeare, and found it so intolerably dull that it nauseated me. I have also almost lost any taste for pictures or music. — Music generally sets me thinking too energetically on what I have been at work on, instead of giving me pleasure. I retain some taste for fine scenery, but it does not cause me the exquisite delight which it formerly did. On the other hand, novels which are works of the imagination, though not of a very high order, have been for years a wonderful relief and pleasure to me, and I often bless all novelists. A surprising number have been read aloud to me, and I like all if moderately good, and if they do not end unhappily — against which a law ought to be passed. A novel, according to my taste, does not come into the first class unless it contains some person whom one can thoroughly love, and if it be a pretty woman all the better.
>
> This curious and lamentable loss of the higher aesthetic tastes is all the odder, as books on history, biographies and travels (independently of any scientific facts which they may contain), and essays on all sorts of subjects interest me as much as ever they did. My mind seems to have become a kind of machine for grinding general laws out of large collections of facts, but why this should have caused the atrophy of that part of the brain alone, on which the higher tastes depend, I cannot conceive.[2]

It is clear to you that the loss of your appreciation of the arts is somehow a consequence of your mind turning into that machine for grinding out general laws. It is also clear that you still consider the arts something noble; you refer to the 'higher tastes'. (There would be a great deal to say, in this context, about your use of the terms 'higher' and 'lower' throughout your work. We will see later that you also ascribe 'higher taste' to birds, reptiles, and fish — or at least, to female birds, reptiles, and fish. But let us leave that for now.) There is no mistaking your sense of regret at having lost access to them. The question that sticks in your mind is why; why, as your mind became a machine for grinding out general laws, it became, as a result, unable to appreciate art.

I am going to allow myself, in a moment of reckless presumption, to try to help you to understand not only why that machine for grinding general laws out of facts should have caused atrophy of the higher tastes, but also how you could have preserved those tastes.

No enterprise could concern me more directly. A century and a half after you wrote those lines, we have all come to believe that general laws ground out of large collections of facts are the archetypical form of truth. Indeed, many of the laws in which we believe most firmly were established by you, following that method. The Darwinian approach to establishing truth is now generally accepted.

2   Ibid., pp. 138–39.

It is also generally accepted that truth is a central value in universities. So if the Darwinian approach logically leads to the loss of music and poetry, then I ought to embrace that loss, and abandon everything I have worked for all my life. The only intellectually honest alternative is what I will now attempt: to demonstrate that you made a mistake. You failed to see how music and poetry could thrive in their own time, which is not the same as that of evolution. There need be no contest between them, despite their incompatibility. And the proof of this can be found in your own writing.

★   ★   ★   ★   ★

The loss of the ability to appreciate music is linked, in your Autobiography, to the loss of your belief in the immortality of the soul, and of the sense, which you had when young, that there is a sublimity in nature which speaks to us of that immortality. Your loss of that sense of natural sublimity, which most people retain, you compare to a kind of late-onset colour-blindness:

> Formerly I was led by feelings such as those just referred to, (although I do not think that the religious sentiment was ever strongly developed in me), to the firm conviction of the existence of God, and of the immortality of the soul. In my Journal I wrote that whilst standing in the midst of the grandeur of a Brazilian forest, 'it is not possible to give an adequate idea of the higher feelings of wonder, admiration, and devotion which fill and elevate the mind.' I well remember my conviction that there is more in man than the mere breath of his body. But now the grandest scenes would not cause any such convictions and feelings to rise in my mind. It may be truly said that I am like a man who has become colour-blind, and the universal belief by men of the existence of redness makes my present loss of perception of not the least value as evidence.[3]

Colour-blind people may regret their colour-blindness on the occasions when they witness other people being able to distinguish nuances they cannot see. You, in your soul-blindness, do not much regret your loss of belief in God. However, you do regret another loss, which seems (in ways you do not analyse but indicate by apposition) to have been, for you, an inevitable corollary of your soul-blindness. You have lost your sense of the sublime; not only in nature, but also in music. Without the immortal soul of divine origin, nature and music lose their power:

> The state of mind which grand scenes formerly excited in me, and which was intimately connected with a belief in God, did not essentially differ from that which is often called the sense of sublimity; and however difficult it may be to explain the genesis of this sense, it can hardly be advanced as an argument for the existence of God, any more than the powerful though vague and similar feelings excited by music.[4]

Before we go any further, let us be absolutely clear about the belief system that has supplanted the old one, and caused your blindness to the immortality of the soul.

3   Ibid., p. 91.
4   Ibid., pp. 91–92.

You express it, simply, thus: 'Everything in nature is the result of fixed laws'.[5] If we accept that everything is the result of fixed laws, then we cannot believe in the immortality of the soul. Nor is there any room for music; for we cannot believe that music is the result of fixed laws. But before we give up on any sense that music and immortality can be salvaged — let me point out that I have just deliberately misrepresented your position.

You did not say, and as far as I know never said, that everything is the result of fixed laws. You said that everything *in nature* is the result of fixed laws. The question then becomes: is everything that is, in nature? Is music in nature? Is sublimity? Or might we be able to give them a place or time beyond your nature, and thus beyond the reach of fixed laws?

For most people at your time and since, it has been possible to lose faith in the immortality of the human soul without losing a sense of the sublime, or an appreciation of music. You did not manage this. Perhaps that is because most people actually, as one can see if one analyses the way they construct their beliefs, maintain a sense that not everything is really in nature; whereas you did not.

★   ★   ★   ★   ★

In *The Expression of the Emotions in Man and Animals*, you take it as a principle that everything that humans naturally do should have a purpose that can be explained in terms of evolution. Music is certainly natural to humans, according to your definition of the natural, since all human societies, as far as we can tell, have always produced music. What evolutionary force gave rise to it? Your own hypothesis is this:

> That the habit of uttering musical sounds was first developed, as a means of courtship, in the early progenitors of man, and thus became associated with the strongest emotions of which they were capable, — namely, ardent love, rivalry and triumph.[6]

In short, music, for you, results from the force which provides the second half of the title of your foundational text on human evolution: *The Descent of Man, and Selection in Relation to Sex*.

Does an understanding of this force help us to appreciate what music is, and the means by which it produces its effects? That is not obvious. Music, for you, seems to be defined rather, in a more traditional way, as it had been since the time of the ancient Greeks, as composed of sounds, referred to as 'tones', of which each has a discrete pitch, related to the pitch of other tones by analysable mathematical proportions:

> That animals utter musical notes is familiar to every one, as we may daily hear in the singing of birds. It is a more remarkable fact that an ape, one of the Gibbons, produces an exact octave of musical sounds, ascending and descending

5   Ibid., p. 87.
6   Charles Darwin, *The Expression of the Emotions in Man and Animals*, ed. by P. Ekman (London: Harper Perennial, 2009), p. 92.

the scale by half-tones; so that this monkey 'alone of brute mammals may be said to sing.'[7] From this fact, and from the analogy of other animals, I have been led to infer that the progenitors of man probably uttered musical tones, before they had acquired the power of articulate speech; and that consequently, when the voice is used under any strong emotion, it tends to assume, through the principle of association, a musical character. We can plainly perceive, with some of the lower animals, that the males employ their voices to please the females, and that they themselves take pleasure in their own vocal utterances; but why particular sounds are uttered, and why these give pleasure cannot at present be explained.[8]

I am certainly not going to take issue with your conclusion that we cannot explain why particular sounds give pleasure. I am, however, going to take issue with the implication of your words 'at present' — 'cannot *at present* be explained'. This suggests that we should aim to produce such an explanation, and will one day be able to do so. On the contrary: I am going to try to persuade you that accepting our inability to explain the pleasure of music is the key to retaining that pleasure.

To explain is to provide a general law, inferred from a collection of facts, that tells us how those facts came about. That faculty of explanation through general laws is what you became a genius at. And it is indeed not a coincidence that as the machine for producing general laws out of collections of facts took over your brain, music quietly slipped away. Gibbons, birds, and human musicians are not possessed of, or at least not possessed by, such a machine. They make music without explaining it in terms of general laws, and without thinking they ought to be able thus to explain it. That is why they have not lost their appreciation of music.

Let us begin from the following working hypothesis: someone for whom truth must always take the form of general laws derived from facts cannot appreciate music. A corollary of this hypothesis would be that the value of music cannot be understood as such a truth. Should this be the case, could it ever be possible to produce any kind of argument that might persuade a rational man, a scientist such as yourself, to believe in music? I think that it could be; but that the argument would have to proceed indirectly, through a reflection on another art.

★   ★   ★   ★   ★

You never mention poetry as a means of expression in *The Expression of the Emotions in Man and Animals*. The word 'poetry' does not occur anywhere in the book, nor 'poetic', nor 'poem', nor indeed 'verse'. You do not appear to consider poetic language as distinct in any way from other uses of language. Which raises the question: why, then, shortly after writing the book, did you find all poetry insupportable, whereas novels you continued to find pleasurable? I shall suggest that the key to the answer lies in the little word 'line': 'I cannot endure,' you wrote, 'to

7   Actually, Darwin more than once took issue with this assertion, pointing out that other creatures, too, could be said to sing, including a rodent, the 'singing hesperomys'. See *The Expression of the Emotions in Man and Animals*, p. 92, n.; also, *The Descent of Man, and Selection in Relation to Sex* (London: Penguin, 2004), pp. 633–35.
8   Darwin, *The Expression of the Emotions in Man and Animals*, p. 92.

read a line of poetry'. There is something about the *line* of poetry that the machine for grinding out general laws cannot stomach.

You also said in your Autobiography that Shakespeare, who in your youth had delighted you, was now 'intolerably dull'. It is all the more remarkable that in *The Expression of the Emotions in Man and Animals*, Shakespeare is, of all writers, the one you quote most often. You credit him with a 'wonderful knowledge of the human mind', and it is to him, in spite of his intolerable dullness, and not to novelists, not Walter Scott for example, nor to the many writers of Shakespeare's time and since who wrote in prose about human passions, that you look for verbal descriptions of the expression of the emotions. Furthermore, it is almost always his verse that you quote; his verse set out, precisely, in lines. You never mention the fact that he writes in verse; yet it is difficult not to suppose that the verse has something to do with the exemplary quality of what he says, something to do with the reason for which you quote him rather than prose writers.

Before I talk about the quality of the verse itself, I should like to point out a very particular characteristic of what Shakespeare actually says in all the major verse extracts that you give. Let me begin with your last quotation, which is in fact the last quotation in the entire book, on the very last page. It is from *Hamlet*; it is Hamlet describing the ability of an actor, who is to perform in the play within a play, to simulate passion:

> 'Is it not monstrous that this player here,
> But in a fiction, in a dream of passion,
> Could force his soul so to his own conceit,
> That, from her working, all his visage wann'd;
> Tears in his eyes, distraction in 's aspect,
> A broken voice, and his whole function suiting
> With forms to his conceit? And all for nothing!'
> — *Hamlet*, ii, 2[9]

All for nothing. The play, the acting, the art of acting, is all for nothing. Is that to be taken simply as a condemnation? Or is that nothing, that absence of purpose, actually the essential distinctive property of the value of art? In any case, what is clear here is that Hamlet is commenting on a *display* of emotion which is not simply an *expression* of emotion. The player does not feel an emotion which he then expresses. The process begins not with an emotion, but with a thought, a conceit, to which the actor forces his soul, in the service of a fiction and of a dream. Central to this process is that word 'soul'; another word which, like poem, poetry, and verse, you never use yourself in the book; it occurs only in quotations, direct or indirect. I think we will see why. I would also like to point out that the soul, here appears as feminine — 'from her working'.

There is one other Shakespeare quotation of similar length in your book. It is from *Henry V*:

9   Ibid., p. 360.

Shakespeare sums up the chief characteristics of rage as follows:

> 'In peace there's nothing so becomes a man,
> As modest stillness and humility;
> But when the blast of war blows in our ears,
> Then imitate the action of the tiger:
> Stiffen the sinews, summon up the blood,
> Then lend the eye a terrible aspect;
> Now set the teeth, and stretch the nostril wide,
> Hold hard the breath, and bend up every spirit
> To his full height! On, on, you noblest English.'
> — *Henry V*, iii, I[10]

Certainly, Shakespeare here lists some characteristics of rage. He lists them, however, not as a set of naturally occurring features, but as a set of actions to *imitate*. Just as in the passage from *Hamlet*, we have here a putting-on of expression, an acting out of a passion. Henry is telling his men what to do. He is instructing them not on what they should feel, but on how to put on the appearance of feeling. That is clear enough from the lines you quote. It is even clearer from the actual passage in Shakespeare, of which you omit some telling lines:

> In peace there's nothing so becomes a man
> As modest stillness and humility:
> But when the blast of war blows in our ears,
> Then imitate the action of the tiger;
> Stiffen the sinews, summon up the blood,
> Disguise fair nature with hard-favour'd rage;
> Then lend the eye a terrible aspect;
> Let pry through the portage of the head
> Like the brass cannon; let the brow o'erwhelm it
> As fearfully as doth a galled rock
> O'erhang and jutty his confounded base,
> Swill'd with the wild and wasteful ocean.
> Now set the teeth and stretch the nostril wide,
> Hold hard the breath and bend up every spirit
> To his full height. On, on, you noblest English.

Note King Henry's injunction to his men to disguise nature, and to become like mineral things, unfeeling.

In our time, Mr Darwin, schoolchildren who study Shakespeare are taught that a main theme, which they ought to be able to find everywhere in his plays, is that of appearance and reality; as if Shakespeare were constantly denouncing artificiality and insincerity. This distresses me. For nothing could be further from the artistic truth of Shakespeare's verse. On the contrary, he is constantly showing how it is the imitation, the putting on, the summoning, the lending, the setting, the bending, in a word the appearance, not the reality, that creates the very movement and spirit of his art. It would be all too easy to read your quotation from Hamlet as saying that putting on emotions, as actors do, is monstrous. In fact, what Hamlet is actually

10   Ibid., p. 137.

calling monstrous, in the context, is his own inability to bend his body to act on his emotion.

But here I must stop myself, for I have been using that word improperly.

★   ★   ★   ★   ★

Shakespeare never uses the word 'emotion', anywhere in his work.

It was quite a new word in his time, and it did not have at all the sense that it acquires in your book, Mr Darwin. I say 'acquires' advisedly: your book is a key point, a pivot, in the history of that word. Now, in our century, it has the sense which you gave to it: an emotion is a specific feeling, such as rage, or grief, or love, or happiness. Very few people today are aware that this is not what it has always meant. But not long before your time, that was absolutely not its meaning, and a perusal of old dictionaries (or indeed of the quotations in the Oxford English Dictionary) makes this perfectly clear. Back in Shakespeare's day, the word had only one meaning, and that was civil unrest, riots, trouble on the streets. Gradually, during the seventeenth and eighteenth centuries, and up to the middle of the nineteenth century, it acquired a second meaning, which was an agitation of the mind or a movement of the soul.

What is, or rather was, the soul? To you, it was primarily a Christian concept. In humanity, it was that immortal part of man which God had given to him, and to him alone. You reject this as incompatible with your belief in the unity of life. You cannot allow man to have a soul that is denied to all other life forms. Man, to you, is part of nature, continuous with and not separate from all other forms of life. It used to be accepted that animals could have no emotions, because they had no souls. This notion you challenged, and indeed succeeded in destroying, by giving to the word 'emotion' a sense which allowed it to be found in animals as well as in man. The emotions of man and of animals, as you saw them, being of the same order, are made manifest in the same ways: through expression, purposeful expression, expression that we can understand as the result of evolution through natural selection. The line of poetry, however, resists that understanding.

I shall now ask the question which you never ask. Why does Shakespeare write in verse? What difference does it make? And the answer I shall give again is this: it is all for nothing.

The primary character of Shakespeare's verse is that the same form can be used for every kind of human experience. Whether he is writing of love, or of rage, or of war, or of happiness, he uses the same basic set of techniques, the same type of verse form. When we find verse forms other than iambic pentameter in Shakespeare's plays, they are normally associated with music, not with particular emotions in the Darwinian sense. In short, the line of verse, the essential character of the line of verse, is not in itself expressive of anything in particular. Having said that, it is almost always *received* as expressive of something in particular, as tutors know only too well from their students' essays. There is, it seems, an irresistible urge to feel the power of verse as being an expressive power. How can we read that passage from *Henry V* without being convinced that the pace of the verse itself is urging the soldiers on to war? Or that passage from *Hamlet* without feeling Hamlet's rage and self-disgust in the very rhythm of his speech? But in fact, there is nothing in the verse itself that provides this expression. We find the meaning first in the sense of the words; then, whether we are acting them out or reading them to ourselves, we transfer that meaning to the rhythm of the verse.

Now, that is a dynamic which accords perfectly with the concept of the soul as it pertained in Shakespeare's day, and up to your time, Mr Darwin, especially in the verse of those Romantic poets who delighted you until the machine for grinding out general laws crushed your delight. What was a soul to Shakespeare and to the Romantics? What is my soul? Is it that part of me which is unique and individual, that marks me, Peter Dayan, out? Or is it on the contrary the part of me that participates in the universal, my point of contact with something that is the same for all times and all people? Poetry at least from the Renaissance to the middle of the twentieth century is built entirely on the refusal to answer or even to recognise this question, because its most fundamental principle is that what is most personal to us is also what is most universal; that the divine is both particular and universal; and that, in the same way, God, to the extent that he exists, must be at once everywhere and in everything, and a specific will, a will which demands to be understood as not simply coterminous with the diverse and fallen world in which we live, but as a precious and unique exception. The soul has to be understood as that part of us which is divine in this sense. Its movements are thus always open to dual interpretation. On the side of the earthly, they appear to relate to specific passions, sensations, desires, and actions. On the side of the divine, they appear to transcend all such specificity. And the secret — but of course, it used to be no secret — of verse is that its movements have precisely this dual face. They lend themselves, like Shakespeare's actor, to the expression of anything we like. But in that very universality, they prove that the particular passions are in art all for nothing, and that it is the pure movement itself, the pure rhythms, which truly make poetry what it is. Fictions, dreams, conceits, and imitations, far from being a threat to poetry, are the breeding-ground of its truth; they show us how art is at once in and beyond reality, at once expressive and a constant flight from expression. For the Romantics, the word 'emotion', just like the word 'soul', was used precisely to evoke this pivot between the expressive and the universal. If I had another hour, I would spend it analysing how some well-known Romantic writers used the words 'soul' and 'emotion', and you would see what I mean: they work in the same way. But in truth, that would be unnecessary. I am sure, Mr Darwin, that you knew full well how they used to work. You knew exactly what you were doing when you abandoned the word 'soul', but diverted the word 'emotion', and saddled it with the unpoetic meaning it still has today.

Now let us turn back to music.

You acknowledge, as we have seen, that we cannot explain the pleasure music gives. This acknowledgement was common in your time. Nonetheless, you imply that one day it should be possible to explain this. Many of your contemporaries, however, especially musicians themselves, knew that it was the very condition of music to escape such explanation. By which I do not mean to say that music in general could not be explained, but rather that the intrinsic value of any particular piece of music is always in the process of escaping from explanation. In the nineteenth century, the classic way of demonstrating this was to point to the illusory nature of the naive general conviction that music expresses the sense of the words associated with it. Composers and music theorists (throughout that century and beyond) were perpetually insisting that a piece of music only appears to express the same sense as a given set of words if we know those words in advance. One can change the apparent meaning of a piece of music by changing the words around it, for example by changing or withdrawing the title or programme associated with it, as so many nineteenth- and twentieth-century composers did, from Beethoven and Berlioz to Mahler and Stravinsky. Music, like poetry, with its lines and its rhythms, has no simple relationship with the expression of the emotions. Whenever we try to explain it, we always find it is, like the line of poetry, in flight from expression. But where is it flying to? Where is it heading as it ceases to express any specific feeling? There was a time when the answer was obvious: it was heading towards the divine face of the soul, and thereby towards God. Certainly, during the course of the nineteenth century, faith in the Christian concept of the immortal soul diminished. But composers did not let that trouble their own souls. Debussy, Stravinsky, Schoenberg, and many others maintained the concept of a movement of the soul which tends to the universal and away from the expressive, that strains away from your concept of the emotions, back towards an earlier, more singular sense of emotion.

Why does Hamlet gender the player's soul as feminine? Would he have done this if the player had been a woman (as, of course, no actor on his stage could be)? I suspect not. The very point of giving him a feminine soul is what we might today call an 'othering': it is to separate the player's soul from the player himself. Poetry is born of the movement of that singular other within us.

That very singularity is what gives the great fact-grinding machine indigestion. It can only swallow facts that are multiple and can hence form part of a collection. Nor can it ever stop collecting. Science conceives of itself as a steady advance towards a goal which it has never quite reached because it is always in the process of collecting more facts and thus refining its general laws. Art, on the contrary, has always already reached a goal which we can never refine.

As you are happy to acknowledge, indeed as you explicitly say at the end of your book, your theories concerning the expression of the emotions can and will be improved by later scientists. More facts will be brought, the machine will grind them, and improved laws will result. Homer, on the other hand, cannot be improved on, and neither can Shakespeare. They are different from each other. However, that difference needs no reconciliation, whereas two different theories of evolution would need reconciliation. You and Lamarck could not both be right. But Shakespeare and Homer can both be right, because their rightness is not in what they say, it is in what happens to what they say as it traverses the forms of their lines. Science proceeds by attempting to grind out general laws from facts; poetry uses facts not to formulate laws that must be or must have been obeyed, but to dissolve those facts through fiction, dream, and simulation, so that they can fall into lines that can take us where explanation cannot go. That is why you could not allow yourself to see the essential quality of Shakespeare's verse, even as you quoted it. You could not help feeling the power of Shakespeare's genius at formulating the generally true; but nor could you admit the condition of that genius, which is the formal material quality of poetry, in Shakespeare manifested in the line, his essential instrument for giving flight to the apparent subject of poetry, letting it turn into a movement of the soul, rather than a mere expression.

★   ★   ★   ★   ★

In your book, you quote poetry, but you do not quote music. Poetry can appear at first, on the surface, as a means to express something specific. It is possible to ignore its poetic form, as you do. This allows you simultaneously to profit explicitly from what the poem expresses, and implicitly, surreptitiously, from the universality to which it tends. You borrow from Shakespeare's immortality that aura of timeless truth towards which science would like to believe it, and it alone, can lead us. You cannot do that with music because music does not appear to contribute, through what it expresses, to that collection of facts from which you grind out your laws. So you cannot blind yourself to its true implications; you cannot pretend it is an expression, as you can pretend that poetry is an expression when you quote it. I think that explains the difference, in your Autobiography, between your reaction to music, and your reaction to poetry.

Music, you find, you cannot appreciate; but it does not nauseate you. You shut your ears to an appreciation of the particular work of music itself, which can no longer delight you because you cannot admit what it is since you have lost your notion of the soul. But music still has a powerful effect on you, which is this: 'Music generally sets me thinking too energetically on what I have been at work on, instead of giving me pleasure'.[11] Why? Why 'too energetically'? Because the power of music is that movement towards the universal which is also the direction of your work. Therefore music inspires you, urging you on as King Henry urged on his men. However, your work must always, for you as a scientist, proceed by slow and careful accumulation, fuelled by collections of facts that can be ground into general laws. Music lacks that ballast. It proceeds too immediately towards the general. It whisks you away, in a tempo that you mistrust.

Poetry, though, is worse still. It is not only methodologically unsound, too energetic and too scornful of fact-collecting; it is also a constant reminder of your own self-imposed blindness to its operation. You know, you have always known, that just like music, poetry is a matter of lines, of forms, of patterns, as much as it is a matter of expression; and you feel the universality those forms exude. But you cannot allow yourself to admit to that musicality of poetry. That is why Shakespeare, now, cannot even inspire you as music does to think of your work. Rather, he interrupts your work. He tells you not to think as you have to think. He stops you; he bores you. That is why you say you have come to find his poetry

11 *The Autobiography of Charles Darwin*, p. 138.

'so intolerably dull that it nauseated me'. Nauseating, because it cannot be digested by the machine for grinding laws out of facts. Shakespeare refuses to be reduced to facts; you are too sensitive to Shakespeare's music to manage not to see this.

★   ★   ★   ★   ★

I said at the beginning that I have been wondering how you could have kept your faith in music and poetry as you developed your scientific method. Most scientists nowadays have little difficulty reconciling the two. However, one might suspect, being uncharitable, that they do this simply by not thinking through the intellectual difficulties involved. It is your powerful and uncompromising integrity that led you both to the power of your insights, and to your inability to swallow what would not fit with those insights. Is there any way you could have retained that integrity without losing your 'higher tastes'? I happen to think there is, and that the keys to it are all in your writing.

You gave us, as we have seen, in *The Expression of the Emotions in Man and Animals*, your theory of the origin of music: 'the habit of uttering musical sounds was first developed, as a means of courtship, in the early progenitors of man, and thus became associated with the strongest emotions of which they were capable, — namely, ardent love, rivalry and triumph'.[12] Music is thus associated from the beginning with love. In the same book, you assert that love is an emotion for which there exists no characteristic expression: 'Although the emotion of love [...] is one of the strongest of which the mind is capable, it can hardly be said to have any proper or peculiar means of expression'.[13] Are we, then, not to believe that music is the proper expression of love? 'Music has a wonderful power [...] of recalling in a vague and indefinite manner, those strong emotions which were felt during long-past ages, when, as is probable, our early progenitors courted each other by the aid of vocal tones'.[14] Music, certainly, has wonderful powers associated with those of love. But perhaps it does not exactly express love. Rather than expressing, it recalls, in a vague and indefinite manner, from a past long lost; and what it recalls is not exactly love itself, but courting, the search for love. Thus love may remain, despite its close association with music, that emotion for which there is no proper or peculiar means of expression. Conversely, music, despite its close association with love, is not the proper or peculiar means of expression for anything.

You write:

> As several of our strongest emotions [...] lead to the free secretion of tears, it is not surprising that music should be apt to cause our eyes to become suffused with tears [...]. Music often produces another peculiar effect. We know that every strong sensation, emotion, or excitement — extreme pain, rage, terror, joy, or the passion of love — all have a special tendency to cause the muscles to tremble; and the thrill or slight shiver which runs down the backbone and limbs of many persons when they are powerfully affected by music, seems to bear the

12   Darwin, *The Expression of the Emotions in Man and Animals*, p. 92.
13   Ibid., p. 212.
14   Ibid., p. 216.

same relation to the above trembling of the body, as a slight suffusion of tears from the power of music does to weeping from any strong and real emotion.[15]

Trembling, like tears and like music, is not the expression of a single kind of emotion. It is, rather, a movement, expressive of emotion in general — poets of your time might have said: of the movement of the soul itself. That kind of movement is indeed the true origin of art. And I think you could have allowed yourself to see that, to realise that the expression of emotion is not necessarily the expression of *an* emotion, had it not been for a mistake you make at the very end of that passage. You distinguish between the effects of music, and those of 'any strong *and real* emotion' (my emphasis). It is that concept of reality which creates the guard-rails channelling the facts to the machine. As poetry could have told you if you had let it, the movements of music and poetry work with what cannot be said to be either simply real or simply fictional. Their rhythms abolish the difference. Shakespeare's lines could have shown you that; and if you had let them do so, if you had allowed the emotion of art to be as real as any other, your backbone would have been able to shiver in your old age, as it did in your youth, to the power of music.

★ ★ ★ ★ ★

Now let us return to the question of the immortality of the soul. This is what you have to say on the subject in *The Descent of Man*:

> He who believes in the advancement of man from some low organised form, will naturally ask how does this bear on the belief in the immortality of the soul. [...] Few persons feel any anxiety from the impossibility of determining at what precise period in the development of the individual, from the first trace of a minute germinal vesicle, man becomes an immortal being; and there is no greater cause for anxiety because the period cannot possibly be determined in the gradually ascending organic scale.[16]

We cannot situate the point at which the soul appears in the development of the individual human. No more can we say where it arises in the historical process of evolution. This makes it difficult to see the soul as an exclusively human attribute. Does that mean it does not exist? Or does it, rather, exist beyond the human sphere to which it had traditionally been confined? Let us remember the association you have always made between belief in the immortal soul, and the ability to appreciate beauty.

You say in your Autobiography, as we have seen, that as you lost your belief in the immortality of the soul, you also lost the ability to feel those 'higher feelings of wonder, admiration, and devotion which fill and elevate the mind' at the sight of nature. But perhaps you did not lose those 'higher feelings' entirely, or all at once. When you wrote *The Descent of Man*, the feeling of wonder, at least, was still present in you. However, what now inspired it was not nature in general. Rather, it was the appreciation of how beauty is perceived by female pheasants:

---

15 Ibid.
16 Darwin, *The Descent of Man, and Selection in Relation to Sex*, pp. 682–83.

> I know of no fact in natural history more wonderful than that the female Argus pheasant should appreciate the exquisite shading of the ball-and-socket ornaments and the elegant patterns on the wing-feather of the male. He who thinks that the male was created as he now exists must admit that the great plumes, which prevent the wings from being used for flight, and which are displayed during courtship and at no other time in a manner quite peculiar to this one species, were given to him as an ornament. If so, he must likewise admit that the female was created and endowed with the capacity of appreciating such ornaments. I differ only in the conviction that the male Argus pheasant acquired his beauty gradually, through the preference of the females during many generations for the more highly ornamented males; the aesthetic capacity of the females having been advanced through exercise or habit, just as our own taste is gradually improved.[17]

Why should the female pheasant's appreciation of the beauty of the male affect you thus? Why should there be nothing more wonderful in nature? Specifically, why should it be more wonderful than any other reason for a creature's appreciation of the attractions of her or his potential mate? There can only be one answer to this question, but it is one you avoid confronting. It is this: you share the female Argus pheasant's 'aesthetic capacity'. What is beautiful to her, is beautiful to you. 'It is undoubtedly a marvellous fact,' you tell us, 'that she should possess this almost human degree of taste'.[18] And somehow, this marvellous fact, this kinship between her taste and yours, comforts you in the unexpressed conviction that beauty is not merely another fact of nature, subject to evolution. It is something that appears to us in a timeless category of its own, one that evolution, and nature herself, seems powerless to change. It strikes us, in a word, as immortal.

In the well-known concluding sentence to the first edition of *On the Origin of Species*, you wrote:

> There is grandeur in this view of life, with its several powers, having been originally breathed into a few forms or into one; and that, whilst this planet has gone cycling on according to the fixed law of gravity, from so simple a beginning endless forms most beautiful and most wonderful have been, and are being, evolved.[19]

'There is grandeur': grandeur, we may recall, is one of the qualities you remember having sensed in the forests of Brazil, though you lost that sensitivity in later life, as the scientific principle came to dominate your spirit. The 'beautiful' and 'wonderful' are also here, in this final sentence of *On the Origin of Species*. Why, we might ask, is there grandeur in this view of evolution, beauty and wonder in the evolved forms of life, as there was in the rainforest? Or rather: what definition of grandeur, beauty, and wonder are we here being offered? The answer is given by the origin of species, which is life 'having been originally breathed into a few forms or into one'. Let us dwell on the word 'originally', in that sentence.

17   Ibid., pp. 686–87.
18   Ibid., p. 449.
19   Charles Darwin, *On the Origin of Species* (London: John Murray, 1859), p. 490.

The origin of species, for you, is actually dual. In one sense, it is the variety wrought by natural selection. But in another sense, the origin is the single life, the single breath, 'originally breathed' in an unfathomably remote past. Our sense of wonder, beauty, and grandeur similarly, necessarily, has a dual origin. For that sense to work within us, we must admire the diversity of forms we see; no habitat on earth is more diverse than the forest that so impressed you. At the same time, we must feel, in all those forms, as you once did, a single original breath.

In *The Descent of Man*, you give us a lengthy and marvellous description of the ornamental feathers of the male Argus pheasant. You describe how they must have evolved. At every stage, what fascinates you is this: the force which must have presided over that evolution, which can only have been the aesthetic capacity of the female pheasants, coincides precisely with the highest artistic tastes of man. Let us note the recurrence of the word 'wonderful' in your description, and the references to human artists:

> The ocelli on the wing-feathers of the Argus pheasant [...] are shaded in so wonderful a manner as to resemble balls lying loose within sockets [...]. No one, I presume, will attribute the shading, which has excited the admiration of many experienced artists, to chance — to the fortuitous concourse of atoms of colouring matter. That these ornaments should have been formed through the selection of many successive variations, not one of which was originally intended to produce the ball-and-socket effect, seems as incredible as that one of Raphael's Madonnas should have been formed by the selection of chance daubs of paint made by a long succession of young artists, not one of whom intended at first to draw the human figure.[20]

The beauty of these feathers is, you say, universally acknowledged: 'these [...] ornaments have been shewn to many persons, and all have admitted that they are beautiful'.[21] All? Would everyone agree? Is taste a universal? Let me remind you of your acquired colour-blindness to the sublime. This 'all' cannot prove the beauty of the feathers, any more than a general belief in redness can prove the existence of redness, or a general religious sentiment prove the existence of God. What it does prove is your belief in the existence of their beauty, and thus in beauty itself; just as the non-colour-blind person's sense that redness is a universal category does not prove that redness exists as such, but does prove it is possible to believe in redness; and the true religious believer's faith does not prove that God exists, but does prove that faith exists.

Beauty exists, then, like redness exists, and like faith exists. The fact-grinding machine cannot admit it as part of the functioning of nature, because it will not march in step with the time of science. So you, Mr Darwin, with that part of your mind which has become a fact-grinding machine, cannot allow yourself to see it. Nonetheless, with another part of your mind, you know it is there. You let us see it, in your evocations of grandeur, wonder, and a shared aesthetic sense. More than that, indeed: you tell us how to perceive its origin, by gazing back into time beyond

20 Darwin, *The Descent of Man, and Selection in Relation to Sex*, pp. 487–88.
21 Ibid., p. 496.

the world we can imagine, to the very origin of the animal kingdom itself:

> Everyone who admits the principle of evolution, and yet feels great difficulty in admitting that female mammals, birds, reptiles, and fish, could have acquired the high taste implied by the beauty of the males, and which generally coincides with our own standard, should reflect that the nerve-cells of the brain in the highest as well as in the lowest members of the Vertebrate series, are derived from those of the common progenitor of this great Kingdom.[22]

There is something in the nerve-cells of the brain which derives from the progenitor of our Kingdom, and which has never changed since the moment of their first creation. That is why we share, so you give us to believe, the 'high taste' of female fish, reptiles, mammals, and birds, including, as we have seen, the female Argus pheasant. We have no other way to explain our perception of the presence of 'high taste' among the lower orders. It does not seem to have been inflected by evolution in the same way as other attributes. I say 'does not seem': I must emphasise, here, again, that I am attempting to describe, not a natural or scientific phenomenon, but a belief system, a perception. In the same way, it may be remembered, redness is a perception, not a fact of nature; and so, going by the analogy you propose, is faith in the immortality of the soul.

The way in which you use the word 'and' in your work is always worthy of note. It performs a dual function. It allows the fact-grinding machine to accumulate parallel facts, from which it grinds out singular conclusions. But it also, surreptitiously, in a secondary parallelism, allows you to set up alternative systems to the fact-grinding one. Nowhere is this more cunningly accomplished than in this passage, towards the end of *The Descent of Man*:

> Courage, pugnacity, perseverance, strength and size of body, weapons of all kinds, musical organs, both vocal and instrumental, bright colours and ornamental appendages, have all been indirectly gained by the one sex or the other, through the exertion of choice, the influence of love and jealousy, and the appreciation of the beautiful in sound, colour or form; and these powers of the mind manifestly depend on the development of the brain.[23]

And the appreciation of the beautiful, in sound, colour or form: the appreciation of the beautiful is not simply to be conflated with the exertion of choice, or the influence of love or jealousy. It is — how? to what extent? we cannot say — a separate category. Beauty resists reduction. It will not feed into the fact-grinding machine. We can, of course, choose or attempt to ignore it. Rationally speaking, perhaps we should be sceptical of it. We should not, perhaps, to be scientific, wonder at the aesthetic sense of the female Argus pheasant. But, Mr Darwin, you did wonder. Nothing in nature (and what, exactly, is not in nature?) has ever seemed to you more wonderful.

To you, that sense of beauty was a fact in natural history. This is not the same as saying that it is a law of nature, or obeys a law of nature. The laws of nature determine evolution, which is a succession in time. Beauty, which refuses time,

---

22   Ibid., p. 687.
23   Ibid.

escapes them. We cannot understand it any other way. If we try to see it in the light of the laws of nature, we simply become blind to it. That is what happened to you; so you tell us. But you never became so blind to it as to be unable to weave into the fabric of your writing its originality, and the consequent dynamics of its appearance and disappearance, to your eyes. That is why you are, forgive me for saying so, a poetic writer.

Like so many poets of the nineteenth century, you cannot see beauty as a true, real property of this world. Nonetheless, you are able to let us see the structures of belief that would allow us to keep faith with it, as something out of this world, something not subject to the laws of nature which govern this world. Following that cunning word 'and' — I will allow myself to repeat after you: and the appreciation of the beautiful, in sound, colour or form — you express the strange truth behind all the arts. It is an intermedial truth. The appreciation of beauty is not of the same temporal order as natural law; but it is of the same order for all media, whether they work with sound (as music is said to do), with colour (as painting does), or form (as do, doubtless, in their different ways, all the arts). I cannot help thinking, any more than you could help thinking you had become colour-blind to the immortality of the soul, that it is because you appreciated that strange intermedial parallel truth that you were also such a great scientist.

CHAPTER 7

❖

The Soul on Repeat:
Poetry

> I look at professional people like comedians in night-clubs, and I'm always
> impressed with their perfect timing, but I could never understand how they can
> bear to say exactly the same thing all the time. — ANDY WARHOL[1]

Poetry is international. It is also old, of course, very old. No one will argue with
me for saying that. But if I say it, and you agree with me, then we are all accepting
that, to some extent at least, we all know what poetry is. Otherwise, how could we
talk about its age, and recognise it in all the cultures where it appears?

So what is it? What do we agree on about it? Until quite recently, no one worried
much about defining it, any more than they worried about defining painting,
sculpture, or architecture. They knew what it was, and they knew repetition was at
its heart. To be more precise: a certain kind of codified repetition was the essential
objective marker of poetry. I will venture to make an assertion as unfashionable as
the idea that we know what poetry is: this codified repetition has been a universal
feature of all human cultures, and it remains present in all of them even now, even
though poetry written recently has often appeared to suggest we do not need it.

This codified repetition has always been of two types. Every culture uses at
least one of them. Most cultures use both. The first type is repetition of sounds;
assonance and rhyme are the archetypes of this. The second type is number:
repetition of segments which one can count. Whether one counts characters, as
in Chinese poetry, or syllables as in French, or quantities, or feet, or stresses, as in
most modern European languages, whatever it is that one counts, one counts them,
up to a normal maximum of fourteen, contained within that larger segment which
we, today, call the line. It is number, in fact, more consistently than rhyme, that
used to define poetry.

In the late nineteenth century, for reasons we will come to shortly, number in
verse began to wobble, and gradually, free verse came into its own. The old kind
of poetry, however, did not disappear, any more than painting disappeared when
photography came along, or the novel when cinema was invented, or the cinema
when television became ubiquitous. A new term had to be found to define the old
poetry, in opposition to its new sibling, free verse. That term was soon settled on. It
was: 'regular'. The poetry that we had always known, poetry as it had always been

1   Andy Warhol, *The Philosophy of Andy Warhol* (London: Penguin, 2007), p. 114.

and indeed remains today, in our reading practice, more often than not, is defined by regularity. But regularity is really nothing more than codified repetition.

As is so often the case in the history of artistic forms, it was as the old principles were being worn away that they were most lucidly explained. In about 1861, in notes for a preface to a new edition of his *Fleurs du Mal*, Baudelaire wrote:

> Qu'est-ce que la poésie? Quel est son but? De la distinction du Bien d'avec le Beau; de la Beauté dans le Mal; que le rythme et la rime répondent dans l'homme aux immortels besoins de monotonie, de symétrie et de surprise.[2]

> [What is poetry? What is its aim? Concerning the distinction between the Good and the Beautiful; concerning the Beauty in Evil; that rhythm and rhyme answer in man to the immortal needs for monotony, for symmetry, and for surprise.]

Monotony and symmetry, those fundamental needs of the human spirit according to Baudelaire, are both formed of regularity, hence of repetition. In poetry, he tells us, they are incarnated by rhythm and rhyme. Let us note the position of rhythm and rhyme in Baudelaire's formulation. They are tucked in, in such a way that we do not question for a moment that they are unquestionably a natural part of the thing called poetry. They correspond to the two kinds of codified repetition I have identified: number, and the repetition of sounds. However, let us also note that by the time he wrote this text, Baudelaire had already embarked on the production of poems with neither rhythm nor rhyme, 'sans rythme et sans rime' as he himself put it, to which he gave the name: 'poèmes en prose' [prose poems].[3] So it was already, objectively speaking, false to suggest that rhythm and rhyme were unproblematically elements of poetry. And yet he does so.

Baudelaire, then, is simultaneously telling us that codified repetition (rhythm and rhyme) is necessary to poetry, and demonstrating by his poetic practice that this is not true. Why? Why write poetry that according to his own definition is not poetry? The impulse was given by a change in the way repetition was perceived.

During the nineteenth century, repetition became a danger to poetry, as well as fundamental to poetry. No one saw that danger more clearly than Baudelaire. The archetypal manifestation of the danger is in a poem he did not write, but that he knew very well, admired, and translated (into prose — it was the only poem he ever translated): 'The Raven', by Edgar Allan Poe. It begins thus:

> Once upon a midnight dreary, while I pondered, weak and weary,
> Over many a quaint and curious volume of forgotten lore —
> While I nodded, nearly napping, suddenly there came a tapping,
> As of some one gently rapping, rapping at my chamber door.
> 'Tis some visitor,' I muttered, 'tapping at my chamber door —
> Only this and nothing more.'

2   Charles Baudelaire, *Les Fleurs du Mal* (Paris: Garnier, 1961), p. 248.
3   Charles Baudelaire, 'À Arsène Houssaye', the 'lettre-préface' he wrote to accompany the publication of several of his prose poems in the journal *La Presse*, in August 1862. It has been more widely read and commented on than any of the poems themselves, and is to be found in all modern editions of his prose poetry. See for example, Charles Baudelaire, *Petits poëmes en prose (Le Spleen de Paris)*, ed. by Robert Knopp (Paris: Gallimard, 1973), pp. 21–22.

On reading out or hearing these lines, no anglophone reader entirely escapes a certain discomfort. There is something wrong with the repetition. The rhythm seems too regular; too much monotony, not enough surprise. As for the rhymes, the second, fourth, fifth, and sixth lines all rhyme, which again seems too monotonous (and the rhyme between the fourth and fifth lines contains too many repeated words); but the first and third lines are orphans. They do not rhyme with any other line. This in itself should, perhaps, bother us. If it fails to, that is doubtless because its oddity is drowned out by the secondary oddity of the internal rhyme (dreary / weary, napping / tapping), which suggests that perhaps the real problem here is that the line breaks are not properly set out. There is such excessive repetition of so many sounds in so many semi-correct places that the noise of the repetition threatens to overwhelm both our expectations of poetry, and the very sense of the words.

That, we later discover, is the story the whole poem recounts. The story of a word that, repeated too often as a sound, turns out to have no meaning at all for the brain that utters it; and for its hearer, a meaning finally determined by its very repetition.

There was no one behind the narrator's chamber door. At his window, there was a raven, who enters, says 'Nevermore', repeats that word another five times, and never says anything else. Our poet realises that the raven knows only that one word, says it in response to every question, and doubtless has no idea that it is a word with a distinct meaning. The bird, one might say, is making a sound, but not really saying a word. Or else one might put it thus: the bird cannot mean what he says. Therefore, our poet ought logically to say to himself that there is no point in engaging in a dialogue with the bird, no possibility of an exchange with the bird of meanings mediated through words. However, he does not follow that logic. He does something entirely contrary to it, something apparently pointless, foolish, and self-destructive, something which can only work because he knows the bird will always repeat the same sound, something which for me represents the first full expression of the crisis of repetition of poetry — which is also the crisis of poetry as such.

He puts a question to the bird, as if he did not know that the bird's reply could only be a repetition of a sound. And that question is not an innocent one. It is, in fact, a question that separates out two world views: one in which the soul can resuscitate after death, and one in which it cannot.

> 'Prophet!' said I, 'thing of evil! — prophet still, if bird or devil!
> By that Heaven that bends above us — by that God we both adore —
> Tell this soul with sorrow laden if, within the distant Aidenn,
> It shall clasp a sainted maiden whom the angels name Lenore —
> Clasp a rare and radiant maiden whom the angels name Lenore.'
>   Quoth the Raven 'Nevermore.'
>
> 'Be that word our sign of parting, bird or fiend!' I shrieked, upstarting —
> 'Get thee back into the tempest and the Night's Plutonian shore!
> Leave no black plume as a token of that lie thy soul hath spoken!
> Leave my loneliness unbroken! — quit the bust above my door!

Take thy beak from out my heart, and take thy form from off my door!'
      Quoth the Raven 'Nevermore.'

And the Raven, never flitting, still is sitting, *still* is sitting
On the pallid bust of Pallas just above my chamber door;
And his eyes have all the seeming of a demon's that is dreaming,
And the lamp-light o'er him streaming throws his shadow on the floor;
And my soul from out that shadow that lies floating on the floor
      Shall be lifted — nevermore!

Let us backtrack a little. There is one question above all to which, one might have thought, our poet would like a positive response: will I meet my deceased lady love in the hereafter? One would have thought, again, that he would resist putting this question in circumstances where he could expect only a negative answer. And yet he puts that question to the raven knowing full well that the raven will answer 'Nevermore'.

But let us note that it is not exactly the narrator himself that seeks the answer to this question. It is his soul: 'Tell this soul with sorrow laden'... And the effect of the answer is to trap that same soul: 'My soul from out that shadow that lies floating on the floor | Shall be lifted — nevermore!'.

Our poet could, one might have thought, even once he had received the answer, have said to himself: ah well, I need not take that reply seriously, since the bird knows not what he says. He utters a sound only, not a word that bears meaning. That way of thinking would have been entirely in accordance with the scientific and philosophical approach to truth, meaning, and intention which came to dominate the nineteenth century. But our poet does not travel that way. He refuses to do so; and he refuses by attributing to the bird a faculty that neither the science, nor the philosophy, nor yet the established religion of his time would have allowed him. He gives the bird a soul. It is the soul, and not the bird, that speaks, knowing what it means. 'Leave no black plume as a token of the lie thy soul hath spoken!'

I think it is fair to say that most modern readers would hardly notice the word 'soul', here, despite its repetition. It occurs six times in the poem (it is doubtless a coincidence that the raven utters 'Nevermore' the same number of times), three of them in the last three stanzas. What is its function here? What is its force? Why say that the raven's soul has spoken a lie, and not the raven himself?

The bird can utter the sound 'Nevermore'; but he cannot tell a lie. To tell a lie is to say something that one knows (or should know) to be untrue. The bird does not know what he is saying; therefore, he cannot tell a lie. His soul, on the other hand, it would seem, does know what he is saying, and therefore it can tell a lie.

But what is the raven's soul? We are not explicitly told. All we know is that it seems to the poet 'as if' the bird's soul were in that fateful word 'Nevermore': 'But the Raven, sitting lonely on the placid bust, spoke only | That one word, as if his soul in that one word he did outpour'. As if the soul could pour out in that one word... pour out, perhaps, never to regain its previous seat within.

The soul, after all, had always, traditionally, before Poe's time, said the opposite of 'Nevermore'. It had been the mark of timelessness, or of eternity; of our eternity, our deathlessness. To have a soul meant to possess a divinity which could allow one to escape mortality. The question of immortality is so obviously at the heart of 'The Raven' that it is all too easy to miss. The poet has lost his beloved. He would like, we think, to believe that they will meet again, in the hereafter; that there will be a repeat elsewhere of their encounter on this earth, that a repeat of him will see a repeat of her. However, he is plainly having difficulty in believing this. In fact, alongside his desire to see her again, he seems to have a contrary urge to believe they can never meet again. That would, at least, explain his insistence on asking the raven the vital question, knowing he will get the answer 'Nevermore'. That answer terrifies him and traps his soul in a shadow (the raven's shadow, a repetition of the raven's form); but he asked for it.

I shall now give, in quite abstract form, the line of reasoning that led him to ask for it, as I see it. We shall see this line of reasoning repeatedly, rhythmically, reflected by other poets, over the following century.

★   ★   ★   ★   ★

According to the Bible, we are made in the image of God. All of us? All humans, male and female? Some of us are tall, others short, some young and some old, some have a big nose or are, as Erik Satie once claimed to be, bald from birth... Do we need to ask whether God is male or female, tall, short, young, old, big-nosed, or bald? That is obviously a stupid question. The reason it is a stupid question has to do with the dynamics of the image, of repetition.

Until the advent of what we now think of as science, an image of something was never an exact reproduction of it. The image contained something of the soul of the original; that was all it could or was expected to do. The actual material of which the image was made was quite naturally and inevitably different from that of the original. The appearance of the image could also be different. So could its position in the scale of values, between the earthly and the divine. Our earthly music did not reproduce the music of the heavens in the same way as, today, one CD can reproduce the music on another CD, or a digital download can reproduce the same track. And yet that earthly music was in the image of heavenly music; that was the only source of its value. Can one say that earthly music repeated heavenly music? Only in the same way as each human was a repeat of the divinity — or each rhyme a repeat of the same sound.

A rhyme is never an exact reproduction. A word never sounds the same twice, and it does not naturally, normally, comfortably, unproblematically rhyme with itself. ('The Raven' plays disturbing games with this principle.) Rhyme always suggests a common soul underlying a different material. The truth, for poetry and music in those times, was always in that dual relation: within the tangible matter of the art, we could sense both the diversity of tangible material forms and the unity of the invisible soul.

But the truth of science is based on exact repetition, material repetition, not on images in the old sense. For something to be scientifically true, it has to be exactly repeatable. Science is the handmaiden of industry. It allows us to produce exact copies, and to value the exact copy. The old dynamics of image and imitation saw always a shared though invisible soul beneath ever-shifting appearances; appearances whose very impermanence is to be valued to the extent that it inspires us always to look elsewhere for the permanent, the true, the immortal. Living in the age of science, we have learned, on the contrary, to look for and to observe the visible reality, the exact repetition; and the exact repetition freezes the soul, sucks the soul out of us, immobilises our soul in shadow.

Baudelaire, as well as translating Poe's 'Raven', wrote 'Les Sept Vieillards' [The Seven Old Men], which is also a poem about repetition. Like 'The Raven', it has a narrator whom it is difficult not to identify as our poet. He tells us the tale of a repetition that crossed his path one day, and of the effect of that repetition on his soul. While he was out walking, he tells us:

> Tout à coup, un vieillard dont les guenilles jaunes
> Imitaient la couleur de ce ciel pluvieux,
> Et dont l'aspect aurait fait pleuvoir les aumônes,
> Sans la méchanceté qui luisait dans ses yeux,
>
> M'apparut. On eût dit sa prunelle trempée
> Dans le fiel; son regard aiguisait les frimas,
> Et sa barbe à longs poils, roide comme une épée,
> Se projetait, pareille à celle de Judas.
>
> Il n'était pas voûté, mais cassé, son échine
> Faisant avec sa jambe un parfait angle droit,
> Si bien que son bâton, parachevant sa mine,
> Lui donnait la tournure et le pas maladroit
>
> D'un quadrupède infirme ou d'un juif à trois pattes.
> Dans la neige et la boue il allait s'empêtrant,
> Comme s'il écrasait des morts sous ses savates,
> Hostile à l'univers plutôt qu'indifférent.
>
> Son pareil le suivait: barbe, œil, dos, bâton, loques,
> Nul trait ne distinguait, du même enfer venu,
> Ce jumeau centenaire, et ces spectres baroques
> Marchaient du même pas vers un but inconnu.
>
> À quel complot infâme étais-je donc en butte,
> Ou quel méchant hasard ainsi m'humiliait?
> Car je comptai sept fois, de minute en minute,
> Ce sinistre vieillard qui se multipliait!
>
> Que celui-là qui rit de mon inquiétude
> Et qui n'est pas saisi d'un frisson fraternel
> Songe bien que malgré tant de décrépitude
> Ces sept monstres hideux avaient l'air éternel!
>
> Aurais-je, sans mourir, contemplé le huitième,
> Sosie inexorable, ironique et fatal
> Dégoûtant Phénix, fils et père de lui-même?
> — Mais je tournai le dos au cortège infernal.

Exaspéré comme un ivrogne qui voit double,
Je rentrai, je fermai ma porte, épouvanté,
Malade et morfondu, l'esprit fiévreux et trouble,
Blessé par le mystère et par l'absurdité!

Vainement ma raison voulait prendre la barre;
La tempête en jouant déroutait ses efforts,
Et mon âme dansait, dansait, vieille gabarre
Sans mâts, sur une mer monstrueuse et sans bords!

[Suddenly, an old man whose yellow rags
Imitated the colour of that rain-filled sky
And whose appearance would have made alms rain down
Had it not been for the cruelty glowing in his eyes

Appeared to me. His eye seemed soaked
In bile; his look would have sharpened a frost,
And his long-haired beard, stiff as a sword,
Stuck out, like that of Judas.

He was not bent, but broken, his spine
Making a perfect right angle with his legs,
With the result that his stick, the finishing touch,
Gave him the aspect and the clumsy gait

Of an infirm quadruped or a three-legged Jew.
He trudged on bogged down by snow and mud
As if crushing cadavers beneath his clogs,
Hostile to the universe rather than indifferent.

Following him was his likeness: beard, eye, back, stick, rags,
No detail distinguished this centenarian twin
Risen from the same hell, and these baroque spectres
Walked with the same step towards an unknown goal.

To what infamous conspiracy was I victim,
Or what cruel chance thus humiliated me?
For I counted seven times, from minute to minute,
This sinister old man who multiplied himself!

Let he who laughs at my troubled state of mind,
He who is not seized by a fraternal frisson,
Reflect on the fact that despite all their decrepitude
These seven hideous monsters appeared eternal!

Could I, without dying, have contemplated the eighth,
Inexorable clone, ironic and deathly,
Disgusting Phoenix, son and father to himself?
— But I turned my back on the infernal procession.

Exasperated like a drunkard who sees double,
I went home, I shut my door, in terror,
Sick, dragged under, my spirit feverish and murky,
Wounded by mystery and by absurdity!

In vain my reason tried to take the helm;
The storm as it played out made short work of its efforts,
And my soul danced, danced, an ancient barge
Without masts, on a monstrous and unbounded sea!]

The seven identical old men, like the raven's identical cries of 'Nevermore', mean nothing in themselves. The effect they produce is generated by their repetition. That is what takes out the poet's soul. To perceive exact repetition is to lose one's sense that this world is one of necessarily shifting appearances whose very shifting invites us to sense the blissfully unchanged soul behind them. When the appearances cease to shift, the soul loses its place within. The poet cannot fight this. He must not. He must embrace it. He must ride the terrifying wave. He must ask the raven to confirm what he already knew. We will never see our loved ones again after death. To resurrect is to repeat. And according to the modern definition of repetition, which has conquered our world, to repeat is to cast out the soul; therefore, resurrection casts out the soul.

We can now see the reason for the disquieting pattern of sound repetition in 'The Raven'. What is the difference between a good old-fashioned poetic rhyme, and the raven's repeated 'Nevermore'? In terms of versification, the answer is simple. 'Nevermore' provides the *only* rhyme in the entire poem, according to the traditional definition of rhyme (a sound at the end of the line, repeated according to an analysable pattern). It is surprisingly easy for the reader to miss that astonishing fact, unique to my knowledge in any poem in English of this length. 'The Raven' has 108 lines. Of those 108 lines, two thirds (the second, fourth, fifth, and sixth of each stanza) rhyme with 'Nevermore'. The other thirty-six lines do not fit into any pattern of end-rhymes. We have, then, on the one hand, an excess of rhyme — such monotony that we can hardly conceive it — and on the other, a disruption of rhyme. What is missing is the shading, the nuance, the subtle variety which used to combine with repetition to produce the essential force, the soulfulness of rhyme. Rhyme, in the old dispensation, kept the soul in poetry as an image, not a reproduction, an echo in which we could hear both the original voice, and the evidence of the journey across space and time which had changed its sound. It symbolised the belief that what we see in this world is a reflection of another life; that other life which belonged to the soul. If excessive repetition takes over from that logic of the image, of the echo, of the reflection, then rhyme loses its magic, and poetry is threatened with death. As are we.

The only way to save poetry is to install a new kind of relation to repetition which relies, not on a general belief in the absolute pre-existence of the soul, but on its generation, which is also a casting out, since the soul can never rest before our eyes. To do so, poetry has to call out the dynamics of scientific repetition. That is what Poe does in 'The Raven', so effectively that many anglophone readers cannot see beyond the repetition. They cannot see how the poem also, at the same time, draws out for us the soul.

⋆   ⋆   ⋆   ⋆   ⋆

I have been calling the narrator of 'The Raven' and 'Les Sept Vieillards': 'our poet'. We cannot, however, see him writing, and there is a reason for this, a reason for which literature, in this period, so often shows us a narrator who can tell a story but never quite write works of art. It, too, has to do with repetition.

The poet, our poet who does not write poetry, is, in both these poems, driven mad by repetition. He sees, he knows, he never disputes that this kind of repetition, the repetition of form, reigns supreme in the world he perceives, and displaces the soul. But in his madness, he refuses to accept that this world, the world in which repetition reigns, is all there is. His soul is driven out of him by it; still, it will not die. It cannot go to heaven, it cannot be resurrected with the body, but it does not die. And perhaps to this day it has still not died, though it may have changed its name and shape.

⋆   ⋆   ⋆   ⋆   ⋆

The danger to art represented by exact repetition continued to exercise critical as well as poetic minds throughout the twentieth century. It was nearly a century after Poe wrote 'The Raven' that Walter Benjamin produced his famous essay 'The Work of Art in the Age of Mechanical Reproduction'. He explains that the artwork loses its traditional form of value when it can be reproduced identically. The quality of what is lost by repetition he defines through the concept of authenticity. He gives to it the name 'aura', whereas I have been calling it the 'soul'. My terminology is more typical of the period up to the 1920s; his, more typical of the later period. (Andy Warhol, for example, writes of a person's unique 'aura', but avoids the word 'soul'.)[4] But in both contexts, the effect of precise repetition is the same. It is to produce an absence of meaning, an *absurdité*, which wounds the spirit of our poet, and wrests the tiller from his reason.

Benjamin writes, for example: 'Von der photographischen Platte z. B. ist eine Vielheit von Abzügen möglich; die Frage nach dem echten Abzug hat keinen Sinn' [Many prints can, for example, be taken from one photographic plate; it is therefore senseless to enquire after the authentic print].[5] In Pierre Klossowski's 1936 French translation, which Benjamin knew and which was instrumental in popularising his essay, this becomes: 'Un cliché photographique, par exemple, permet le tirage de quantité d'épreuves: en demander l'épreuve authentique serait absurde' [A photographic negative, for example, allows one to produce a number of prints; it would therefore be absurd to ask for the authentic print].[6] Why senseless? Why absurd? It is worth answering this question carefully. It requires us first to meditate on the authentic, in Benjamin's German: *echt*.

---

4   See, for example, Warhol, *The Philosophy of Andy Warhol*, p. 77.
5   Walter Benjamin, 'Das Kunstwerk im Zeitalter seiner technischen Reproduzierbarkeit', in *Gesammelte Schriften. Band 1 Teil 2* (Frankfurt: Suhrkamp, 1980), pp. 471–508 (pp. 481–82).
6   Walter Benjamin, 'L'Œuvre d'art à l'époque de sa réproduction mécanisée', trans. by Pierre Klossowski, *Zeitschrift für Sozialforschung*, 5.1 (1936), 40–68 (p. 45).

Authenticity, like the concept of the soul, demands of us that we conceive of an original which can be perceived through multiple images, all materially different, but can never itself be imitated precisely, in any material perceptible to our senses; like the music of the spheres, like the face of God. This authenticity, this inimitable inner self, is what we, generally, still today believe in as the defining quality of the human being, as well as of the work of art. If the human being can be imitated precisely, as the seven old men are precise repetitions of each other, as each photographic print (Benjamin's 'Abzug', Klossowski's 'épreuve') is exactly like another, then the soul, the aura, the authenticity is lost. The same applies to the work of art, though in a far more complex way because the relationship between the spirit of the artwork and its physical manifestation is less straightforward than the relationship between the soul and the physical human body, especially in the case of music.

However, our modern concept of reason is based entirely on the possibility and indeed the valorisation of precise reproduction. That is what reason itself has become: the ability to understand a phenomenon by identifying how it could, at least in theory, be repeated. Its opposite is the absurd, a word which acquired its modern sense — the sense it has in Baudelaire, as in Benjamin according to Klossowski — in the nineteenth century. It follows that belief in the soul or in authenticity is itself absurd. The poet of 'Les Sept Vieillards' sees absurdity in the procession of seven identical old men because it seems to prove he is wrong to believe in the uniqueness of every human being. The same absurdity, as the nineteenth century knew well, is produced by the notion that science could create a mechanism, a robot, an android, indistinguishable from a given human. Villiers de l'Isle-Adam's astonishing novel *L'Ève future* is based entirely on that sense of absurdity. It tells the tale of how the inventor Thomas Edison produces a female android apparently able to fool Edison's friend Lord Ewald into thinking that she (or it) is the woman with whom he had fallen in love. Is this absurd? Only if one believes, as Lord Ewald does, in the soul. His belief in the soul is, as Edison effortlessly demonstrates, ridiculous, absurd, from the point of view of science. What on earth can prevent a scientist from constructing an exact replica of a real human being? Surely, in principle, nothing. But somehow, somewhere, like Lord Ewald, we know that something must prevent it. We continue to believe in that unrepeatable authenticity which had always been called the soul. Without it, there is no poetry. The question then becomes: how can we persuade ourselves to believe in something that science proves to us is unreasonable? The only way is to embrace our absurdity; to play repetition at its own game, and beat it.

Excessive repetition stalks the art of the twentieth century. Andy Warhol is perhaps its greatest exponent in the field of the visual arts. Erik Satie's *Vexations*, a short piece to be repeated 847 times, haunts modern music. Ionesco's rhinoceroses stridently amplify the multiplication of Baudelaire's old men, while the empty repeated words of his *Cantatrice chauve* [The Bald Prima Donna] echo the raven's 'Nevermore'. In all these cases, as with Baudelaire, Poe, and Benjamin, a sense of absurdity emerges from the tension between the repetition, and the continued belief in the unique, the authentic, the inimitable: the soul. It is never the case that the capacity for repetition establishes itself as the one true value. Repetition is always at once incontestable, contested, and valued above all: incontestable, because it alone is reasonable; contested, because its effect on us is to suck out of us our soul; valued, because as it sucks out the soul, the poet can give us a glimpse of the sucked-out soul as it passes before our eyes. It becomes fleetingly and unstably visible, itself incontrovertible, as it is consumed in its very absurdity and in our own madness.

I will conclude by examining one shining example of how this plays out in the art of the twentieth century.

★   ★   ★   ★   ★

Tristan Tzara, like Ionesco, was a Romanian who wrote in French. As one of the founders of the Dada movement, he is often seen as a poet of absurdity. Indeed he is, of an absurdity rife and chuckling with repetition, as we shall see. As with Ionesco, Baudelaire, Poe, Benjamin, and Warhol, absurdity, in his work, always serves to prove our belief in the existence of what escapes repetition. Just as Poe's repetitive raven, taking prisoner the poet's soul, left that soul forever in view upon the floor; just as Baudelaire's seven old men, making his soul dance like an old barge, left us forever witness to that dance of the soul; so Tzara's absurd repetitions serve at once to drown Tzara in their flood of inhumanity, and to invite us to believe, however unreasonably, however absurdly, in a Tzara who eludes repetition and maintains his own lovable uniqueness with all the force of his soul.

Benjamin tells us that it is senseless to ask for the original copy of a photograph that has been printed multiple times. Is it senseless to ask for the original copy of a poem that has similarly been printed many times? We shall see that the answer to this question is not as obvious as it might seem.

I am fortunate enough to be the owner of a copy of the original edition of Tzara's book *Lampisteries, précédées des sept manifestes dada*, published in 1963, only a few months before Tzara's death.[7] Here is what we read on the last page:

> *Cet ouvrage,*
> *comportant la réédition des*
> SEPT MANIFESTES DADA
> *parus en 1924 chez Jean Budry et Cie à Paris*
> *et tirés à 300 exemplaires*
> *et l'édition originale de*
> LAMPISTERIES [...]
> *a été achevé d'imprimer le 10 octobre 1963*
> *sur les presses de la Société*
> *d'Impressions publicitaires à Montreuil.*
> *30 exemplaires numérotés*

---

7   The word *lampisteries* is not easy to translate. Its normal meaning is a place where lamps or lanterns are manufactured or stored. Should one take it, in Tzara's title, as indicating that his essays are repositories of light? It is difficult to resist the temptation to sense alternative derivations, from the verb *lamper* meaning to knock back a drink, or *lampiste*, a worker at the bottom of the chain of command.

ont été imprimés sur Hollande van Gelder
contenant chacun en hors-texte
une eau-forte gravée par Jean Arp
et tirée sur un collage original
exécuté par l'artiste.
Le cuivre a été rayé après tirage.
Tous ces exemplaires ont été signés
par l'auteur et l'illustrateur.[8]

[*This volume,*
consisting of the republication of
SEVEN DADA MANIFESTOS
originally published in 1924 by Jean Budry and Co in Paris
in a limited edition of 300 copies
and the original edition of
LAMPISTERIES [...]
the print run was finished on 10 October 1963
on the presses of the Société
d'Impressions publicitaires in Montreuil.
30 numbered copies
were printed on Van Gelder Holland paper
each containing as a separate print
an etching engraved by Jean Arp
on an original collage
created by the artist.
The copper plate was cancelled after printing.
All of these copies have been signed
by the author and by the illustrator.]

Almost all of Tristan Tzara's numerous books were published thus, in the form of artist's books, *livres d'artiste*. My copy contains, after the title page, a list of no fewer than fifty books published by Tzara, between 1916 and 1963. Almost all are illustrated, and the artists include Janco, Arp, Picabia, Juan Gris, Louis Marcoussis, Joan Miró, Paul Klee, Max Ernst, Salvador Dalí, Kandinsky, Giacometti, Matisse, Henri Laurens, Suzanne Roger, Yves Tanguy, Fernand Léger, Pablo Picasso, Georges Braque, Jacques Villon, Nejad, Sonia Delaunay, Jean Hugo, Camille Bryen... I am sure that no other writer has ever assembled such an extraordinary catalogue of visual artists as collaborators. The print runs of most of these books were limited. Not infrequently, as with my edition of *Lampisteries*, a small number of copies were printed on better paper and with an extra work of visual art, for sale of course at a higher price. My copy, alas, is not one of the thirty with an engraving by Arp. But it does have many startling illustrations by Picabia, including a portrait of Tzara as frontispiece.

Why the limited print runs and the luxury editions? Why the 'rayé après tirage'? Why the beautifully reproduced portrait? Why the signatures? One might certainly interpret all these as strategies for claiming authenticity by limiting repetition. But

---

8   Tristan Tzara, *Lampisteries, précédées des sept manifestes dada, quelques dessins de Francis Picabia* (Paris: Jean-Jacques Pauvert, 1963), p. 153.

like Poe, like Baudelaire, Tzara knows that in the modern world, authenticity only passes before our eyes after repetition has driven us mad. And he was a master of the art of that madness.

Here is a poem from the same book:

hurle hurle hurle hurle hurle hurle hurle hurle
hurle hurle hurle hurle hurle hurle hurle hurle
hurle hurle hurle hurle hurle hurle hurle hurle
hurle hurle hurle hurle hurle hurle hurle hurle
hurle hurle hurle hurle hurle hurle hurle hurle
hurle hurle hurle hurle hurle hurle hurle hurle
hurle hurle hurle hurle hurle hurle hurle hurle
hurle hurle hurle hurle hurle hurle hurle hurle
hurle hurle hurle hurle hurle hurle hurle hurle
hurle hurle hurle hurle hurle hurle hurle hurle
hurle hurle hurle hurle hurle hurle hurle hurle
hurle hurle hurle hurle hurle hurle hurle hurle
hurle hurle hurle hurle hurle hurle hurle hurle
hurle hurle hurle hurle hurle hurle hurle hurle
hurle hurle hurle hurle hurle hurle hurle hurle
hurle hurle hurle hurle hurle hurle hurle hurle
hurle hurle hurle hurle hurle hurle hurle hurle
hurle hurle hurle hurle hurle hurle hurle hurle
hurle hurle hurle hurle hurle hurle hurle hurle
hurle hurle hurle hurle hurle hurle hurle hurle
hurle hurle hurle hurle hurle hurle hurle hurle
hurle hurle hurle hurle hurle hurle hurle hurle
hurle hurle hurle hurle hurle hurle hurle hurle
Qui se trouve encore très sympathique

                                    Tristan Tzara.[9]

[howl howl howl howl howl howl howl howl
howl howl howl howl howl howl howl howl
howl howl howl howl howl howl howl howl
howl howl howl howl howl howl howl howl
howl howl howl howl howl howl howl howl
howl howl howl howl howl howl howl howl
howl howl howl howl howl howl howl howl
howl howl howl howl howl howl howl howl
howl howl howl howl howl howl howl howl
howl howl howl howl howl howl howl howl
howl howl howl howl howl howl howl howl
howl howl howl howl howl howl howl howl
howl howl howl howl howl howl howl howl
howl howl howl howl howl howl howl howl
howl howl howl howl howl howl howl howl
howl howl howl howl howl howl howl howl
howl howl howl howl howl howl howl howl

9   Ibid., p. 75.

> howl howl howl howl howl howl howl howl
> Who still finds himself most likeable
>   Tristan Tzara.]

If, for the moment, we set aside the last two lines, which take us back to the author and his opinion of himself, this poem seems to be about nothing much apart from repetition. It has no concrete subject. It describes and narrates nothing. The word 'hurle' becomes at least as meaningless as the raven's 'Nevermore'. Let us allow Benjamin to explain to us why modern poetry can thus allow itself to be apparently about nothing much:

> Als nämlich mit dem Aufkommen des ersten wirklich revolutionären Reproduktionsmittels, der Photographie [...] die Kunst das Nahen der Krise spürt, die nach weiteren hundert Jahren unverkennbar geworden ist, reagierte sie mit der Lehre vom l'art pour l'art, die eine Theologie der Kunst ist. Aus ihr ist dann weiterhin geradezu eine negative Theologie in Gestalt der Idee einer 'reinen' Kunst hervorgegangen, die nicht nur jede soziale Funktion sondern auch jede Bestimmung durch einen gegenständlichen Vorwurf ablehnt. (In der Dichtung hat Mallarmé als erster diesen Standort erreicht.)[10]

> [It was with the arrival of the first genuinely revolutionary means of reproduction, photography [...], that Art felt the approach of the crisis, which after another hundred years has become impossible to ignore. Art reacted to it with the doctrine of art for art's sake, which is a theology of art. Out of that, a negative theology later evolved, which took the form of the idea of 'pure' art, which refused, not only any social function, but also any determination by any concrete subject. (In poetry, Mallarmé was the first to occupy this position.)]

Mallarmé was also the inventor, with Manet, of the *livre d'artiste*. The very first *livre d'artiste*, published in 1875, in a limited edition of 240 copies, signed by the author and illustrator, was Mallarmé's translation of Poe's 'The Raven'. That was the foundation of the tradition which Tzara followed all his life. The artist's book is pure art, according to Benjamin's definition, because it is not determined by any subject from outside. Its only true subject lies within: between the words, and the visual art.

Similarly, the Dada movement in general, in accordance with Benjamin's formulation, refuses to allow its works to be determined by any concrete subject. A Dada poem represents nothing. It repeats nothing from the world outside it. This does not exactly mean that Dada poetry has no subject. It reproduces no subject, certainly. Nonetheless, it projects one. It throws one out, as the raven in its lie, its meaningless repeated word, revealed its soul and drew out the poet's soul, leaving it trapped on the floor.

This allows us to understand something that readers have always found difficult to formulate: the relationship between the Dada poet and the Dada poem. The Dada poet never becomes the concrete subject of the poem. We cannot see the poet in the poem. The poem does not reproduce the poet. We cannot find or settle the link between them; 'hurle' is not Tristan Tzara's expression of his soul. On the contrary; it seems a trap, from which we struggle to escape. But as we struggle

---

10 Benjamin, 'Das Kunstwerk im Zeitalter seiner technischen Reproduzierbarkeit', p. 481.

(try reading the poem out loud and see how far you get!), we may find ourselves desperately trying to imagine or to desire the ever-elusive poet, to bring the poet to life; to a kind of life that cannot be repeated. In the same way, I imagine and desire the engraving by Hans Arp that I do not have. The Dada poem does not speak its author, but it makes us dream of its author, and the dream is all the more powerful, obsessive, beautiful, for the strength of the poem's resistance. It mocks us. It tells us: you cannot see through me to the authentic soul of the poet. The soul is not within. And that is how it frees the soul.

The copper plate has been scored through after the print run. The book has only been signed thirty times. The word *hurle* has only been repeated 298 times. After which, Tzara finds himself still 'très sympathique'... So do I. I love Tristan Tzara (what does it mean to love a dead person? perhaps I should ask Poe's raven) because he draws out the soul of poetry without ever repeating it.

My beautiful book also contains Tzara's 'Note sur la poésie' [Note on poetry]. I quote:

> L'esprit porte de nouveaux rayons de possibilités: les centraliser, les ramasser sous la lentille ni physique ni définie, — populairement — L'âme. [...]
> Le poème n'est plus sujet, rythme, rime, sonorité: action formelle [...].
> Le rythme est le trot des intonations qu'on entend; il y a un rythme qu'on ne voit et qu'on n'entend pas: rayon d'un groupement intérieur vers une constellation de l'ordre. [...]
> Le reste, nommé *littérature*, est dossier de l'imbécillité humaine pour l'orientation des professeurs à venir.[11]

> [The spirit carries new rays of possibilities: the task is to centralise them, to bring them together under that lens which is neither physical nor definite, — commonly known as — The soul. [...]
> The poem is no longer subject, rhythm, rhyme, sonorities: a formal action [...].
> Rhythm is the trotting of audible intonations; there is a rhythm that one cannot see or hear: the ray of an interior grouping towards a constellation of order. [...]
> The rest, popularly known as *literature*, is a compilation of human stupidities for the guidance of future professors.]

Formal repetition, of sound in rhyme or of number in rhythm, no longer determines the poem, any more than subject. For us today, the true rhythm of poetry is one that we cannot hear. We cannot hear it because it is not actually there, in the form of the poem. What can be there, in the poem, is a repetition which denies its own value, with the aim of allowing new possibilities to be regrouped under a lens which physically does not exist, for which there is today no appropriate name, but which used to be popularly known as: the soul.

Repetition was poetic when an image was not a precise reproduction. Now, in the era of mechanical reproduction, repetition drives us mad because it drives out the soul. But we may still fancy the driven-out soul passes before our eyes, borne on an unheard rhythm.

11   Tzara, *Lampisteries*, pp. 105–06.

How can we recognise a poetic rhythm which cannot be seen or heard, which has no concrete existence? The answer is: between poetry and another medium. The artist's book, like all Tzara's books of poetry, projects the beauty of its poetry in an invisible space between the verbal and the visual. The same intermedial dynamic is at work in Baudelaire's famous evocation of the urge to create prose poetry. The soul is there; the absence of rhythm and rhyme are there; but so is music:

> Quel est celui de nous qui n'a pas, dans ses jours d'ambition, rêvé le miracle d'une prose poétique, musicale sans rythme et sans rime, assez souple et assez heurtée pour s'adapter aux mouvements lyriques de l'âme, aux ondulations de la rêverie, aux soubresauts de la conscience?[12]

> [Which of us has not, in his moments of ambitiousness, dreamt of the miracle of a poetic prose, musical without rhythm and without rhyme, both sufficiently supple and sufficiently disjointed to adapt itself to the lyrical movements of the soul, to the undulations of dream, to the joltings of conscience or of consciousness?]

The prose poetry of our dreams will be musical, even though it has no rhyme or rhythm. Music had always been, of course, even more than poetry, an art of sounds repeated (as rhyme is), and an art of rhythm. The repeated rhythms of poetry were perceived, indeed, as originally musical. If music is essentially rhythmical, and the new prose poetry has no rhythm, in what sense can that new arhythmic poetry be musical? In the same sense as that in which the raven's 'Nevermore' is a lie, spoken by the bird's soul.

Let us remember that the repeated appearances of the old men in 'Les Sept Vieillards' set the soul of our poet to dancing. Dance, like music, is traditionally an art of rhythmic repetition. The word *dansait* is the only verb in 'Les Sept Vieillards' which is immediately repeated.

Tzara, in his note on poetry, situates the inaudible rhythm of his new poetry not in dance or music, but in a constellation. Any reader of Mallarmé will recognise and appreciate the manoeuvre. What, after all, is a constellation? To begin with, is it a visual or a verbal construct? Like the artist's book, it is between. It consists of visible stars; but those stars only become a constellation when they are grouped, by the human imagination, by means of a story told in words, and a name attached to them. Nor is the image of the constellation the only Mallarmean feature of Tzara's formulation. Let us note the preposition *vers*: *towards* a constellation of order. We will never have arrived there. If we did arrive, if we installed ourselves in order, we would have lost our souls. Again.

Since we ceased to believe in the kind of image which would allow us to see ourselves as in the image of God, the repetition of the tangible has threatened the sanity of anyone who has a soul. Poetry shows us why, and how. It not infrequently stages that threat. Baudelaire, Poe, and Tzara thrust in our faces that repetition which drives us mad. They show us how this madness is the purported truth of the new humanity whose logic tells it that everything can be reproduced. No, they say; do not believe this. You cannot and do not believe it. You believe in the soul. Your

---

12   Baudelaire, 'À Arsène Houssaye'.

perception that repetition is madness proves it. True, you cannot say what the soul is, nor how it echoes in the poem. That is why you have difficulty in allowing its existence, when you are being reasonable. But if you can see that a poem resembles its author rather as it might resemble a constellation, or a dance, or a piece of music, or as each individual human used to resemble a divinity, then perhaps you will manage not to betray what poetry exhausts itself in repeating.

PART IV

❖

Gender Inequality, and Three Women's Voices

In this part, we encounter three women writers of the long nineteenth century: George Sand, Mathilde Mauté de Fleurville, and Cécile Sauvage.

Their literary status could hardly be more diverse. Mathilde Mauté wrote only one book, an autobiography centred on her marriage with the poet Paul Verlaine. It was not published in her lifetime, it has been little read since, and its real power and interest have never been recognised. Cécile Sauvage has been slightly better served. She published two volumes of poetry when she was in her twenties, which have been twice re-published since. But the print runs were never large, her many later poems were not published until after her death, and academia has taken no notice of her. George Sand, on the other hand, became in her lifetime one of the most famous and best-selling novelists in Europe. Her work was underestimated for much of the twentieth century, but her name has always been well known, many of her once neglected novels are once again being read, and she has an ardent academic following. Still, all three have one thing in common: their writing defines itself, from within and without, by its difference from a central literary tradition that is gendered as masculine.

Of course they did not accept the idea that women could not or should not write. When M. de Kératry told George Sand that, being a woman, she should make children and not books, she laughed, and shut the door in his face; both that laughter and that door-shutting resound through the century.[1] Nor, however, did they think that women could or should write in the same way as men.

Christine Battersby's wonderful book *Gender and Genius* gives us, among many other precious insights, an explanation of how women are both central to the art of the nineteenth century, and unable to identify themselves with the figure of

---

1   George Sand: 'Croyez-moi, me dit-il gravement comme j'ouvrais la dernière porte de son sanctuaire, ne faites pas de livres, faites des enfants. — Ma foi, monsieur, lui répondis-je en pouffant de rire et en lui fermant sa porte sur le nez, gardez le précepte pour vous-même, si bon vous semble' ['Believe me,' he said to me gravely as I opened the last of the doors to his sanctuary, 'do not make books; rather, make children.' 'Upon my word, sir,' I replied, unable to suppress a laugh, and shutting his door in his face, 'you may take the precept for yourself, if that takes your fancy'] (*Histoire de ma vie*, in *Œuvres autobiographiques*, ed. by Georges Lubin, 2 vols, Bibliothèque de la Pléiade (Paris: Gallimard, 1970–71), II, 150).

the Creator which looms over it.[2] Men, like the God of the Bible, create without giving birth, and what they create does not separate itself from them in the way that children separate themselves from their mother; it does not grow up to independent self-willed adulthood in the same way. George Sand, when she shut the door in M. de Kératry's face, already knew what it was to be a mother. She also knew that he would never know, or even want to know. That, for him, was his strength. It was what gave him the right to write; to create as only non-mothers can. But for her, it was also an opportunity to create a new kind of writing, in which a kind of love which M. de Kératry would never have experienced finds its place.

The three essays in this part all show how women's creativity was compressed or suppressed by the cultural establishment. In the late nineteenth and early twentieth centuries especially, that suppression was often founded on explicitly misogynistic principles. It worries me that even today, this misogyny is often not noticed. Paul Verlaine beat his wife tirelessly until she left him, and he tried to murder both her and his mother. Yet his poetry repeatedly tells us that she was a monster for having abandoned him. Verlaine's message is that a woman should always stay and let her husband beat her. She has no right to escape. Do Verlaine's readers today realise how knottily that misogynistic message is entwined with the values of his poetry? I fear not. They should.

His wife certainly knew. She read every line of verse he published with careful attention, including the revolting insults he addressed directly to her. Her response was not to contest the beauty of his poetry. She never ceased to admire it. She did not see in Verlaine's misogyny a reason for rejecting his poetry. On the other hand, she did not want to allow his dishonest portrayal of her to stand. She wanted her perspective also to be written out, and published. She did not want it to suppress or replace his verse; she just wanted it to have its place. The cultural and critical establishment, at the time, foiled her.

The cultural misogyny of that time also severely damaged Sand's reputation, and crushed the literary ambitions of many women writers apart from Mathilde Mauté. We like to think it has abated. Few European lovers of art would now say out loud that women's writing is not only essentially different from men's writing, but also essentially inferior. And yet, at the same time, the way in which we love art tends still to give a vital privilege to the kind of creativity that is associated with the figure of the non-maternal Creator, whose natural[3] identification is with the male.[4] My own sense, which I will not attempt here to justify or articulate, is

2   Christine Battersby, *Gender and Genius: Towards a Feminist Aesthetics* (London: The Women's Press, 1989).
3   I choose the word 'natural' carefully. On the question of what it might mean, please see Chapters 1 and 3 of this book.
4   The most magnificently and admirably honest expression of this natural identification remains, for me, Naomi Schor's unique book *George Sand and Idealism*. In a way that more modern critics, I suspect, simply would not dare to emulate for fear of being accused of making unacceptably gendered value judgements, she allows herself to give voice both to her admiration for Sand, and to her visceral feeling that Sand's writing can be so bad it makes her physically sick, whereas Flaubert's never is. The reason is not, we might say, the subject-matter. She writes of her reaction to one of Sand's later novels: 'it was almost literally nauseating [...] I can think of no other work I have read in my life as

that slowly, very slowly, an evolution in our love of art is taking place, which can only happen alongside a parallel evolution in our art of love, in the way we love our partners and our children; especially, in the way that parents of both genders relate to children of either gender. The complex and often contradictory pressures driving this dual evolution can, certainly, be discerned in much modern writing. However, the force of gendering in art persists. To see clearly how it works, it pays to look at the writing of the period before the 1960s, when there was much less political pressure to claim to believe in gender equality in the cultural realm. Both inequality and difference were nearer the surface, more visible, more often taken or asserted as unavoidable; their relation to art could therefore, in a sense, be thought through and represented more directly.

At the heart of the evolution of the gendering of art and of love is the question of equality. We all know, if we are honest with ourselves, that the realm of art is utterly unequal. There are songs, books, paintings that we love; these beloved works are only a tiny proportion of what has been produced. We have no time for the inferior productions of footsoldiers and epigones. Love, of course, is similarly unequal. We do not love everyone equally. To love is to distinguish. But on what grounds? And how can that distinction compose with the noble principles of equality? These are questions which used to be answered in ways determined by gender. As that determination fades, so the way in which we distinguish the objects of our love is changing. It is a slow, tortuous process, never clearly visible, in which our sense of justice and our loving instincts are not always comfortably in harmony.

The first of these essays is based on a talk given in July 2006, in Dublin City University, at the 17th International Conference of the George Sand Association, and originally published in French in the proceedings of that conference.[5] The second, on a paper given (also in French) at a conference entitled 'Valeurs plastiques, valeurs mobiles: la configuration des valeurs dans la littérature et les arts au 19e siècle', at the University of Geneva in October 2019. The third is woven around a modest contribution I would have made to the 6th Biennial Conference of the Word and Music Association Forum, in September 2020, on the theme of 'Words, Music, and Marginalisation', had I been able to attend.

---

a reader of fiction that provoked in me such a physical sense of repulsion, based not on its content but on its very form — or, rather, formlessness' (*George Sand and Idealism* (New York: Columbia University Press, 1993), p. 214). One may sense a curiously comparable combination of admiration juxtaposed with repulsion based on a gendered critique of style in Virginia Woolf's reactions to the writing of George Eliot. Woolf writes, in *A Room of One's Own*, of the type of sentence used by 'all the great novelists' (naming only men in her list of them), and tells us that it is 'a man's sentence [...] unsuited for a woman's use'. Unfortunately, no other type of sentence was available for great novel-writing. This created an eternal problem for women novelists, which they did not always solve successfully: 'George Eliot committed atrocities with it that beggar description' (*A Room of One's Own; Three Guineas*, World's Classics (Oxford: Oxford University Press, 1992), pp. 99–100).

5   Peter Dayan, 'L'Absence de la polyphonie dans les romans de George Sand', in *George Sand: intertextualité et polyphonie*, ed. by Nigel Harkness and Jacinta Wright, 2 vols (Oxford: Peter Lang, 2011), II, 93–109.

CHAPTER 8

❖

On the Absence of Polyphony in the Novels of George Sand

In the mid-1990s, I nearly managed to turn into a George Sand specialist. I had only recently discovered her. (She had been completely invisible to me when I was a student in Oxford, between 1976 and 1984; no one, as far as I can remember, ever mentioned her.) Her writing fascinated me. I went through a phase of reading almost nothing but her novels. No writer had ever given me to think so much. Alone among novelists, she seemed to me to have that rare intelligence which engenders humility and tolerance because it knows how to map the limits of intelligence. More specifically, she gave me the beginnings of an answer to a question which had always nagged at me.

How can we write about music? Why do we have such difficulty writing about what music actually is, about what makes music musical, about what distinguishes music from non-music? It was obvious enough that to address this question, I would have to think through the relationship between music and writing. But I could not see where or how to begin — until George Sand showed me the way.

As I read *Un hiver à Majorque*, *Histoire de ma vie*, *Les Maîtres sonneurs*, and *Consuelo*, I gradually began to realise that there exists a style of writing, always associated with a specific, coherent, and recognisable thematic matrix, which, once one knows how to read it, demonstrates how literature creates music by persuading us that it depends on music, and vice versa. Thus it was Sand who opened up, for me, the possibility of pursuing a vast project, an unlimited project, to explore how writers (whether themselves musicians or not) make music, create music, engender the thing we call music, in the grain of their writing. I climbed through that opening. At the same time, the field of enquiry known as 'Word and Music Studies' was beginning to emerge, with the constitution of the association of that name. I became a 'Word and Music' scholar, rather than a Sand expert.

But I remained ever grateful to Sand. At every stage of my voyage of discovery through the writing of music in literature, I have always asked myself: how would this idea work itself out if one tried to find or apply it in the context of Sand's writing? The answers have been consistently unexpected and illuminating.

If one wants to gain an understanding, the kind of understanding that can be expressed in words, of what music is, then one has to be prepared to examine closely, carefully, rigorously, the logic and the history of the words and expressions we use when we talk and write about music. It is the failure to do this which has allowed shallow and misleading notions to prevail for so long. The results of such an examination have a habit, I have always found, of upsetting received opinion, often in quite radical and concrete ways. This is certainly the case with polyphony. What follows is the record of my attempt at a close reading of the novels of George Sand, looking in them for polyphony.

★   ★   ★   ★   ★

For at least two centuries now, writers and literary critics have been in the habit of borrowing words from the musical lexicon, in order to borrow with them the aesthetic legitimacy of music. Does the literary critical use of the word 'polyphony' follow this pattern? When applied to novels, as it so often is, should we read it as an evocation of an originally musical technique or concept? How, when, and why did it enter the literary vocabulary? At least to the question of 'when', there is, I think, a generally accepted answer: the term 'polyphony' became popular in literary studies, and particularly in writing about novels, when Bakhtin became fashionable, in the last third of the twentieth century. However, as we shall see, it did not at all mean to Bakhtin what it is now generally taken to mean.

Nowadays, when critics or, indeed, students use the word 'polyphony' in relation to novels, they intend it simply to convey the sense of a multiplicity of independent voices, woven together in the texture of the novel. If we accept this sense, then it would be fair to say that George Sand's novels are, today, generally perceived as polyphonic. It is true that they have not always been so perceived, and even now, there is not unanimity on this point.[1] Nonetheless, contemporary Sand experts almost all see, and are often concerned to describe, such a multiplicity of voices in her novels.

Bakhtin himself, however, gave a far more specific sense to the word 'polyphony', a sense more clearly linked to the musical origin of the term. Polyphony for Bakhtin is absolutely not synonymous with a multiplicity of independent voices in the novel. We shall return to this point. But first, let us investigate the origin of the term, and ask what, if anything, it might have meant for Sand herself.

★   ★   ★   ★   ★

I feel able to assert with confidence, to begin with, that *polyphonie* is totally absent

---

1   See, for example, Éric Bordas, 'La Contre-polyphonie sandienne de *Consuelo*', in *Lectures de 'Consuelo, la comtesse de Rudolstadt' de George Sand*, ed. by Michèle Hecquet and Christine Planté (Lyon: Presses universitaires de Lyon, 2004), pp. 22–37. Bordas maintains that Sand's novels are not polyphonic, that on the contrary they produce a strangely monodic effect, 'effet étrangement monodique', because in them, one single voice predominates, 'celle du conteur sandien' (p. 34). I would say, rather, that the apparent single-voicedness which Bordas perceives is the result of a certain novelistic standardisation which Sand was always conscious (often explicitly so) of applying to the many voices of her characters, and that through this stylisation, if one lends an ear, one can hear an extraordinary diversity of voices in Sand, corresponding to the vast social diversity of her characters, who range from absolute monarchs to paupers, from gypsy orphans to self-satisfied aristocrats, from bourgeois intellectuals to illiterate peasants. Such is Sandian heterophony.

from the novels of George Sand. The reason is simple. *Polyphonie* would have meant nothing to her. It is a word she probably never encountered.

It is a far more recent coinage than most people realise. It hardly existed in Sand's lifetime. It is true that the first documented occurrence of *polyphonie* in French dates from the 1860s, when Sand was still alive and writing. But it was then a rare technical term, whose meaning would have been very unlikely to interest Sand. It had nothing to do with music. It was a philological term, designating graphic signs which could correspond to more than one sound. This is the only sense given by the *Grand Dictionnaire universel Larousse du XIXe siècle*, in the relevant volume which appeared in 1874, two years before Sand's death.

In the 1870s, however, the word was beginning to acquire a new sense, which, unlike the philological one, managed to enter general circulation, and soon became its primary meaning. 'Polyphony', from the 1880s, had become a musical term. It designated a musical style which originated in the sixteenth century, and whose emblematic exponent was Palestrina. The distinctive characteristic of this musical style was its use of *equal* voices. In polyphonic music, each voice sings the same words, and each voice uses the same musical material. This point is absolutely central. In fact, it is the reason for the creation of the term.

There is, of course, a reason for which a word was needed, around 1875, to designate that style, as opposed to all others. It was needed as part of a campaign which sought to redefine music history for the contemporary cultural needs of the French nation. The aim was to inspire belief in a first non-Germanic golden age of pure music.

There were aesthetic as well as nationalistic motivations behind this move. The years following 1871, in France as elsewhere (including Germany), saw the culmination of an anti-Wagnerian aesthetic movement which sought to situate the true value of music in music's formal, absolute, and (to use a term that became current a few decades later) abstract nature. This movement was to acquire an institutional base. In 1894, the Schola Cantorum de Paris was founded, with the express intention of reviving appreciation of the polyphonic style of Palestrina as an essential component of the composer's education. Among its pupils were many of the central figures behind the evolution of music in the early twentieth century, including Erik Satie, Gabrielle Buffet, and Edgard Varèse. They all studied under Vincent d'Indy. They learned that the birth of pure music, which was also by definition the one true religious music, dated from the time of Palestrina, in the sixteenth century, when the Council of Trent required composers to abandon the style of church music that was then dominant, in which one of the voices in the choir sang a well-known and often profane tune (whose profane words might be only too well known to the congregation), while the other voices wove around it different musical motifs in counterpoint. The Church objected to the evocation of profane words, but even more to the obscuring of the liturgical texts. In the new style, of which Palestrina was from the beginning the greatest master, every voice in the choir was to be given the same musical material, setting the liturgical text in the same way. All voices were to be henceforth equal. All sang the same words to the same tunes. For the anti-Wagnerians of the late nineteenth century, this Palestrinian music was more pure, more purely musical, than the style it replaced, because it relied, not on old tunes, but on the relations, the structures, the composition of the composer's own musical motifs. They gave to it the new name 'polyphony' in order to distinguish it from other styles, before and since, in which the voices were not all equal. I will allow myself to insist on this point: polyphony, from the moment when the term was invented in musicology, never meant, and never has meant, a multiplicity of different voices. On the contrary: polyphony replaced a style in which there was a multiplicity of different voices. Polyphony means a multiplicity of voices which are all in an essential sense the same as each other, all equal, all of equal importance, all equally working with the same material. Thus, an operatic ensemble is not polyphonic. A Haydn quartet is not polyphonic (give or take the occasional fugue). A song or a sonata with basso continuo is the very opposite of polyphonic. Even a mass by Lassus is not polyphonic. Polyphony is in the first place Palestrina and his school, and later, for example, Bach fugues minus their episodes.

Sand never knew the word in this sense. She died too soon. Nonetheless, she was alive during, and very much alive to, its prehistory, to the gradual blossoming since the 1830s of the concept of music which led to the need for the term 'polyphony'. A music more pure, more abstract, more egalitarian, a music of which Palestrina was both the fount and the apogee: this notion is to be found in many of her novels, but most explicitly of all in *Consuelo* and its sequel *La Comtesse de Rudolstadt*, written in the early 1840s. George Sand's way of thinking about music made her a natural ally of the musicological school which was working towards the creation of the concept of polyphony.

It is known that while she was writing *Consuelo* and *La Comtesse de Rudolstadt*, Sand looked for information on music history by consulting the *Biographie universelle des musiciens* of François-Joseph Fétis, first published in 1837. This immense, encyclopaedic project is unmistakably underpinned and driven by an entirely coherent and quite explicit set of principles concerning the evaluation of music history, and these principles are unmistakably the same, in essence, as those that were to fire the anti-Wagnerists and the founders of the Schola Cantorum half a century later. Fétis makes Palestrina the unique, emblematic master of the true ideal of music, and more specifically of the only genuinely religious music, precisely because only in the musical tradition he created are all voices rigorously equal. And already for Fétis, it is the birth of opera which betrayed music by poisoning this ideal equality.

Palestrina, Fétis tells us, 'fut le créateur du seul genre de musique d'église qui soit conforme à son objet' [the creator of the only type of church music which is adequate to its object].[2] This affirmation is at the heart of his work; and that work has a unique place in the history of French musicology. It remained for many years the most thorough, the richest, the most intellectually and philosophically coherent, the most respected, and the most consulted work of music history ever published in French, covering music from antiquity to the present. Its influence was immense. That work told the French nation that the only true church music was in the style

2   Fétis, art. 'Palestrina', in *Biographie universelle*, VII, 146.

created by Palestrina. To see how deeply rooted this conviction was in Fétis's view of music, one has only to note how he describes Bach. Bach was for Fétis, as for most musicians of his time, undeniably a great composer of religious music. Fétis calls him 'le Palestrina de l'Allemagne' [the German Palestrina].[3] Bach's virtue was to have revived the style that Palestrina had inaugurated; and to have written no operas.

The ideal Palestrinian style was created, as we have seen, in reaction against a compositional model in which only one voice carried the principal melody. From the seventeenth century, opera became the new vehicle for that anti-Palestrinian model, in which one voice stands out from the musical texture. According to Fétis's narrative, the fashion for opera led to the contamination of church music, which gradually lost the egalitarian purity conferred on it by the Palestrinian style.

Let us return to the birth of that ideal style, later to be baptised 'polyphony'. Here is how Fétis describes it:

> L'usage de composer des messes entières et des motets sur le chant d'une antienne ou sur la mélodie d'une chanson profane s'était introduit dans la musique d'église dès le treizième siècle [...]. Cet usage était d'autant plus ridicule, que pendant que trois ou quatre voix chantaient en contrepoint fugué *Kyrie-Eleyson*, ou *Gloria in excelsis*, ou *Credo*, la partie qui chantait la mélodie disait ou les paroles de l'antienne, ou même celles de la chanson italienne ou française, quelquefois lascives ou grossières. [...] [L]'indécente et ridicule conception du mélange du profane et du sacré dans la musique d'église, fut l'objet des censures du concile de Bâle, puis de celui de Trente. [...] [I]l fut décidé: 1° qu'on ne chanterait plus à l'avenir les messes et motets où des paroles différentes étaient mêlées; 2° que les messes composées sur des thèmes de chansons profanes seraient bannies à jamais. [...] Cependant, à l'exception des messes des anciens compositeurs appelées *sine nomine*, parce que les auteurs en avaient imaginé les thèmes, il n'existait pas de modèles pour la réforme qu'on voulait opérer.[4]

> [The tradition of composing motets and entire masses on the melody of an antiphon or on the tune of a secular song had been established in church music as early as the thirteenth century [...]. This tradition was all the more ridiculous in that, while three or four voices were singing in fugal counterpoint *Kyrie Eleison*, or *Gloria in excelsis*, or *Credo*, the voice which sang the melody was singing the words of the antiphon, or, worse, those of the Italian or French song, which could be coarse or lascivious [...] The indecent and ridiculous idea of mixing the sacred and the profane in church music was censured by the council of Basel, then by that of Trent. [...] It was decided that: 1° in future, no masses or motets would be sung in which different sets of words were mixed; 2° masses composed on the tunes of secular songs would be banned forever. [...] However, with the exception of those masses by old masters entitled *sine nomine*, because their composers had invented their own themes, no models were in existence for the reform that was proposed.]

Palestrina was called for, and he created, as if by a miracle, the model that the

3   Fétis, 'Résumé philosophique de l'histoire de la musique', in *Biographie universelle*, I, ccxlviii.
4   Fétis, 'Palestrina', pp. 141–43.

Church had imagined, the model of true church music, in which both the words and the musical material are the same for all the voices, and in which the total effect is one of unity, simplicity, and intelligibility.

Unfortunately, this ideal and egalitarian unity lasted but a few decades. The composer who overthrew them was another Italian: Claudio Monteverdi. Certainly, Fétis sees Monteverdi as a uniquely important composer. His innovations in harmony and instrumentation laid the groundwork for all of modern music, by introducing into music the means to express the full diversity of human passions. This expressive diversity was the fruit of a new freedom introduced into music by Monteverdi: the freedom to separate the instruments from the voices, to give to the instruments their own distinctive musical material and style, and to give to each singing voice its own material, which could have its own specific character. Thus was opera born, and thus was the Palestrinian style corrupted:

> Dès lors le caractère de la musique religieuse fut changé, et peut-être est-il permis de dire que celui qui lui convenait le mieux fut perdu. Les variétés de sonorité des instruments sont un des moyens d'expression des passions humaines, qui ne devraient pas trouver place dans la prière. Palestrina avait mieux compris qu'aucun autre le style convenable pour l'église et l'avait porté à la perfection; après lui, on a fait de belles choses d'un autre genre, mais où il y a moins de solennité, de dévotion et de convenance.[5]

> [From that moment on, the character of religious music changed, and perhaps we may say that the character which suited it best was lost. The variety in sonority of musical instruments is one of the means of expression of human passions, and these should have no place in prayer. Palestrina had understood better than anyone else the style suited to the church, and had brought it to perfection; after him, beautiful things have been wrought of a different type, but in which we find less solemnity, less devotion, less propriety.]

We see, then, that while Fétis does not use the word *polyphonie* since it did not yet exist, he clearly does have in mind the concept which that word will later name: the concept of a music for several equal voices, equal both in the words and in the musical material they develop, which is the only religious music truly adequate to its purpose, and whose tutelary figure is Palestrina. Before and after Palestrina, music, including most church music, is impure because of the distinctions made between voices, between parts, between voices and instruments; in short, because of inequality. After Palestrina, in the seventeenth and eighteenth centuries, the fertile breeding-ground for this inequality is opera. This interpretation of music history is what we find in Sand's novel.

★   ★   ★   ★   ★

Consuelo-La Comtesse de Rudolstadt is a novel well anchored to the historical and musical period in which it is set. Its action takes place between 1744 and 1774. The political regimes its characters inhabit, whether in Italy, Germany, Austria, or Bohemia, are all aristocratic, and generally despotic. The dominant musical genre

---

5   Fétis, 'Résumé philosophique de l'histoire de la musique', p. ccxx.

for the elite in these societies is opera. Church music does have an important place; true musicians take a keen interest in it, as do Consuelo herself and her teacher, the composer Nicola Porpora. But the music we witness being sung in the churches of Venice, including by Consuelo under Porpora's direction, is not of the school of Palestrina.

When, in the tenth chapter of the novel, Consuelo sings in public for the first time, she is not performing polyphony. She sings an accompanied solo. The text is religious (it is a psalm, set by Marcello). However, the song is perceived by all who hear it, not as religious music, still less as liturgical, but rather as a vehicle for the wonderful talent of Consuelo herself. Those who hear the song, when they wish to praise what they have heard, praise the singer; they praise the voice of Consuelo. They appreciate the music only through that one voice.

The composer of the song, Marcello, is himself present. He expresses his reaction using exclusively operatic terms of comparison. He compares Consuelo's singing to that of the most famous stars of the operatic stage. 'J'ai entendu la Faustina, la Romanina, la Cuzzoni, toutes les plus grandes cantatrices de l'univers; elles ne te vont pas à la cheville' [I have heard Faustina, Romanina, Cuzzoni, all the greatest singers of the universe; they are mere sparrows compared to you].[6] This listing of famed operatic sopranos is telling. It fits perfectly into the narrative that Fétis provides. Marcello's psalms were settings, for voice with basso continuo, of Italian paraphrases of biblical psalms (Sand gives the words sung by Consuelo in Italian). They were generally written, like operatic arias, as vehicles for the display of beautiful solo voices. How different from the character of Palestrina's music! The reason for the evolution is plain. True religious music, the music of Palestrina, is egalitarian. It does not allow for distinction. It therefore does not suit an aristocratic society which seeks in all things superiority, the exceptional, in a word: the star. Opera created the diva. The diva's fans then demanded the same kind of thrill from church music. And they got it.

Consuelo opens in the Republic of Venice. Being a republic, it has certain institutions which had been founded with egalitarian principles. One of those is the school of singing directed by Porpora. Consuelo is one of its pupils. We are told, in the novel's second chapter, that the Venetian state paid for their education, and in principle, only girls from poor families were admitted. However, by Consuelo's time, this principle was no longer rigorously applied. Some of the pupils came from socially superior families, and considered themselves above the others: 'Toutes ces jeunes personnes n'étaient pas également pauvres. [...] C'est pourquoi quelques-unes se permettaient d'oublier les saintes lois de l'égalité' [Not all these young ladies were equally poor [...]. That is why a certain number of them allowed themselves to forget the sacred laws of equality] (1, 46). One might ask why our narrator presumes that in this context, the laws of equality are sacred, despite the obvious fact that no such laws continued to apply in Venetian society in Consuelo's time. The answer is not explicitly given, but it soon becomes plain.

---

6   George Sand, *Consuelo; La Comtesse de Rudolstadt*, 3 vols (Meylan: L'Aurore, 1983), 1, 101. All future references to this work will be to this edition. They will be given in brackets, with the page number preceded by the volume number.

At another church service, Consuelo sings an aria by Pergolesi. Count Zustiniani, a rich and influential aristocrat, hears her, likes what he hears, and asks Porpora for the name of his talented pupil. Porpora refuses to give it. He is determined that his pupil should remain anonymous. The reason for this is that if he gave her name to the Count, it would be, for her, the first step on the road to a career as an opera singer. Pure church music should not distinguish its individual singers. But opera, of course, works on the star system.

Porpora's attempt to keep Consuelo nameless and in the bosom of the Church fails. The first chapters of *Consuelo* tell us how, despite clear and well-motivated misgivings, Consuelo does become an opera singer, eventually famed throughout Europe. The last chapters of the sequel, *La Comtesse de Rudolstadt*, mirror this: we see how and why she definitively quits the operatic stage, and returns to anonymity. For opera is, in the novel, where names are made, as equality is undone.

Consuelo begins thus:

> Oui, oui, Mesdemoiselles, hochez la tête tant qu'il vous plaira; la plus sage et la meilleure d'entre vous, c'est... Mais je ne veux pas le dire; car c'est la seule de ma classe qui ait de la modestie, et je craindrais, en la nommant, de lui faire perdre à l'instant même cette rare vertu que je vous souhaite. (I, 41)

> [Oh yes indeed, young ladies, you may shake your heads as much as you like: the wisest and the best of you is... But I shall not say it; for she is the only one in my class who has any modesty, and I might fear that by naming her I would cause her instantly to lose this rare virtue which I wish you shared.]

La Comtesse de Rudolstadt ends in the same way: with a refusal to name Consuelo. The last part of the immense work is entitled: 'Lettre de Philon à Ignace Joseph Martinowicz, Professeur de physique à l'université de Lemberg'. This letter is a good thirty pages long. Consuelo's husband Albert is named (all his many names are given). Their children are all named. But Consuelo, despite her central part in the narrative, is never named. Philon, the author of the letter, calls her only 'la Zingara' [the Gypsy]. He never seeks to know her name.

Without name, *sine nomine*: that, let us remember, is the term Fétis uses for the musical style which was the predecessor to what was to be called polyphony. The music of Palestrina, the one true religious music, is born of the nameless. But two centuries later, in Porpora's Venice, this namelessness no longer has a secure home in music. It is under threat even in liturgical music. The operatic taste of the aristocratic public thirsts even in church services for a soloist, a star, a famous name. Count Zustiniani is not to be frustrated. He discovers the name of the singer who had charmed him. Her career develops as he would have predicted and hoped. She sings in his theatre. Porpora sees it cannot be helped, and accepts the situation. After all, he is also a composer of operas. He knows full well that only the operatic system can bring the public adulation and remuneration that he himself, a child of his time, craves, and he sees that opera provides the only socially viable future for Consuelo. But as he accepts the inevitability of that future, he curses it, in the name of Palestrina.

I shall allow myself to quote at length the exchange between Porpora and Zustiniani. It sets out with admirable clarity the opposition between opera and polyphony; an opposition which turns out to define two diametrically opposed views of society and morality. Opera is the expression of a corrupt and inegalitarian society. The style of Palestrina, the proper and pure music of the Church, is the expression of an egalitarianism which no longer has its place in the contemporary world, but remains an aesthetic as well as a moral ideal:

> — Son nom? reprit le comte.
>
> — Quel nom? dit le malin professeur.
>
> — Eh, *per Dio santo!* celui de la sirène ou plutôt de l'archange que je viens d'entendre.
>
> — Et qu'en voulez-vous faire de son nom, seigneur comte? répliqua le Porpora d'un ton sévère.
>
> — Monsieur le professeur, pourquoi voulez-vous m'en faire un secret?
>
> — Je vous dirai pourquoi, si vous commencez par me dire à quelles fins vous le demandez si instamment.
>
> — N'est-ce pas un sentiment bien naturel et véritablement irrésistible, que celui qui nous pousse à connaître, à nommer et à voir les objets de notre admiration?
>
> — Eh bien, ce n'est pas là votre seul motif; laissez-moi, cher comte, vous donner ce démenti. Vous êtes grand amateur, et bon connaisseur en musique, je le sais: mais vous êtes, par-dessus tout, propriétaire du théâtre San-Samuel. Vous mettez votre gloire, encore plus que votre intérêt, à attirer les plus beaux talents et les plus belles voix d'Italie. Vous savez bien que nous donnons de bonnes leçons; que chez nous seulement se font les fortes études et se forment les grandes musiciennes. Vous nous avez déjà enlevé la Corilla; et comme elle vous sera peut-être enlevée au premier jour par un engagement avec quelque autre théâtre, vous venez rôder autour de notre école, pour voir si nous ne vous avons pas formé quelque nouvelle Corilla que vous vous tenez prêt à capturer... Voilà la vérité, monsieur le comte: avouez que j'ai dit la vérité.
>
> — Et quand cela serait, cher maestro, répondit le comte en souriant, que vous importe, et quel mal y trouvez-vous?
>
> — J'en trouve un fort grand, seigneur comte; c'est que vous corrompez, vous perdez ces pauvres créatures.
>
> — Ah ça, comment l'entendez-vous, farouche professeur? Depuis quand vous faites-vous le père gardien de ces vertus fragiles?
>
> — Je l'entends comme il faut, monsieur le comte, et ne me soucie ni de leur vertu, ni de leur fragilité; mais je me soucie de leur talent, que vous dénaturez et que vous avilissez sur vos théâtres, en leur donnant à chanter de la musique vulgaire et de mauvais goût. N'est-ce point une désolation, une honte de voir cette Corilla, qui commençait à comprendre grandement l'art sérieux, descendre du sacré au profane, de la prière au badinage, de l'autel au tréteau, du sublime au ridicule, d'Allegri et de Palestrina à Albinoni et au barbier Apollini?
>
> (I, 48–49)

['And her name?' the Count asked.

'Whose name?' countered the cunning master.

'Why, *per Dio santo!* the name of the siren, or rather the archangel, whom I have just heard.'

'And what do you intend to do with her name, my lord?' replied Porpora sternly.

'For what reason, Master Porpora, do you wish to keep it secret from me'?

'I will tell you the reason, if you begin by telling me why you are so anxious to know it.'

'Is it not a very natural and indeed irresistible impulse that drives us to want to know, to name, and to see that which we admire?'

'Come now, that is not your only motivation; allow me, dear Count, to dispute what you have said. You are a great lover and a fine connoisseur of music, this I know; but above all, you are the owner of the San-Samuel theatre. It is for you a matter of pride, even more than of self-interest, to bring to your theatre the finest talents and the most beautiful voices in Italy. You know that here, we teach well; that only in our school are girls given a solid training, and educated so that they may become great musicians. You have already taken Corilla from us; and since she may be taken away from you any day by a contract with another theatre, you prowl around our school, to see whether we might not have trained up some new Corilla, which you are ready to take as your next prey... That is the truth, Count; admit that I have spoken the truth.'

'And even if that were so, dear maestro,' answered the Count, smiling, 'what would it matter to you, and in what would you find it objectionable?'

'I find it most objectionable in this, my lord: that you corrupt these poor creatures, you lead them to perdition.'

'Goodness, o severe schoolmaster, what might you mean thereby? Since when do you deem yourself the paternal guardian of these fragile virtues?'

'I mean thereby no more than I should, Count, and my care is neither for their virtue not for their fragility; it is for their talent, which you denature and debase in your theatres, by giving them music to sing which is vulgar and tasteless. Does it not bring grief and shame to see Corilla, who was beginning to develop a fine understanding of serious art, fall from the sacred to the profane, from prayer to banter, from the altar to the stage, from the sublime to the ridiculous, from Allegri and Palestrina to Albinoni and Apollini the barber?']

Serious art, sublime art, is synonymous for Porpora with sacred art. The true sacred music is that written by Palestrina, and by Allegri in whom Fétis praises the same qualities as in Palestrina. The art of the theatre, of opera, is, on the contrary, by definition not only profane, but ridiculous. Palestrina, according to Fétis, composed only religious music; Albinoni and Apollini composed no religious music, and made their reputations as opera composers for the Venetian stage. We find, then, the same systematic opposition in Fétis, in the words of Sand's Porpora, and in the movement that created the term polyphony. True music is always religious; and the purest religious music is the genre inaugurated by Palestrina, in which no one voice stands out. It was to honour that pure music that the term 'polyphony' came into being. Born of the *sine nomine*, it is opposed to the operatic star system; egalitarian in essence, it cannot satisfy the aristocratic taste for distinction. Its polar opposite, the most false of music, is opera.

But George Sand wrote novels; and she was acutely aware that novels work like operas. There is no novel *sine nomine* — or at least, it was impossible in Sand's time to write such a novel, a novel with no named parts. It is true that Beckett, a century later, would attempt precisely that; Flaubert (later to become Sand's privileged literary interlocutor) dreamt of doing so; and, as we shall see, there is a point of view from which Dostoevsky (who loved Sand) might be seen as having aimed at that mark. Still, in all novels as Sand knew and wrote them, there is, as in an opera, a multiplicity of contrasting voices, with a matching multiplicity of names. These names and voices designate characters who are not at all equal. Characters in novels are different from each other, they speak in different ways, and indeed we often judge novelists by their talent in giving voice to these differences. Furthermore, we generally look, in a novel, among the throng of characters, for one or two exceptional ones, whom we will distinguish and who will stir our emotions. That is the novelistic version of the operatic star system. The opera and the novel are faithful reflections of the tastes of a society in which inequality and exceptionality are positive values, where Porpora's 'saintes lois de l'égalité' are foolish pipe-dreams, where Palestrinian polyphony seems at best an archaism. The novel, then, cannot be polyphonic. Like the opera, the novel incarnates the polar opposite of the polyphonic.

★   ★   ★   ★   ★

And yet we read that Bakhtin writes of the novel as polyphonic.

One might be tempted to dismiss this by suggesting that Bakhtin must simply be using the word 'polyphony' in a sense different from that which it originally had, in the late nineteenth century. That would, however, be very misleading. For Bakhtin knew full well what the word originally meant, and used it himself in that original sense.

The source of the misunderstanding may be traced back to the fact that Bakhtin uses two different words in Russian which have both been translated by 'polyphony'. One of these two words (which one might transcribe as *polifonija*) corresponds to the musicological sense of the French word *polyphonie*: it refers to the distinctive characteristics of the style of Palestrina. For the other Russian word, *raznogolosie*, 'hétérophonie est une traduction plus exacte que *polyphonie*, parce que l'accent porte non sur la pluralité mais sur la différence' [heterophony is a more precise translation than *polyphony*, because the emphasis is not on plurality but on difference]. I quote here a seminar entitled 'Le Sens exact de la polyphonie chez Bakhtine' [The Precise Meaning of Polyphony in Bakhtin] , in which we learn how the word 'polyphony' acquired for Bakhtin's epigones a sense that it did not have for Bakhtin himself, and that is wrongly attributed to him.[7] Alain Rabatel, in a splendid article entitled 'La Dialogisation au cœur du couple polyphonie/ dialogisme chez Bakhtine', arrives at the same conclusion.[8] Bakhtin, we realise, maintained the vital distinction between polyphony as a musicological concept evoking a multiplicity of *equal* voices, and heterophony, which is a linguistic or literary critical concept evoking a multiplicity of *different* voices, and which not only valorises their difference, but allows a hierarchy to be established between them.

Among Bakhtin's published works, the only one which puts to use the musical

---

7   I found this article on <http://www.anthropologielinguistique.fr/spipanthling/spip. php?article33> in 2010, but the link no longer works. The text is that of a seminar given by Francis Zimmerman in February 2006 on the concept of polyphony at the École des Hautes Études en Sciences Sociales in Paris.

8   Alain Rabatel, 'La Dialogisation au cœur du couple polyphonie/ dialogisme chez Bakhtine', *Revue Romane*, 41 (2006), 55–80.

term 'polyphony' is his book on Dostoevsky.[9] In every other case where we encounter 'polyphony' in translations of Bakhtin's writings, the word he had used was not *polifonija*, but usually, *raznogolosie*. What Bakhtin has to say about polyphony in his book on Dostoevsky is of the greatest interest for us here. The word itself appears precisely at the point where Bakhtin wishes to persuade us that between the many voices in the novel by Dostoevsky, we should perceive a certain equality. He is concerned to build a clear distinction between on the one hand, dialogism, which requires a number of different, distinctive voices, which he finds in Shakespeare as well as in Rabelais, and which characterises the novelistic style in general; and on the other hand, polyphony, which requires not only a number of voices, but a vital equality between those voices. Dostoevsky, he tells us, is the inventor of the latter, of polyphony in the novel. Just as Palestrina is the first polyphonist in music for Fétis (if I may allow myself this anachronistic use of the term), so, for Bakhtin, Dostoevsky is the first polyphonist in literature.

Bakhtin, however, never loses sight of the fact that he is borrowing a musical term. He reminds us of its metaphorical status in his literary critical discourse, and of the problems that leaves in the air. Stephen Benson brings this out beautifully in his essay 'For Want of a Better Term? Polyphony and the Value of Music in Bakhtin and Kundera'. Benson quotes Bakhtin as translated by Caryl Emerson:

> It must be noted that the comparison we draw between Dostoevsky's novel and polyphony is meant as a graphic analogy, nothing more. The image of polyphony and counterpoint only points out those new problems which arise when a novel is constructed beyond the boundaries of ordinary monologic unity, just as in music new problems arose when the boundaries of a single voice were exceeded. But the material of music and of the novel are too dissimilar for there to be anything more between them than a graphic analogy, a simple metaphor. We are transforming this metaphor into the term 'polyphonic novel,' since we have not found a more appropriate label. It should not be forgotten, however, that the term has its origins in metaphor.[10]

Bakhtin reminds us that the term, borrowed from music history, is here used metaphorically, and the analogy is rather loose. Novels do not work in the same way as choral church music. Why, then, use the term? Why invite us to think metaphorically about novels, as if they could be like music when in fact they cannot? The answer to that question is one of very wide application in literary studies. It reveals a dynamic fundamental to the reasons driving the endless recycling of terms that originate in other art forms.

Is the novel, indeed, an art form, or is it merely a kind of writing? The half-hidden motive of the analogy with music is to answer 'the former'. The novel is an art form. The strategy is to imply that it has more or less secret affinities with the

---

9   I am most grateful to my colleague Lara Ryazanova-Clarke, who has confirmed to me what Rabatel says on this topic.

10   Stephen Benson, 'For Want of a Better Term? Polyphony and the Value of Music in Bakhtin and Kundera', *Narrative*, 11.3 (2003), 292–311 (p. 296). Benson is here quoting Mikhail Bakhtin, *Problems of Dostoevsky's Poetics*, trans. by Caryl Emerson (Manchester: Manchester University Press, 1984), p. 22.

way that other arts — music, or the visual arts — operate; affinities that bind it to a community of genres whose core values go beyond their material substance, and which march together under the banner of art. This is what Bakhtin does when he tells us that the evolution of the novel has encountered issues similar to those encountered by music. But that general bringing together of the artistic media is always to be nuanced. Not all novels are equal; not all are equally artistic. The most artistic of them, the most valuable, are distinguished by the depth of their connection to the other arts. Dostoevsky's novels are like Palestrina's music not only because both can be described as polyphonic, but also because both represent similar regenerations of their genres. That is the reason for which Dostoevsky's novels deserve to be distinguished by the metaphorical link to music.

That regeneration, as we have already seen in the case of Palestrina and as we will shortly see in the case of Dostoevsky, is achieved by weaving together many equal voices. There is, certainly, here, an idealisation of 'les saintes lois de l'égalité'. Equally certainly, there are strict limits to the territory within which those sacred laws apply. Sand's Porpora, Fétis, Dostoevsky, and Bakhtin may all admire equality between the voices within the work; but they certainly do not think that all artistic voices are equal. Their exaltation of equality is always accompanied by an equally powerful exaltation of the exceptional. Palestrina and Dostoevsky are unique geniuses; they have no equals. Nor does Consuelo. (As for Porpora, he is tormented by the fact that he is not generally perceived as having that exceptional status.) Within the domain of art, as within the Church, a weaving together of equal voices remains the ideal, the purest form of composition. But that weaving can only be done, precisely, by a composer; a composer of genius. As we saw earlier, the unique purity of the Palestrinian style is a product of the fact that within it, composition is everything. The words are absolutely standard. All reference to words outside the liturgy is banned. Evocation of music from outside the composition in question is banned. Everything in the music is determined by the compositional process. The work is, one might say, nothing but composition.

Bakhtin makes it perfectly clear that this is the virtue he admires in Dostoevsky, just as Fétis admired it in Palestrina. The composition of the novel is what matters. That is the source of its aesthetic value. There remains, certainly, an obvious difference, on the surface, between polyphonic music, and the novel as Dostoevsky composed it. In musical polyphony, all the voices use the same musical material, whereas Dostoevsky gives to each voice in his novel a distinctive tone and character. But it is not this distinctiveness, this heterophony, that for Bakhtin gives Dostoevsky's novel its exceptional value. It is that he finds a way of composing with these very differences in order to ensure that, at the vital level of the structure of the word, the voices can be felt to have a certain equality between them. It is on this that Bakhtin insists.

He begins his book with a powerful condemnation of the critical tradition on Dostoevsky's novels. The error of the critics has been, he tells us, that they have been content to analyse the different voices in the novels, as if the individual character of each voice was what mattered. No; what matters is not each voice, nor its character, nor what it says, but the composition between voices that their plurality makes possible. 'The important thing in Dostoevsky's polyphony is precisely what happens *between various consciousnesses*, that is, their interaction and interdependence'; what creates the value of the novel 'is not so much the *ideological* multi-voicedness of Dostoevsky's novels as the specifically compositional application of counterpoint'.[11]

Here again, we see how Bakhtin belongs to the same grand old tradition as Sand herself. He weaves into his literary writing evocations of music, of polyphony, counterpoint, and the concept of composition (which he carefully flags as musical) in order to encourage us, indirectly and while always acknowledging the radical difference between the two arts as social phenomena and creative practices, to believe that what matters in literature is not what is said or represented, but rather a kind of force or ambition which draws us towards the compositional value of music. That same force gives a unique privilege to composition. And for Bakhtin as for Sand, that privilege given to composition is also a privilege of equality. Not equality between works; but equality of voices within the work, '*equal rights*' for each.[12] How does this equality within the work relate to the desire for equality in society, political equality? That is a fascinating and highly complex question. It lies at the heart of the plot of *Consuelo*. The driving force of the whole immense work is the question of the relationship between art, despotism, and revolutionary ambitions. No question is more fundamental. I have not space to do it justice here; but I will allow myself to point to one distinctive way in which Sand follows its ramifications.

In the society described in *Consuelo-La Comtesse de Rudolstadt*, just as in the society in which Sand lived, women could not be the equals of men when it came to composing music. That was a social fact. Consuelo herself does at one point compose music: when she is alone in a prison cell, incarcerated by arbitrary order of the King of Prussia. But she writes few of her compositions down, preferring to memorise them. Even when she acquires a stock of paper, she uses it to write diaries rather than to note her compositions. When she escapes from prison, she seems to leave those compositions behind. They are never mentioned again in the novel. No one ever hears them while she is in prison, and no one ever hears them afterwards. They are all lost; and she never tries to write music again.[13]

On the other hand, in that same society, women could perfectly well be the equals of men as singers. In Sand's novel, we meet women, castrati, and men who are all magnificent singers, and seen as such; gender does not operate as a determinant of musical skill in singing. The world of singing allows a certain equality that is not allowed in society in general. It is doubtless true, historically, that Palestrina's polyphonic style was created for boys and men rather than for women and men; but to give equality to children's voices is itself a gesture which should give us pause for thought, and by Consuelo's time it had become well established that women, too, could inhabit the egalitarian space of polyphony. Consuelo experiences from the beginning, then, a contradiction. Within her art as performer, she need recognise no superiors. But outside that sphere, as a woman of no social status, she is constantly

11   Bakhtin, *Problems of Dostoevsky's Poetics*, pp. 36, 42.
12   Ibid., pp. 6, 37.
13   See Sand, *Consuelo; La Comtesse de Rudolstadt*, III, 143–207.

reminded of her radical inferiority and of the infinitely gradated hierarchy that is the society of her time. No king is her musical superior; but a king can always put her in prison, and any king would deny her the right to publish her compositions.

The dramatic tension, and I would say the tragic undertow, in *Consuelo-La Comtesse de Rudolstadt*, is an echo of the dramatic tension in Sand's political life. The novel aims both to be a work of art, and to tell the truth about society. But equality does not function in the same way in art as in society. There seems to be no way to describe within the texture of the novel a society in which the 'saintes lois de l'égalité' function as they do within the work of art. Life is not polyphonic in the Palestrinian sense. In musical polyphony, a woman's voice (or a child's) is equal to that of a man. In Sand's social reality, that was certainly not the case. Those who dream of social equality, and even more so those who try to realise it by political action, appear in the novel either to be mad, as is Consuelo's husband Albert, or to be misled visionaries whose well-meaning projects can only lead to disaster, as are the Invisibles, the revolutionary sect which conscripts Consuelo, and whose fine-sounding ideals will, we are only too well aware, end in warfare and bloodshed.

Polyphony, then, cannot be represented in the society evoked by the novel. And yet the genius of the novelist can compose with the voices of the novel, and make them of equal weight, thus creating a kind of ideal, non-realist polyphony within the novel itself. I would contend that this, if one knows how to read her, is what Sand did, before Dostoevsky. He admired her immensely (as he made clear in the essays on her which he published in *A Writer's Diary*), and his admiration was never dissociated from his fascination with her approach to social equality. But although the voices may be woven in a manner that reminds us, as it reminded Bakhtin, of polyphony, the perspectives they represent, the things they say, remain stubbornly heterophonous. Polyphony can be composed in the novel; but it cannot be represented.

As I indicated towards the beginning of this essay, the word 'polyphony' is absent from Sand's novels. That is hardly surprising since the word barely existed in her day. What is more extraordinary, so extraordinary that we can only take it as the expression of a deep-seated principle, is that polyphony itself, the music that came to be called polyphonic, is similarly absent from her novels. Sand's characters never perform it, and never hear it performed. Many of her novels, including *Consuelo-La Comtesse de Rudolstadt*, are full of musical performances in a magnificent range of styles, from folk fiddling and rustic piping to grand opera and church psalms. They are also full of references to composers; and these composers include both Palestrina and Bach, who was, it will be remembered, according to Fétis, the German Palestrina, thanks to his ability to compose in polyphonic style. But never, in any of her novels, do we witness a performance of polyphonic music. Palestrina is never performed. Despite her master Porpora's praise of him, Consuelo never sings his music, as far as we are aware. She does sing Bach; but never the polyphonic, contrapuntal, choral Bach; only accompanied arias, in which she sings the solo part, and in which her performance is invariably described in operatic terms.

Thus the music we hear in Sand's novels has had excised from it an entire genre which is, at the same time, presented within the novel as the purest music of all. Its very purity seems to condemn it to inaudibility. This applies in all of Sand's novels, including, for example, *Les Maîtres mosaïstes* and *Rose et Blanche*. Sand admires and idealises polyphony and the 'saintes lois de l'égalité' that it epitomises, and there is a level at which we can find in her novels an emulation of those laws, a profound equality of voice similar to the *'equal rights'* Bakhtin finds in Dostoevsky. However, that level, the level at which the novel can be thought of as working like polyphonic music, is deep below the surface, at the level of composition, which even the critical genius of Bakhtin can only evoke indirectly. What we see on the surface of the novel is always a representation of society. Society is fundamentally unequal. Therefore, novelistic writing can never present to us directly that sense of ideal, pure, divine equality that we hear so immediately in polyphonic music. Polyphony symbolises an ideal. The writing of the novel can make us feel this, but we see all too clearly that novelistic writing itself would have to die before the novel could show us socialised human beings living in that ideal state.

★   ★   ★   ★   ★

I shall now offer two conclusions. The first is a summing up of the preceding argument. It concerns the use of the word 'polyphony' and the concept to which it corresponds in Bakhtin and Sand.

Bakhtin uses the Russian word which properly signifies 'polyphony' only in one context: when he wants to persuade us of the equality between the voices in the novels of Dostoevsky. A completely unconnected Russian word used by Bakhtin, with a different meaning and a non–musicological etymology, has also often been translated into English as 'polyphony' (and into French as *polyphonie*). It would be better to translate it as 'heterophony'. Bakhtin himself never confuses the two terms. They have very different applications. Heterophony is to be found in all novels. Perhaps it is a necessary condition of novelistic writing. Polyphony, on the other hand, is only to be found in its proper sense in music. Bakhtin applies it in a metaphorical sense to the novel, but in order to tell us that only one writer has achieved it. In the domain of the novel, 'Dostoevsky alone can be considered the creator of genuine polyphony', for it is only in Dostoevsky that Bakhtin finds an equality between voices such that it allows them to be the material of a composition as pure as polyphonic music.[14] Dostoevsky's voices are, to him, different from each other in tone, and in that sense they are unlike the voices in musical polyphony; however, they are like the voices in musical polyphony in the sense that the value of the work is in the composition between the voices, and in that composition, different voices have equal weight and equal rights. He remains conscious of the musicological origin of the term, which allows him both to profit from the implication of a profound affinity between art forms, and to acknowledge the equally profound differences between their materials and procedures.

George Sand, as we have seen, never used the word 'polyphony', and doubtless never came across it. Nonetheless, her novels, and in the first place *Consuelo-La*

14   Bakhtin, Problems of Dostoevsky's Poetics, p. 34.

Comtesse de Rudolstadt, show an acute awareness of the network of concepts that was shortly to result in the creation of that word. At the centre of this network is the figure of Palestrina. He created the only kind of religious music that is truly adequate to its function. The reason for that unique status is the perfect equality between parts, which means that the value of the music is in the composition between those parts. The equal relationship between the parts in this music symbolises an ideal which our inegalitarian societies are unable to realise. Indeed, we seem unable even to imagine or dream of a social state that would place men and women, and a fortiori adults and children, on the same level, as true polyphony does. The novel, like opera, is in its very essence the expression of the inegalitarian social construct in which we live, and in which the divine laws of equality remain nothing more than an aspiration, a vision destined to frustrate those who pursue it. Polyphony, in the novels of George Sand as in all novels, is therefore never immediately present. It can only be represented as an inaccessible ideal, a horizon of the novelistic genre, at which that genre would collude in its own dissolution.

My second conclusion concerns the origin of Palestrina himself. After all, although polyphony is never named in Sand's novels, Palestrina certainly is named, and his name is much praised.

That name was not the composer's birth name. It comes from the town called Palestrina, near Rome, whence the composer was thought to come. In Sand's time, this name was frequently rendered in French as 'Palestrine' (one finds it in that form, for example, in Stendhal). A town of that name is to be found in *Consuelo*. It is, however, confusingly, near Venice, not near Rome. Are we to take it as the town which gave the composer his famous name? Simone Vierne, in her edition of the novel, provides the following note on this subject:

> Il s'agit du village de Pellestrina, qui ferme avec Chioggia la lagune de Venise au Sud. G. Sand l'appelle aussi Palestrine dans les *Lettres d'un voyageur*. Y a-t-il confusion avec la petite ville de la campagne romaine, Palestrina (d'où était originaire le compositeur du même nom, ou plutôt surnom, cité par G. Sand à plusieurs reprises dans le roman)? (I, 485)

> [The reference is in fact to the village of Pellestrina, which, with Chioggia, guards the southern entrance to the lagoon of Venice. G. Sand also refers to it as 'Palestrine' in *Letters of a Voyager*. Might she be confusing it with Palestrina, the little town of the *campagna romana* (whence came the composer of the same name, or rather pseudonym, mentioned several times by G. Sand in the novel)?]

What, though, could have inspired or motivated such a confusion? Why might Sand have wanted to attribute to that Venetian village the name of the father of polyphony?

'Palestrine', in *Consuelo* as, for example, in *Lettres d'un voyageur*, is, for Sand, the port to which one travels when one leaves Venice, heading for terra firma. This allows for the creation of a highly charged musicological topography. Venice is the birthplace of opera. It was in Venice that Monteverdi — I quote, somewhat at random, the *Robert 2* encyclopaedia — 'abandonne définitivement la polyphonie du XVIe s. pour une expression lyrique du drame humain' [definitively abandoned

16th-century polyphony, replacing it with a lyrical expression of human drama]. In Chapter xx of *Consuelo*, Consuelo finally leaves Venice, because she is disgusted by its human dramas, which are also its operatic intrigues. She travels over land, towards Bohemia, in search of a different kind of music and of a divine social equality, which she will never see realised (except, perhaps, in the madness of her husband Albert). Her departure from Venice thus represents the rejection of an entire social and artistic system, which is also the system which the novel will come to represent. That departure is described to us in the following terms: 'Elle s'est embarquée pour Palestrine au jour naissant' (I, 176–77) [She embarked for Palestrina as the day dawned]. In the novel, we never see her arrive there.

CHAPTER 9

❖

Hearing Music, Past Misogyny:
Mathilde Mauté and Paul Verlaine

Back in the 1980s — in the days of Mrs Thatcher — when I was a postgraduate student, then a Junior Research Fellow, then a fresh-faced lecturer in French, it was a generally accepted principle, in the academic circles I knew, that the values of literary study were compatible with our moral, political, and social values. Reading literature, we thought, was a progressive thing to do. I myself wanted to believe this was true, in spite of what Baudelaire and Flaubert proclaimed, in spite of the plain fact that the creators who have most powerfully influenced our conception of the arts are also those who require us most insistently to reflect on the abominable possibility that art does not serve the ends of progress.[1] Gradually, over many years, I learned to admit to myself the truth: all too often, the values that drive the art we find most precious seem to be in an unholy alliance with the most unpleasant social attitudes. This discovery was particularly painful to me because of the gender politics associated with it.

I have inherited from my mother a deep-rooted intolerance of sexism. She particularly taught me to abominate that kind of misogyny that orders women, because they are women, to be silent and not to rebel when they are mistreated by men. As I studied the literature of the end of the nineteenth century in France, I was fascinated and revolted to observe how this strain of misogyny was gaining in strength and in self-confidence at that time. I certainly found it easier to enjoy and admire the work of artists who, at the very least, did not participate actively in this intensification of misogyny. But I had to be honest with myself: I saw that often the art that had the most lasting influence, the art which still, today, we find most self-evidently, incontestably beautiful, seemed to be fed by a subterranean channel linking it to that misogyny. I wanted to understand how and why. One case seemed to me, and still seems, exemplary: that of Verlaine and his music. It is exemplary both because of what we can see in Verlaine's own writing, and because his wife

---

1   To give just one example of the endless uncompromising assertions of this opposition between art on the one hand, and morality and science (those allies of progress) on the other: 'La poésie ne peut pas, sous peine de mort ou de déchéance, s'assimiler à la science ou à la morale' [Poetry cannot assimilate itself to science or to morality; to do so would lead to its downfall or death]: Charles Baudelaire, 'Théophile Gautier', in Œuvres complètes, ed. by Claude Pichois, 2 vols, Bibliothèque de la Pléiade (Paris: Gallimard, 1975–76), II, 113.

Mathilde Mauté, who (along with his mother) was the victim of his murderous violence, left her own memoirs, of admirable lucidity, which we can compare with his.

★   ★   ★   ★   ★

Everyone who knows anything about French poetry knows that Verlaine is a great poet.

Everyone similarly knows that he numbers among the poets for whom poetry must be musical. Poetry, for Verlaine, is defined, is marked out from other uses of language, by its profound affinity with music. 'De la musique avant toute chose' [Music before any thing]: thus begins his 'Art poétique'.

There is something else that everyone knows about Verlaine: he was not always saintly. He drank a great deal, he had many lovers of both sexes whom he did not always treat kindly, he shot Rimbaud and was imprisoned for that act in 1873. This is all true, certainly. Who remembers that he was imprisoned again, in 1885, for assaulting his mother and threatening to murder her? He had, indeed, previously attempted to kill her, so the threat deserved to be taken seriously. He had also attempted to murder his wife. And he tells us — 'admits' would not be the right word, for he appears not in the least ashamed of it — that he slapped and kicked his wife regularly for most of their married life together. In short, he had a long record of violence against women. It has never been a secret. But it is not much discussed, and when it is mentioned by biographers and critics, it is generally ascribed, as we shall see, to his alcoholism.

There is nothing surprising about that. Violence against women is often attributed to alcohol, as if that were a self-sufficient stand-alone motivation. If one actually reads the autobiographical writings of Verlaine and his wife, however, one discovers a different truth. I find that different truth echoed in Verlaine's verse. In fact, it is a fundamental principle of his art.

Verlaine's wife, Mathilde Mauté de Fleurville, was a most remarkable woman; not at all the naive bourgeois snob that his biographers have usually portrayed. She had indomitable strength of character. She was not the kind of woman to allow herself to be maltreated without reacting. Both her parents similarly had pride and strength of character, and they supported her fully when she revolted against the violence of Verlaine. The Mauté family, once the evidence that Verlaine could not be trusted became incontrovertible, went to court and secured, not only a legal separation, but what we might call a banning order, forbidding Verlaine to enter the house in which Mathilde lived with their young son Georges. And when, a decade and a half later, divorce became legal, she divorced him. Verlaine found all this outrageous and incomprehensible. How dare they tell him that he did not have the right to take back his wife? It was ridiculous, it was childish, it was a fundamental misrecognition of what he was, he, Paul Verlaine, a man and a husband. He never showed the least trace of understanding that the reason she left him was to escape from his violence.

Certainly, up to that point, there is nothing unusual in his reaction. Millions of husbands have believed they had the right to beat their wives, and when their wives revolted, they found that revolt not only intolerable but impossible to understand. Their values were clear, and they did not admit for a woman to leave a man just because he beat her. But what is exceptional, exemplary, and particularly troubling in the case of Verlaine is the clarity of the connection he establishes between those values, the values of the man who cannot allow for his wife to defend herself against him, and the value of music in poetry.

★　★　★　★　★

Here is how Verlaine, in his *Confessions*, describes the first time he hit his wife. The scene is during the Franco-Prussian War, in January 1871. Paul and Mathilde Verlaine are living in Paris, as are Mathilde's parents, while the city is besieged and bombarded by the Prussian army. Paul's day job is as a bureaucrat for the Paris city council:

> Le lendemain [...] je rentrais de meilleure heure que d'ordinaire, mon travail à l'Hôtel de Ville terminé, ma femme n'y était pas.
> 'Madame a dit en partant qu'elle reviendrait juste pour dîner: elle est chez ses parents.'
> Or, ses parents, par une étrange stratégie en vue d'éviter le bombardement, avaient quitté leur maison de Montmartre pour prendre un appartement boulevard Saint-Germain [...] je fis le mauvais geste d'aller là [...]. Bien entendu, je trouvai ma femme qui m'accueillit même avec un plaisir sans nul doute sincère, mais qui, dans les dispositions d'esprit où je me trouvais, me parut comme ironique, — et le soir, chez nous, après un dîner, brûlé, de cheval et de conserves de champignons, se produisirent la seconde scène et — la première claque. [...]
> Ç'allait, parbleu! ne plus finir. Qui a bu boira [...] ce fut toujours à recommencer. Tel un jeu de balles, — de *foot ball* car cela en venait trop souvent jusqu'au trépignement.[2]

> [The next day [...] when I came home, earlier than usual since my work at the town hall was finished, my wife was not there.
> 'Madame, when she left, said she would come back just in time for dinner: she has gone to her parents' house.'
> Now her parents, as a bizarre strategy to avoid the bombardment, had left their house in Montmartre, and taken a flat in the boulevard Saint-Germain [...] I went there, not perhaps from the best of motives [...]. Naturally, I found my wife, and she welcomed me, indeed with a pleasure that was certainly sincere, but which, given the current disposition of my spirits, seemed to me ironic, — and that evening, when we had returned home, after a burned dinner of horsemeat and preserved mushrooms, came the second scene and — the first slap. [...]
> There was to be no end to that. He who has tasted of that wine will always return to it [...] it was always ready to start up again. Like a ball game, — a football game, since too often it ended up with stamping feet.]

This was true. Once he had begun, he never stopped. Nor did he limit himself to

---

2   Paul Verlaine, *Confessions* (Paris: Magnard, 2002), pp. 180–82.

slapping and kicking her. As we shall see, a year later, on 13 January 1872, when they were living with her parents, he tried to strangle her (as he had already tried to strangle his own mother), and she might well have died if her father, roused by her cries, had not pulled Verlaine away. That episode was a turning point. Verlaine had also flung their baby son against the wall, and Mathilde feared for both her life and that of the child. A doctor was called to take note of the injuries to Mathilde's neck. Over the following six months, Mathilde did her best to believe in the possibility that Paul might change his ways. He did not. They met for the last time in July 1872, in circumstances we will shortly examine; after that, she began the legal process which led to separation.

The determination of Mathilde and of her parents to secure and maintain this separation may seem legitimate and comprehensible to us. But it never seemed so to Verlaine. For more than fifteen years, he expressed in his published verse his incomprehension, indignation, and contempt for the woman who had dared to do this. One of the first in the long series of poems in which he told his readers what he thought of his wife's behaviour was 'Child Wife' (the original title is in English), from *Romances sans paroles* [Songs without Words]. It is worth bearing in mind that, as he knew, she read everything he published. She was, we might note, a highly cultured woman with a remarkable understanding of contemporary literature and music.

> Vous n'avez rien compris à ma simplicité,
>   Rien, ô ma pauvre enfant!
> Et c'est avec un front éventé, dépité,
>   Que vous fuyez devant.
>
> Vos yeux qui ne devaient refléter que douceur,
>   Pauvre cher bleu miroir,
> Ont pris un ton de fiel, ô lamentable sœur,
>   Qui nous fait mal à voir.
>
> Et vous gesticulez avec vos petits bras
>   Comme un héros méchant,
> En poussant d'aigres cris poitrinaires, hélas!
>   Vous qui n'étiez que chant![3]

> [You have not understood my simplicity at all,
>   Not at all, my poor child!
> Hence with featherbrained disappointment on your brow
>   You flee before us.
>
> Your eyes which should have reflected nothing but sweetness,
>   Poor dear blue mirror,
> Have taken on a tone of bile, o lamentable sister,
>   Which it pains us to see.
>
> And you gesticulate with your little arms
>   Like a nasty hero,

3   Paul Verlaine, 'Child Wife', in *Œuvres poétiques complètes*, Bibliothèque de la Pléiade (Paris: Gallimard, 1962), p. 207.

Emitting shrill consumptive cries, alas!
You who were nothing but song!]

To understand the place of music in Verlaine's poetry, we must begin by carefully noting the verb tenses in this poem, present and past. It is in the present that she gesticulates and squeaks contemptibly. It is in the past that she was nothing but song.

Paul and Mathilde agree, at least, that in their relationship, there were two separate phases, a happy 'before' and a miserable 'after'. The 'before', idyllic, is famously described by Paul in *La Bonne Chanson*, his third volume of poetry, completed and printed shortly before their marriage in the summer of 1870. It is dedicated to Mathilde. In it, she is constantly identified with music. This is not because she herself played or sang. She loved music, but unlike her mother, who was a truly exceptional pianist (she was Debussy's first piano teacher, and he always said that he had learned more about piano-playing from her than from anyone else), Mathilde was not a practising musician. Rather, to Paul's ears, Mathilde herself, physically, and all that emanated from her, actually was, materially, music. She does not need to sing, for her voice is always already music. Indeed, she does not even need to make a sound, for everything about her, from her heart to her appearance, is always already song. Here are a few examples of that identification of Mathilde with music in *La Bonne Chanson*:

I

[...] cette jeune fille,
Blanche apparition qui chante et qui scintille,
Dont rêve le poète et que l'homme chérit [...].

[[...] this maiden,
This white apparition which sings and scintillates,
Of whom the poet dreams and whom the man cherishes [...].]

III
[...]
Sa voix, étant de la musique fine,
Accompagnait délicieusement
L'esprit sans fiel de son babil charmant
Où la gaîté d'un bon cœur se devine.

[Her voice, being delicate music,
Was a delicious accompaniment
To the guileless spirit of her charming chatter
In which the gaiety of a good heart can be divined.]

VIII
Une Sainte en son auréole,
Une Châtelaine en sa tour,
Tout ce que contient la parole
Humaine de grâce et d'amour;

La note d'or que fait entendre
Un cor dans le lointain des bois,
Mariée à la fierté tendre
Des nobles Dames d'autrefois!

[A Saint in her halo,
A Lady of the castle in her tower.
All that human language can contain
Of grace and love;

The golden note that a horn
In the forest's distance gives us to hear,
Wedded to the tender pride
Of the noble Dames of yesteryear!]

XI
[...]
Mon oreille avide d'entendre
Les notes d'or de sa voix tendre [...].

[[...]
My ear eager to hear
The golden notes of her tender voice [...].]

XVII
[...]
Nos deux cœurs, exhalant leur tendresse paisible,
Seront deux rossignols qui chantent dans le soir.[4]

[[...]
Our two hearts, breathing out their peaceful tenderness,
Will be two nightingales singing in the evening.]

Paul hears Mathilde as music: as a nightingale, a song, a horn heard in the woods, as a singing apparition, or simply as song. He does not, on the other hand, hear her as a person who speaks. There is no sign, here or anywhere else in his verse, that he hears or listens to any words she utters. He certainly never quotes what she says. The beloved woman's voice, to him, cannot be a vehicle for words. It must be, only and absolutely, music. It should be, like the voice of the nightingale, a continuous song without words. (The next volume of poetry he published was entitled, precisely, *Romances sans paroles*, which is the usual French translation for Mendelssohn's 'Lieder ohne Worte'.)

But what is song? What is music? Programming our reaction to that question is what defines Verlaine's entire aesthetic. Just as Mathilde's music, her musicality, is dependent on a refusal to listen to her words, so music itself, as Paul conceives of it, depends on a refusal to listen to words, to any words. Mathilde is music; and music simply is, before as well as beyond words. His well-known 'Art poétique', as I said earlier, begins: 'De la musique avant toute chose!' 'Before' in every sense, and before every *thing*, which also means before those words which tell us what things are. Verlaine plays, here, that intermedial game which was so popular among poets at the time. To keep the value of poetry out of the reach of quibblers and critics, one identifies poetry with music — and one refuses to say what music is. The one thing one can safely say about music is the same as the one thing one can safely say about Mathilde as the addressee of *La Bonne Chanson*: it should not speak, and if

4   Paul Verlaine, *La Bonne Chanson*, in *Œuvres poétiques complètes*, pp. 142, 143, 147, 149, 152.

it seems to, we should not listen to its words. Let all songs be received as without words! Let verse, if it be like music, always escape from our words:

> De la musique encore et toujours!
>   Que ton vers soit la chose envolée
> Qu'on sent qui fuit d'une âme en allée
>   Vers d'autres cieux à d'autres amours.[5]

> [Music again and forever!
>   Let your verse be the thing that has flown
> That one senses in its flight from a soul that has gone
>   Towards other skies to other loves.]

And what of Mathilde? Does the same condition apply to her? If she is to be music, does she also have to be: 'la chose envolée | Qu'on sent qui fuit d'une âme en allée | Vers d'autres cieux à d'autres amours'? Perhaps that would have been the condition of her continued idealisation. But it is a condition she failed to fulfil.

What, then, was Paul supposed to do when he found that Mathilde had flown, not towards alternative skies or loves, but to her parents' house, because she felt like going to see them? When she seems to think that all she needs to do, when he comes to find her, is to natter amiably? When she serves him a dinner that tastes only too clearly of the here and now, during the siege of Paris, when horsemeat replaced beef and lamb, and preserved mushrooms replaced fresh? Not only that, but the food was marked by her own material incompetence, being burnt. All of this meant that Mathilde was not living up to her duty to be music, music before all else. She needed to be punished for that dereliction of duty. Paul was willing to provide that punishment. Slap.

This is not at all how the tale has always been presented in biographies or articles on the topic. It is always said that two factors caused Verlaine to treat his wife less than well: Rimbaud and, above all, alcohol. A typical example is this, from Stefan Zweig's *Paul Verlaine*, published in 1913: 'Verlaine began to drink again during his activities in the Commune. Recriminations and scenes rose as the result of this relapse. Suddenly came the decisive act of the drunkard; he struck his wife the first blow'.[6] This directly contradicts Verlaine's own account (and Mathilde's, as we shall see). Verlaine situates the founding episode of domestic violence before the Commune, and does not mention alcohol as a factor in that episode. But it is Zweig's version of events which has always been the generally accepted one, although there is no evidence for it.

Not infrequently, a third factor is more or less subtly evoked, alongside Rimbaud and alcohol: it is insinuated that Mathilde to some extent asked for what she got, because she was a silly, snobbish, small-minded girl who could not appreciate his greatness; and that it really was quite unreasonable of her to have subsequently abandoned him. That was the opinion of Paterne Berrichon, Rimbaud's brother-in-law and self-appointed guardian of his memory. He wrote, in an article published in 1910: 'les causes de la fatale irritation de Paul Verlaine, on les trouve uniquement

---

5   Paul Verlaine, 'Art poétique', in *Œuvres poétiques complètes*, p. 326.
6   Stefan Zweig, *Paul Verlaine*, trans. by O. F. Theis (Boston, MA: Luce, 1913), p. 36.

dans l'attitude, à tort ou à raison assumée, de Mme Mathilde Mauté vis-à-vis de son amoureux et malheureux mari' [the causes of Paul Verlaine's fateful irritation are to be found exclusively in the attitude which Mme Mathilde Mauté assumed, whether wrongly or not, towards her unfortunate and loving husband].[7] It was, according to this widespread point of view, really Mathilde's fault that her husband assaulted her. Although later in the century it would become less fashionable to say so directly, the idea persisted that she provoked him by her character faults. Here, for example, is what readers were told in 1971, in the Twayne's World Authors book on Verlaine:

> She had a streak of snobbery in her nature: it was the worst failing of an otherwise decent woman [...] with his exquisite poetic sense he had no difficulty in perceiving that her interest in literature was so much idle chatter; she could not tell good verse from bad.[8]

There is no evidence whatever for this assertion (none is offered by the author of the book, A. E. Carter). No one who knew Mathilde Mauté ever said this of her. Like the notion that drunkenness was solely responsible for that 'first blow', it is a myth invented to explain away misogynistic violence.

Such myths had already begun to usurp the truth in the biographical writings of men who knew Verlaine personally. Some are to be found in *Paul Verlaine: sa vie, ses œuvres* by Verlaine's friend Lepelletier, first published in 1907. Although he had read (and cites) Verlaine's *Confessions*, Lepelletier, like Zweig, contradicts Verlaine's version of events. According to him, Mathilde ran off to her parents because she was upset by Verlaine's drunkenness and excessive amorous advances. Hers was a 'cœur juvénile et frivole' [juvenile and frivolous heart]. She allowed herself to be unnecessarily upset by 'les scènes pénibles [...] que l'ivresse multipliait' [the painful scenes [...] that multiplied due to drunkenness]: note that it is drunkenness, and not Verlaine himself, which is said to have caused these scenes.[9] Mathilde should, Lepelletier tells us, here agreeing with Verlaine, have been more patient, more gentle, more understanding and forgiving: 'Verlaine était bon, aimant, et c'était comme un souffrant qu'il fallait le traiter. On a des ménagements pour les malades. On leur passe bien des éclats, et leurs boutades, leur mauvais moments, sont oubliés; leurs violences même sont pardonnées' [Verlaine was kind, loving, and he should have been treated as someone suffering from an illness. With the sick, patience and gentleness are called for. One lets their outbursts pass, and their whims, their surly moments are forgotten; even their violence is forgiven].[10] It was Mathilde's duty, according to Lepelletier, to forgive and forget Paul's constantly repeated violence, and return to live with him when he requested it.

7   Quoted in: Ex-Madame Paul Verlaine, *Mémoires de ma vie*, ed. by Michael Pakenham (Seyssel: Champ Vallon, 1992), p. 23. All future references to this work will be given in brackets in the main text. The publication history of Mathilde Mauté's autobiography is a fascinating tale of twentieth-century French cultural misogyny at its most small-minded. Michael Pakenham's remarkable 1992 edition was the first attempt to present the work in its context in any kind of objective way, and contains a wealth of carefully researched contextual detail.
8   A. E. Carter, *Paul Verlaine*, Twayne's World Authors (New York: Twayne, 1971), pp. 40–42.
9   E. Lepelletier, *Paul Verlaine: sa vie — son œuvre* (Paris: Mercure de France, 1907), p. 273.
10   Ibid., p. 274.

Verlaine's more recent biographers do not go so far. Most accept that since her husband was beating her, it is understandable that Mathilde should have left him. But I have yet to find a modern version of these events that does not blame alcohol for the beatings from the beginning, and Rimbaud for the culmination of hostilities. The typical version remains that we find in Wikipedia, of a Verlaine 'ruinant son mariage avec Mathilde qu'il frappe après s'être saoulé à l'absinthe' [ruining his marriage with Mathilde, whom he hits after becoming drunk on absinth]. This convenient explanation is designed to dissuade us from looking for any other factors contributing to Verlaine's treatment of Mathilde, and most notably, from attempting to understand why he never considered that his violence towards her (which he did not deny) could constitute a possible or even her real motive for leaving him.

When Paul and Mathilde last saw each other, in 1872, they had known each other for less than four years. For the next fourteen years at least, Mathilde remained an obsession for Paul. He constantly repeated his incomprehension that she would not return to him. His collection *Amour*, published in 1888, contains three poems directly addressed to her, bearing dates from 1873 to 1886. They are not among his most well-known poems. They do not have that delicate immateriality, that unreal melancholy, which characterises his best-remembered poems, those which are described as musical. They are, on the contrary, direct, forthright, and full of bile and resentment. Paul presents himself as a poor adoring lover, spurned and rejected for no reason. Mathilde he presents to us as a spiteful woman who takes pleasure in being nasty to him. He absolutely never even hints at the reason for which she left him in the first place: his physical violence.

The last of these poems is entitled 'Adieu'. At the end, the date is given as 'Novembre 1886'. Mathilde, after their divorce, had re-married on 30 October 1886. 'Adieu' expresses Paul's indignation at this event. He tells Mathilde that her mother (now deceased) would not have approved, and predicts that their son Georges (whom he had hardly ever met) would one day despise Mathilde for it. (He did not.) It begins thus:

> Hélas! je n'étais pas fait pour cette haine
> Et pour ce mépris plus forts que moi que j'ai.
> Mais pourquoi m'avoir fait cet agneau sans laine
> Et pourquoi m'avoir fait ce cœur outragé?
>
> J'étais né pour plaire à toute âme un peu fière,
> Sorte d'homme en rêve et capable du mieux,
> Parfois tout sourire et parfois tout prière,
> Et toujours des cieux attendris dans les yeux;
>
> Toujours la bonté des caresses sincères,
> En dépit de tout et quoi qu'il y parût [...].[11]
>
> [Alas! I was not made for this hatred
> Or for this scorn which I cannot help feeling.
> But why did you turn me into this shorn lamb

11   Paul Verlaine, 'Adieu', in *Œuvres poétiques complètes*, p. 424.

And why did you give me this outraged heart?

I was born to please every soul with any pride,
A kind of man in a dream and capable of the best,
Sometimes all smiles and sometimes all prayer,
And always the heavens moved to pity in my eyes:

Always the kind-heartedness of sincere caresses,
In spite of everything, in spite of appearances [...].]

'Toujours la bonté des caresses sincères'? Let us remember that Paul remembered perfectly well how he had, in fact, repeatedly beaten and kicked Mathilde, and did not shrink from writing candidly about it. But he was unable to see the connection between that behaviour and her rejection of him, which in turn resulted in his negative feelings towards her. The violence was irrelevant. What mattered was the poetry — his poetry:

Je n'étais pas fait pour dire de ces choses,
Moi dont la parole exhalait autrefois
Un épithalame en des apothéoses,
Ce chant du matin où mentait votre voix.[12]

[I was not made to say such things,
I whose words in an earlier time breathed out
An epithalamium in apotheoses,
This song of the morning in which your voice lied.]

The syntax of this stanza, the seventh of the poem, deserves careful study.

What we are told is this: Paul's 'parole', his words, once upon a time, used to breathe out that morning song in which Mathilde's voice lied. The words breathing out the song are Paul's. Of course; he was, after all, the poet of *La Bonne Chanson*. But in that song, he tells us, was Mathilde's lying voice. Paul's words and poetry; Mathilde's voice and lies.

Let us remember that, in *La Bonne Chanson* as in all Paul's verse, there is never any direct speech from Mathilde, never a single word spoken by her. All the words are his. It is only *in song* that her voice lies. Is the song, then, hers, even though the words are his?

Rather we should say: the words are his, and she must be the song. That is the only way to understand her presence in his poetry. This is as clear in *La Bonne Chanson* itself as it is in 'Adieu'. Paul's words produce the poem. The condition of its musicality is that Mathilde should be music, should be song itself, song as a substance, and not produce any specific words to which we can listen. Her role is to incarnate an essence, not to speak in her own name. This explains why, in *Amour*, Paul perceives her voice as having lied. Originally, in the time of *La Bonne Chanson*, she had said nothing; she had simply been music. That had been fine. Later, she had spoken. Her voice had become a wordy one, rather than a purely musical one. That was not fine. It meant that her initial musical appearance had been dishonest. He had seen her as a perfect musical muse. But she was not. She turned out always to have had her own words in her head. That was a betrayal.

12   Ibid., p. 425.

This way of interpreting their relationship is not the one we find in biographical accounts of Verlaine's life and works. It is, however, by no means an original perspective on the literature of the time. Feminist criticism has been pointing out for seventy years, since Simone de Beauvoir's *Le Deuxième Sexe*, how women are consigned to the role of the absolute Other, and punished if they presume to occupy the space of the active speaking subject. Building on the principles of that feminist analysis, I should like to pose a question that Beauvoir does not address directly.

As I said at the beginning, we all know that Paul Verlaine is a great poet, and a musical one. We love his poetry.

Unfortunately, the music in Paul's poetry turns out to depend on the same misogynistic principles that led not only to his violence against his wife, but to his inability to understand her refusal to accept that violence.

We do not like, today, to think that the qualities we admire in poetry might be umbilically connected to that kind of attitude towards women. But are we not deceiving ourselves? Should we not accept that the great poetic tradition, stretching from Baudelaire to Ponge, at the centre of which Verlaine stands, creates its music by a misogynist dynamic? Man produces, woman is. The woman is song as a substance; the man writes the specific song with its words. If a woman refuses to know her place, if her voice turns from music to words, she threatens the order of poetry herself. She deserves her punishment.

Christine Battersby, in her eye-opening book *Gender and Genius*, first published in 1987, describes this dynamic beautifully. She shows how, in the nineteenth and twentieth centuries, genius, the writing of genius, had a necessary feminine element, but this feminine element could not be that which produced the work of genius. The woman always *was*, while the man *produced*. Women writers always had to compose with this model, and it could never be simple for them to find their voice. Verlaine's portrayal of Mathilde at least has the virtue of helping us to understand why music was, of all the arts at the time, the most gendered. It was possible for a woman to write poetry, provided she showed an appropriate awareness, in her writing, of the confusion of gender roles that this writing entailed. Such was the case of Marceline Desbordes-Valmore, whom Verlaine admired greatly, because her poetry always seemed to say: 'Les femmes, je le sais, ne doivent pas écrire. | J'écris pourtant' [Women must not write, I know. | And yet I write].[13] But music left no room for such subtleties. Only a man could *write* music; a woman could only *be* music. That is why, until well into the twentieth century, it was far more difficult for a woman to publish music than to publish poetry or novels. During all the long reign of the notion of poetic genius, it was simply impossible to believe that a woman could be a composer of genius. Women composers only began to achieve equality of opportunity as, in the twentieth century, the very notion of genius was contested.

This suggests that if we care about equal rights for women in the domain of the arts, we should embrace that contestation. We should junk genius, as an

---

13   Verlaine quotes these famous lines in his essay on Desbordes-Valmore, in *Les Poètes maudits* (Paris: Vanier, 1888), p. 58.

irredeemably patriarchal and misogynistic principle. We should find other values in poetry, values that do not display solidarity with those that led Paul to beat Mathilde unrepentantly. And of course, this search for other values has indeed taken place, never more so than in the 1980s, when Christine Battersby wrote her book and cultural studies were beginning their ascendancy.

Unfortunately, a third of a century later, it has become plain that this strategy has not triumphed over the old enemy. For whatever we do, if we are honest with ourselves, we cannot help feeling that the musical verse of Paul Verlaine is beautiful. He remains a great poet. Worse: yes, we find women writers whose verse is also beautiful, and male poets who are less horribly misogynist than Verlaine. But — I will allow myself to say this although I have not space to demonstrate here how it happens — if we enquire carefully into the reasons for which we admire their poetry, we find ourselves uncomfortably often once again on the trail of that musicality which is also a gendering of roles in art.

The example of Paul Verlaine thus continues to cast doubt on the compatibility between my moral and social principles, and my sense of artistic value. That doubt contaminates, at the very least, all the poetry of the artistic century at the centre of which he lived. Mallarmé, for example, was certainly not as viciously misogynistic as Verlaine. He did not beat his wife. And yet he could not help admiring Verlaine's life as a man, precisely because, unlike Mallarmé, Verlaine had dared to live out concretely the consequences of the poetic state. That is why Mallarmé saw Verlaine as the father of the new generation of poets. Unfortunately, he was right:

> Mais le père, le vrai père de tous les Jeunes, c'est Verlaine, le magnifique Verlaine dont je trouve l'attitude comme homme aussi belle vraiment que comme écrivain, parce que c'est la seule, dans une époque où le poète est hors la loi: que de faire accepter toutes les douleurs avec une telle hauteur et une aussi superbe crânerie.[14]

> [But the father, the real father of all the Young Ones, is Verlaine, the magnificent Verlaine whose attitude as a man I find truly as admirable as his attitude as a writer, because it is the only one, in an age when the poet is an outlaw: to require acceptance of every kind of suffering with such courageous ostentation and such aristocracy of spirit.]

Those 'douleurs' which Verlaine required to be accepted included those he inflicted physically on his wife and mother.

One almost has the sense that Mallarmé regarded himself as something of a coward for not having dared to live out his aesthetic principles as Verlaine had done. I have often felt I was myself something of a coward for not having dared to let my moral principles question my aesthetic principles. Can the two co-exist? Or should I accept that great art is so deeply rooted in misogyny that I should not allow myself to love it?

I have found myself quite unable to answer that question for myself. I lack a sense of the position from which I could do so. Instead, I turn to others who have more of a right to address it, because of the suffering that people like Verlaine forced

---

14   See Jules Huret, *Enquête sur l'évolution littéraire* (Paris: Charpentier, 1891), p. 62.

upon them. And chief amongst them, for me, is Mathilde Mauté. It is time to listen to Mathilde's voice. Let us see what she has to say, both about Verlaine's violence against her, and about the value, the musicality, of his poetry.

★   ★   ★   ★   ★

Her account of how the violence began does not correspond exactly to his, as she says. (In *Mémoires de ma vie*, she is always careful to point out where her version of events differs from those of Verlaine, in his *Confessions*, and of Lepelletier in his biography.) She situates the beginning of it several months later than he does, in October 1871, shortly before the birth of their son Georges (62). I should like, however, to point to a similarity between the two accounts. She describes, as he does, a first scene of violence after which violence became a habit for Paul; and in that first scene, there is no mention of the influence of alcohol. As far as we can tell, Paul was not drunk when he first assaulted her.

Mathilde agrees with Verlaine's biographers that Rimbaud and absinthe can be considered causes of the breakdown of her marriage (76). However, during the happy days of their courtship and early marriage, he drank little. There were always periods of his life when he regularly became drunk, and others when he did not. We are entitled to ask, then, why he began drinking again after a long period of abstinence.

The direct, immediate trigger for the first assault, as described by Mathilde, is of the same order as the trigger for the more serious, life-threatening assault which, as we have seen, in January 1872 set in train the events that led to their legal separation. It was this: Mathilde dared to say to her husband, in her own voice, something that he could construe as critical of his preference for the society of men, and as an affirmation of her own family values over his right to do as he pleased.

In the first episode, in October 1871, she had criticised Rimbaud for stealing books. There followed three months of regular assaults. Then, one day the following January, Paul returns home just as dinner is ending. Mathilde is upstairs in her room. He eats, then goes up and asks her for money to go out to a café because, he says, the coffee he had been given after dinner was cold.

She makes it clear to him that she is not fooled by this excuse. She knows that what he really wants is to avoid being left in her company. He wants to be with his male friends:

> — Tes parents, me dit-il, m'ont fait servir du café froid; donne-moi la clef du tiroir, que je prenne de l'argent pour aller en prendre une tasse au café.
> — Il n'est pas nécessaire de chercher un prétexte pour sortir, lui répondis-je très doucement; tous les jours tu me laisses de plus en plus seule, et aujourd'hui je ne t'ai pas vu de la journée.
> Quoique cette observation fût faite avec beaucoup de calme, elle eut le don d'exaspérer mon mari qui bondit sur moi et, saisissant notre petit Georges, qui avait trois mois, le jeta brutalement contre le mur. [...] Il aurait pu être tué, et ma frayeur fut si grande que je poussai un cri déchirant, qui fut entendu de mes parents. Ils étaient encore au rez-de-chaussée, montèrent quatre à quatre les deux étages et entrèrent dans ma chambre. Quel triste spectacle les attendait!

Paul, que mon cri avait rendu plus furieux encore, m'avait renversée sur le lit et, à genou sur ma poitrine, me serrait le cou de toutes ses forces. Déjà, je ne pouvais plus respirer, lorsque mon père entra et, d'une brusque secousse, empoigna son gendre et le remit sur ses pieds. (152–53)

['The coffee your parents had served to me,' he said to me, 'was cold; give me the key to the drawer, so I can get some money to go and have a cup in the café.'

'You don't need to find a pretext to go out,' I replied, very calmly. 'Every day you leave me alone more and more, and today I have not seen you all day.'

Even though this remark was made quite gently, it managed to exasperate my husband, who jumped upon me, took hold of our little Georges, who was three months old, and flung him brutally against the wall. [...] He might have been killed, and I was so frightened that I cried out piercingly. My parents heard me, from the ground floor. They dashed up the stairs to the second floor where we were, and came into my room. What a sad spectacle awaited them! Paul, whose fury had been exacerbated by my cry, had thrown me backwards onto the bed. Kneeling on my chest, he was squeezing my neck as hard as he could. I was already unable to breathe when my father entered, forcefully took hold of his son-in-law, and with a powerful shove, placed him upon his feet.]

That was the moment from which Mathilde began to envisage separation from her husband. Hence the decision to request the family doctor to take a note of the injuries Paul had caused to her neck.

Let us recapitulate the similarities between the scenes of violence that we have seen described by Mathilde and Paul. To begin with, they agree that she did nothing physical to provoke it. All he had to complain about were her words, and his dissatisfaction with the food and drink he was served. Their accounts are also compatible concerning the role of alcohol. They both say that often he was drunk when he assaulted her, especially towards the end of their time together; and yet in their descriptions of specific foundational episodes of violence, there is no suggestion that he had been drinking. The resumption of his alcoholic habits might seem more a consequence of the rift between him and his wife than its cause.

In all their accounts, it is clear that Paul's violence is spurred by irritation with Mathilde's continuing attachment to her family and its values. He is fond of his mother-in-law and brother-in-law, both highly artistic people who appreciated (as did Mathilde) his verse. But he hates the thought that she might have loyalty to them rather than to him. And he hates even more the thought that he might be expected to have any duties to his wife and child. He felt, as he said a couple of months after the violence started, to the assembled guests (including his boss) at a dinner party organised by his mother: 'que les femmes et les enfants, c'était dégoûtant; qu'on était bien bête de se marier; que, quant à lui, il en avait assez du mariage, etc., etc.' [that women and children were disgusting; that getting married was a stupid thing to do; that for his part, he had had enough of marriage, etc., etc.] (149). Paul and Mathilde, in short, disagree about when the violence started. But they agree on most of the factors that appear to have triggered it. Paul wanted both total control over his wife and the freedom to associate with his male friends as he wanted. He refused to let her continue with the social life of her family; but he was not willing to share his own social life with her. He did not want to hear her speaking voice.

In July 1872, Mathilde and her mother went to Belgium, where Paul had been staying with Rimbaud. Paul agreed to return to Paris with them, and they took the train together as far as the border. But there, Paul got out and refused to travel further. Paul and Mathilde never saw each other again. It is clear from the letter he subsequently sent her that he felt he had to choose between loyalty to Rimbaud and loyalty to his wife; and he chose the former. This is often presented as a choice between homosexual and heterosexual attractions, or between bohemian and bourgeois lifestyles. But it is also a choice between living with the words of a man and living with the words of a woman. It is perhaps worth pointing out that while, over the following fifteen years, he frequently expressed his desire for Mathilde to return to him, he never did this in a way that implied he actually missed her or would have liked to spend time with her. It seems clear enough that he did not really want to live with her. How could he? He could not see her as a social companion. He did not want her words.

In that letter he sent her after their final parting on the Franco-Belgian border, he accuses her of trying to make him betray Rimbaud. He addresses her as a fairy-vegetable, a mouse-princess, or a bedbug; what she clearly cannot be, to him, is a human, speaking woman. Mathilde quotes the letter:

> 'Misérable fée carotte, princesse souris, punaise qu'attendent les deux doigts et le pot, vous m'avez fait tout, vous avez peut-être tué le cœur de mon ami; je rejoins Rimbaud, s'il veut encore de moi après cette trahison que vous m'avez fait faire.' (170)

> ['Miserable carrot-fairy, mouse-princess, bedbug for whom the two fingers and the chamber pot are waiting, you've played every trick on me, you may have killed the heart of my friend; I am going back to Rimbaud, if he will still accept me after the act of treachery which you made me commit.']

Her reaction to the letter was an irrevocable decision to leave her husband: 'Cette fois, mon parti était pris: après avoir remis cette lettre à mon père, je lui déclarai que j'étais décidée à demander la séparation' [This time, my mind was made up: after giving this letter to my father, I told him I had decided to ask for a separation].

This was not the first time that Paul had called Mathilde a 'fée'. In *La Bonne Chanson*, he had written:

> Aussi soudain fus-je, après le semblant
>   D'une révolte aussitôt étouffée,
> Au plein pouvoir de la petite Fée
>   Que depuis lors je supplie en tremblant.[15]

> [Thus of a sudden I found myself, after a feint
>   Of a revolt at once stifled,
> Entirely in the power of the little Fairy
>   Whom since that day I tremblingly implore.]

15   Verlaine, *La Bonne Chanson*, p. 143.

At other points in *La Bonne Chanson*, as we have seen, Mathilde appears, if not as a princess, at least as a 'châtelaine', and as a 'sainte'. What has changed between *La Bonne Chanson* and Paul's last letter is that she is no longer a real fairy but a carrot-fairy, no longer a real damsel but a mouse-princess. Her magic has become contaminated with the monstrosity of the woman who refuses to remain in the place assigned to her by the poet. A woman who has descended into reality deserves only to be squashed like a bedbug and plopped in the chamber-pot.

It was not, then, in the end, Paul's violence alone that drove Mathilde to separate from him. It was the proof that she could not have the status, to him, of a fellow human being, with whom he was content to share his company. She had ceased to be his fairy; the only role he could now allow her was that of a monster, who could be beaten when it suited him. She was, as I have said, a woman of firm character. Once she had taken her decision, she stuck to it unswervingly. She had determined, then, that his character was not one she could live with. But what of his poetry?

She never ceased to consider him a 'poète de génie' [poet of genius] (183), indeed the 'plus grand poète moderne' [greatest modern poet] (221). However, she did not consider all his poems equally admirable. It is worth thinking through why she prefers some poems to others, and how this relates to their properties that might be called musical.

No one will be surprised to discover that she does not find anything positive to say about 'ces vers pleins de haine' [these hate-filled lines] from *Bonheur*, which she quotes:

> — Mais quoi! n'est-ce pas toujours vous,
>   Démon femelle, triple peste,
> Pire flot de tout ce remous,
>   Pire ordure que tout le reste,
>
> Vous toujours, vil cri de haro
>   Qui me proclame et me diffame,
> Gueuse inepte, lâche bourreau,
>   Horrible, horrible, horrible femme! (192)
>
> [— But what have we here? Is it not you again,
>   Female demon, threefold plague,
> A tide worse than all this backwash,
>   A more foul filth than all the rest,
>
> Still you, vile and vilifying cry
>   Proclaiming and defaming me,
> Inept harlot, cowardly torturer,
>   Horrible, horrible, horrible woman!]

Here we find her addressed, not only as a demon, as a plague, as a torturer, and as filth, but also, supreme insult (not to be found in *La Bonne Chanson*), as a woman, 'femme'. Naturally, that status is incompatible, for Verlaine, with the love he used to feel for her. One can, as far as he is concerned, love a fairy, a saint, a 'châtelaine'; one cannot love a woman. For him, as we have seen, 'les femmes et les enfants, c'était dégoûtant'.

Mathilde does, on the other hand, admire these lines from *Sagesse*, finding them 'une de ses plus belles choses':

> Ecoutez la chanson bien douce
> Qui ne pleure que pour vous plaire;
> Elle est discrète, elle est légère;
> Un frisson d'eau sur de la mousse! (186)

> [Listen to the gentle song
> Whose tears aim only to please you;
> It is discreet and it is light,
> A quivering of water over moss!]

It would, of course, be easy to say that she likes these latter lines because they do not insult her. That is true enough. But we can also see the difference in their relationship to music.

By 'music', here, I do not mean in the first place the sound of the poems, indeed any audible sound at all. I mean the way that the poems evoke their own relationship to an unheard, imaginary 'music off', like the music which poetry must be according to 'Art poétique'. Obviously, no such music is to be found in the poem from *Bonheur*. It is a poem of words, with a message to convey which words are well able to transmit. The poem from *Sagesse*, on the other hand, asks Mathilde to listen to a song, a weeping song, a song without words, discreet, light, a quivering of water... She is not being asked to listen to his words, but only to that immaterial song. Verlaine, as he had two different ways of treating Mathilde, had two different ways of writing poems addressed to her. Of the two, only one is musical. And that is not the one that attacks her.

I said at the outset that everybody who knows anything about French poetry knows that Verlaine is a great poet. He is cited alongside Baudelaire, Mallarmé, and Rimbaud, as one of the geniuses of his time. However, his reputation is unlike that of Baudelaire, Mallarmé, and Rimbaud in one important respect. The tendency has long been to treat every poem they wrote as touched by the hand of genius. Verlaine's poetry, on the other hand, has always been seen as of very uneven quality and interest. And the curious fact is that it is precisely his most musical poetry, according to the definition given above, that has always been most often read, including, for example, by Mallarmé: the poetry of the *Fêtes galantes*, of *La Bonne Chanson*, *Romances sans paroles*, of certain pages of *Jadis et naguère* and of *Sagesse*. Mathilde's taste in Verlaine's poetry thus corresponds pretty well to what has always been received critical wisdom. It is worth asking why.

★   ★   ★   ★   ★

The depiction of violence against women is of course common in the most admired poetry of the late nineteenth century in France. To take two well-known examples: Lautréamont's *Chants de Maldoror* and Baudelaire's *Fleurs du Mal* contain some revolting scenes of attacks on women. The former presents with almost caricatural directness the dynamic I have described at work in Verlaine: love lasts as long as its object can be conceived of as an otherworldly ideal, but if that object tries to take its place in the everyday world of the male narrator, especially by engaging in conversation, violent retribution follows.

That violence is sometimes resisted. In the second canto of *Les Chants de Maldoror*, Lautréamont's narrator finds himself admiring a young girl whom he regularly sees in the street, but does not talk to. He feels sympathy for her. Then one day, she speaks to him, asking for the time. From that moment on, his sympathy vanishes. His thoughts of her are always violently murderous, and he avoids her. Let us note the duality of his impulses: not only to murder her, but also to avoid her. This duality corresponds to a profound conflict of values which is at the root of a powerful sense of tragedy in Baudelaire's writing as in that of Lautréamont. That conflict and that sense of tragedy are absent from Verlaine.

Les Fleurs du Mal and *Les Chants de Maldoror* contain in their very titles the word *mal*: pain, but also and above all evil. (None of Verlaine's titles contains that word.) The cruelty that they depict is never allowed to remain innocent. Its perpetration is always accompanied, preceded, or followed by a sense of its morally indefensible destructiveness. Constantly woven into the structure of the work is the interrogation of cruelty, of its motives, its results, its gendering, and its relation to the very matter of poetry. Misogyny appears deeply rooted in the poetry; but at the same time, the poetry compulsively digs around its own roots, at the risk of uprooting itself. It points to the evil at its own heart, and does not simply justify it. It is this interrogation which is missing from Verlaine's poetry. He has the ability to see himself as innocent, as justified; hence, as entitled to treat his wife as he sees fit.

Mathilde saw Paul as a poet of genius with two sides to his character: 'on a affaire à un poète de génie, tour à tour bon et détestable, brutal et doux, aimant et haineux' [we are dealing with a poet of genius, by turns kind and detestable, brutal and gentle, loving and hate-filled] (183). The distinctive feature of Verlaine's doubleness, compared to that of Baudelaire or Lautréamont, is indeed the 'tour à tour', the separation, alternation, and lack of engagement between the two halves. In the writing of Baudelaire and Lautréamont, one can always sense the power of a certain irony, a constant consciousness that whatever they are now saying, another perspective is possible, which might have the right (moral or aesthetic) to condemn the path on which they are engaged. That irony and power of self-condemnation are missing from Verlaine. He is able to see himself as a sinner, certainly. But his sins he always presents, as do his biographers, as the passing consequence of an understandable human weakness, and eminently forgivable; never as the perverse and ineluctable result of his own deeply-held principles. In *Les Chants de Maldoror* as in *Les Fleurs du Mal*, cruelty is an active and powerful force fed not only by our instincts, but by our values. Verlaine has no such awareness concerning his own cruelty. He sees no evil in his own misogyny. That is why he takes no responsibility for the causes of Mathilde's decision to leave him, and never to return. He always presents that decision as the result of her mean-mindedness. But Verlaine's refusal of responsibility comes at the price of music.

The Verlaine that Mathilde describes as 'détestable', 'brutal', and 'haineux' is the Verlaine who can no longer see any music in his love; and when he cannot see music in his love, his poetry ceases to be musical. We have seen how in both 'Adieu' and 'Child Wife', he situates the musicality of his muse in the past. That musicality is absent from the time when he feels absolutely justified in abusing her. When what Paul sees is a Mathilde who is a mere 'femme', and therefore an 'ordure', the music vanishes both as theme and as style. His poems insulting Mathilde lack, very plainly, those qualities of indirectness, of vagueness, of otherworldliness, of the ear always open to what cannot be physically heard, in which he himself situates the musical character of poetry, and which we, like Mathilde, admire in many of his other poems. When the voice we hear is directly that of Paul expressing his poor opinion of his wife as a speaking woman, his voice does not reach us as that of a poetic genius. It has not that musicality which manifests itself through shimmering images and dreams, in white apparitions, in flights towards skies other than those which our vulgar eyes can see.

To recapitulate: there is a difference between Verlaine's misogyny and that which we find in the other admired poetic geniuses of his time. He lacks the sense that there might be anything seriously wrong with it. He really cannot see why anyone might find wife-beating problematic. This is as clear from his verse as from his autobiographical prose. His case therefore presents an exemplary challenge. Can we admire the poetry of a man whose values are so closed to those we claim?

Mathilde Mauté's answer to that question is firm. It is: not all Verlaine's poetry is the same. We can admire those poems that do not express unrepentant misogynist values. And in this judgement, moral and aesthetic values are not in opposition.

One might say: but Mathilde is allowing herself to be duped. Verlaine's musical poetry, which she admires, is built all too clearly on those sexist principles which underpin the gendering of genius at that time. He could never treat her as an equal, as a partner, as a fellow human being; even when he loved her and was kind to her, it was always on condition that she remain confined to the role of muse, of fairy or saint, of incarnation of music — and that she keep her speaking mouth shut. Should Mathilde not have seen the danger implicit even in his most adoring verse? And even if she could not, should not we, more than seventy years after *Le Deuxième Sexe* and more than thirty after *Gender and Genius*, refuse to be taken in? We can see, now, how the role he gives to Mathilde in *La Bonne Chanson* is one that can only end badly for her.

That is true enough. Nonetheless, I find it hard to resist the impulse to take Mathilde as my guide. To begin with, as I read her courageous and lucid account, as I admire her character, intelligence, and firmness, I find it impossible to give myself the right to judge her judgement. My own social position and gender history do not entitle me to do so. They incline me to listen with respect to those who have been through what she went through. And as I ponder her continued love of his verse, persisting unchanged over decades during which she suffered constant verbal abuse following on from his physical abuse, I do find myself seeing in it, as she did, something that — yes, I will use the word — transcends his misogyny.

In her essay *Three Guineas*, which she wrote in 1938, Virginia Woolf drew a vivid portrait of the misogynist principles at work in the society of her own time. She showed why women's struggles and values could not and should not be the same as men's struggles and values. What seemed good and right to men would certainly not necessarily be good and right for women. The whole text is structured as a response to a letter from a man who, she implies constantly, would have been blind to that gendering of values. To him, what was right for men would naturally have been right for all humans. Her aim was to demonstrate how false that view was. And yet, in the very last paragraph of the work, she evokes a value which would be universal, not marked as masculine or feminine, but rather as human, as if the human could be beyond gender. Could the poetry of the time convey that value?

> Your letter tempts us [...] to listen [...] to the voices of the poets, answering each other, assuring us of a unity that rubs out divisions as if they were chalk marks only; to discuss with you the capacity of the human spirit to overflow boundaries and make unity out of multiplicity. But that would be to dream — to dream the recurring dream that has haunted the human mind since the beginning of time; the dream of peace, the dream of freedom.[16]

Those 'voices of the poets' known to Woolf were, as Woolf herself had shown us (not least in her famous portrayal of Shakespeare and his mythical sister, in *A Room of One's Own*), predominantly those of men; moreover, of men content with the artistic superiority assigned to their gender, rarely concerned to contest the sexism of society. How can those gendered voices assure us of a unity that 'rubs out divisions', 'overflows boundaries', 'makes unity out of multiplicity'? The answer is in the following sentence. To hear this in 'the voices of the poets' is to dream. The poets do not actually rub out divisions or make unity of multiplicity. They cannot; they are themselves caught up in division and multiplicity. What they can do, what they have done, is to give us the opportunity to dream 'the dream of peace, the dream of freedom', which is also a dream of unity (the word is tellingly repeated, on either side of a semi-colon).

Mathilde, for Paul, when he loved her and she loved him, was a dream. That dream was a dream of togetherness, of unity. It could only be sustained, in our divided world, by the voice of the poet, by the voice of a poet answering the voices of other poets. We cannot live always in dreams, of course. When Paul Verlaine woke up to reality, he found himself in a world where the divisions between men and women could not be rubbed out, as if they were chalk marks. That was the world in which his social life had always been led. He felt as keenly as Mathilde, I have no doubt, the loss of the unity he had dreamt of. To say this is neither to excuse nor to justify his disgusting behaviour towards her. But it is, perhaps, to allow us to separate, as both Virginia Woolf and Mathilde Mauté did, the dynamics of the dream as we are tempted to hear it in the poets' voice from what happens to that voice when it expresses the social dynamics of a misogynist society.

Towards the beginning of this essay, I posed the question: should we not accept that the great poetic tradition, stretching from Baudelaire to Ponge, at the centre of which stands Verlaine, creates its music by a misogynist dynamic? The answer is that we should. And yet we do not need to receive the music thus created as itself

16   Woolf, *A Room of One's Own; Three Guineas*, p. 365.

misogynist. We can hear it, as in a dream, echoing between voices, rubbing out divisions. As soon as we ask how it relates to concrete social relations, we find it following the channels into which it was made to flow by the misogynist mores of the time. Can we allow ourselves to hear it without asking about that? No... and yet perhaps we can still follow the lead of Mathilde Mauté and Virginia Woolf. We can refuse to justify misogyny in society, we can see how it permeates art, and yet at the same time we can dream of finding something precious in the voices of the poets that is not thereby disqualified. Indeed, we can turn Paul's misogyny against him. He fossilised the distinction between music and speech into a structure built on fixed roles assigned to male and female. That corresponded to a profound and growing tendency in the society of his time. But to fix boundaries thus is actually a betrayal of the dream that we can share if we listen to the echoes between the voices of the poets. He was punished for that betrayal, not only by the loss of his love, but also by the loss of music from his poetry.

This is not to say, of course, that after his separation from Mathilde he wrote no more musical poetry. That is obviously not the case. But the musical verse he did write thereafter is not to be found in the poems where his misogynist principles re-assert themselves. On the contrary, we find it in a bewildered interrogation of his own principles and motivations, and frequently a statement of incomprehension, most notably in the famous verses he penned when in prison after shooting Rimbaud. To take a famous example:

> Le ciel est, par-dessus le toit,
>   Si bleu, si calme!
> Un arbre, par-dessus le toit
>   Berce sa palme.
>
> La cloche dans le ciel qu'on voit
>   Doucement tinte.
> Un oiseau sur l'arbre qu'on voit
>   Chante sa plainte.
>
> Mon Dieu, mon Dieu, la vie est là,
>   Simple et tranquille.
> Cette paisible rumeur-là
>   Vient de la ville.
>
> — Qu'as-tu fait, ô toi que voilà
>   Pleurant sans cesse,
> Dis, qu'as-tu fait, toi que voilà,
>   De ta jeunesse?[17]
>
> [The sky is, above the roof,
>   So blue, so calm!
> A tree, above the roof,
>   Waves its frond.
>
> The bell in the sky that one sees
>   Softly rings.

17   Verlaine, *Sagesse*, in *Œuvres poétiques complètes*, p. 280.

A bird in the tree that one sees
   Sings its complaint.

My God, my God, life is there,
   Simple and tranquil.
Those peaceful murmurs there
   Come from the town.

— What have you done, o you who are here
   Weeping without cease,
Say, what have you done, you who are here,
   With your youth?]

Life is there, in the world of blue skies, trees with their fronds, ringing bells, and singing birds. He is separated from it. Why this separation? It must be the result of something he has done. But he cannot tell what. He can only weep. If we wanted to take a crass biographical approach, we might say to him: Paul, face the facts. You beat and insulted your wife, so she left you. You shot your friend and lover, and he called for help because he feared you would kill him. That is why you ended up in prison, unloved. But we know better than to want to enlighten him thus. For the musicality of the poem results from his incomprehension. As long as he cannot understand what he did, we can hear the echo of the dream of unity in the voice of the poet. If he lost that incomprehension, he could only settle back into the clear misogynistic principles of the man who believes he has the right to beat his wife; then the dream and the music would be lost, too.

Yes, Verlaine's concept of music is gendered. Via the opposition between the woman who is music and the man who writes it, that gendering of music colludes in the creation of a wellhead of misogyny. Where that misogyny surfaces in his writing, it brings with it a cruelty that is never challenged or questioned, and that absence of questioning destroys the music. That is what makes Verlaine's poetic output so uneven. Verlaine lacks the lucid, vivid, tormented, ironic awareness of the evil of cruelty which gives the writing of Baudelaire and Lautréamont its constant suffocating power. Nonetheless, there are times when Verlaine does have an indirect awareness, so indirect that it is uniquely conducive to music in his verse, beyond any concept, be it of music or of relations between the sexes, of the terrible consequences of his cruelty. Thus it is that, in the *Fêtes galantes* as in those wonderful poems written in prison, the words of his verse can speak of division and lack of unity in a way that makes us weep and dream with him of their opposite: a rubbing out of boundaries, which no voice can express directly, but which echoes between the voices of the poets. Since Mathilde Mauté and Virginia Woolf could be tempted to dream they heard such things, I will allow myself to succumb to the same temptation.

CHAPTER 10

❖

The Place of Cécile Sauvage

The theme of the Word and Music Studies Forum conference in September 2020, held online because of the coronavirus travel restrictions that year, was: Words, Music and Marginalisation. Wondering what I might contribute to it, I thought of Cécile Sauvage (1883–1927). She is a wonderful poet whose work has always been almost totally unknown, in academia at least, so she would count, I thought, as marginalised; and many kinds of music are woven into her words. She seemed to fit the bill perfectly.

Then it occurred to me that I ought to ask myself: unknown, certainly; but does that entitle me to think of her as marginalised? After all, there are millions of poets who are unknown. Should they all be considered marginalised? My mother wrote poems which were never published except by her, for private circulation; does that make her marginalised? I would not have said so. I realised I needed to dig back to find the presuppositions behind my sense that I could present Sauvage as marginalised, but not my mother.

The primary reason, I soon found, is this. I consider Sauvage to be a great poet, who deserves to be widely read and studied in universities. I do not consider my mother to be a great poet who deserves to be widely read and studied in universities. To me, Sauvage's poetry is vastly superior to that of many male poets of her period whose names are much better known. Therefore, I presume that sexist social forces are responsible for the fact that her poetry has not been properly recognised. In the case of my mother, I do not blame sexist social forces at all. Her poetry I love, because it is hers; however, I can see no compelling reason why it should be read or studied by people who never knew her.

Certainly, social forces, or, to put it plainly, prejudice and gender stereotyping, worked on the reception of Sauvage's poetry in a way which is likely to give rise to a weary sigh of recognition in anyone familiar with the history of literary sexism in twentieth-century France. We are told everywhere, whether on Wikipedia or on the back cover of the paperback edition of her complete works, that she is the poet of maternity and of nature; we should be interested in her because her son (who features in her poetry) became one of France's greatest composers, and because the menfolk around her, substantial cultural figures in their own right, appreciated her poetry.[1] Poetry by women presented in this way has always been relegated to the

1   Cécile Sauvage, *Œuvres complètes*, ed. by Claude-Jean Lannay, with a preface by Olivier Messiaen (Paris: La Table Ronde, 2002). All page numbers in brackets in this essay refer to this

second division of the second sex. It can never be part of the great central tradition of French poetry. But that has been the common lot of the women poets of her time in France. It continues to be, in many circles, the default attitude to poetry written by women in France, especially between 1850 and 1970. One only has to read the blurb on the back cover of volumes of their verse to see this all too clearly. Why pick out Cécile Sauvage, rather than any of the others?

To such a question, one of the answers that often occurs to students has to do with the importance of a poet. A poet who is historically important but little valued today may be thought of as marginalised. The concept of importance, however, will not help me here. What is importance, after all? Influence, actual or potential, on society, or what we might today call 'impact'? I suspect Sauvage had almost none, and can never have much. A key place in the development of poetry? I cannot say I feel Sauvage might have had one; the history of French poetry in many ways bypassed her. A message of social or political value? An account of historically interesting events? No, none of that, really. But perhaps that in itself helps to explain why, to me, Sauvage can help us to think through marginalisation.

A comparison with Marie Krysinska (1857–1908) is illuminating. Krysinska was a magnificent poet, who was the first person to publish free verse in French. Her *Rythmes pittoresques* were received with extraordinary critical enthusiasm when the book was first published in 1890. But her fame was not allowed to last. She was subjected to a deliberate campaign of denigration and ostracism by male poets motivated by a combination of misogyny, xenophobic nationalism (Krysinska was of Polish origin), and professional jealousy, with the result that it became steadily more difficult for her to publish her work and have it fairly assessed. This left her feeling embittered, and, we may safely say, marginalised. After a century of misrecognition, her verse and her pioneering role in literary history were re-discovered, thanks largely to the work of Seth Whidden. She now has a small but proud academic following. We seek, one might say, to restore her to her rightful place.

Cécile Sauvage, on the other hand, was never famous, and never sought fame. Unlike Krysinska, she was never at home in Parisian literary society. She has no claim to have inflected French literary history. She was culturally at home, and at her most productive, living in the provinces, ploughing her own furrow. I have come across no unambiguous evidence that she felt her talent was not recognised as it should have been. She did not seek or desire a central place in the poetic life of the nation. Nor did she claim to speak for any oppressed group. On the contrary: one senses she felt herself quite privileged, despite her frequent melancholy. It is therefore understandable that her cause should not have been taken

---

edition. This invaluable volume, which made Sauvage's poetry available to a wide audience for the first time, reproduces the poetry and other texts in the posthumous edition of her works published by Mercure de France in 1929. On the back cover, we read: 'La poésie de Cécile Sauvage est vouée au bonheur, aux joies de la maternité et à la simplicité de la nature' [The poetry of Cécile Sauvage is devoted to happiness, to the joys of maternity and to the simplicity of nature]. As we shall see, this is at the very least a simplification. It seems strange, to begin with, to assert that her poetry is 'vouée au bonheur' given that one of her five collections is entitled *Mélancolie*, and many poems in the other collections evoke death, loss, and sadness.

up, as Krysinska's has been. There is no academic critical literature on her poetry, although, unlike Krysinska's, it has been relatively accessible.[2] Simone de Beauvoir, for example, read and admired her work; but she had little distinctive to say about it. She is content to present it as an expression of the female condition at the time, quoting only passages that directly concern maternity.[3]

Krysinska was actively, deliberately marginalised. She was removed, by card-carrying misogynists, from the central position that should have been hers, and it is an act of academic and cultural justice to restore her to that position. I do not think, however, that we can attempt anything similar with Sauvage. It is not just that she was not as egregiously victimised as Krysinska was. It is also that the centre was never the place for her. Her work contests the very concept of centrality. If we take marginalisation to be a state from which poets are to be rescued, it seems somehow wrong to put Sauvage in that category.

★   ★   ★   ★   ★

One of the grand central narratives in French literary history into which Cécile Sauvage does not fit concerns versification. She was born as the ancient monolithic tradition of regular verse was being challenged for the first time (by Krysinska and others), and she wrote her poetry in an era of titanic cultural struggles between poetic traditionalists and revolutionaries, closely interwoven with the equally polarised politics of the time. Her own versification, however, stages a different kind of drama.

Cécile Sauvage's prosody has, I suspect, never been closely analysed, but it deserves to be. It is extremely subtle, deft, careful, precise, and knowing. She rarely writes verse that is as free as that of Krysinska; but nor does she entirely follow the rules of traditional verse. Her rhythms and rhymes are in constant dialogue with the ancient, central tradition and its rules. Of all those rules, the one that she plays with most insistently is one of the least known. It concerns a single inaudible written letter: the last consonant of the line, when it is unpronounced.

Sauvage's second collection of poems, dated 1908, is entitled *L'Âme en bourgeon* [The Soul in Bud]. The poems in it tell a tale, in chronological order. The first-person voice is that of a woman who is pregnant, then gives birth to a son. It begins with three magnificent alexandrines, lines perfect in their rhythm and rhyme according to the most hallowed canons of French verse. Victor Hugo or Charles Baudelaire could not have written better from the point of view of prosody — though certainly neither would have expressed for himself the sentiment these lines convey:

2   The only writer who has conducted sustained research of academic value into Cécile Sauvage is Béatrice Marchal, who has published two books concerning her. Both, however, centre on her relationships with the men in her life, rather than on her poetry. One, *Écrits d'amour* (Paris: Cerf, 2009), concerns her relationship with Jean de Gourmont; the other, *Les Chants du Silence* (Paris: Delatour, 2013), her relationship with her son Olivier Messiaen.

3   See Simone de Beauvoir, *Le Deuxième Sexe II*, Collection Folio (Paris: Gallimard, 1976), pp. 359–65.

Nature, laisse-moi me mêler à ta fange,
M'enfoncer dans la terre où la racine mange,
Où la sève montante est pareille à mon sang. (47)

[Nature, let me blend myself with your filth,
Dig myself into the earth where roots eat,
Where the rising sap is like unto my blood.]

Our poet seeks to blend with a nature which is not merely flowers and birdsong. It is nature as earth, as soil, as muck, as the source of nourishment for something else, something that grows according to its own laws. She is asking, in the first two lines, not to be a pretty plant, but to be one with the soil that feeds the plant. Then, in a shift typical of many in her verse, the third line displaces the identification. The sap rising from the soil is, she says, like her blood. This suggests not that she will be the plant, but that the plant will take something of hers. We soon understand the parallel between this image, and her feelings in pregnancy. The child within is not her — he is himself (the child's gender is always given as masculine, and indeed, when born, we see he is a boy).[4] She is the ground from which he grows. But at the same time, there is a vital sharing and communication between them: a communication without words, without sound, without sight. In this sharing, the mother takes a unique delight. This delight is constantly (though usually implicitly) contrasted with the drudge and dullness of normal communication, which passes through language and gesture, sound and sight.

She consistently uses, from the title of the collection on, a single, simple word to designate that part of the human being whose mode of being and of sharing is beyond words: it is the soul, *l'âme*. As I have said earlier in this book, it is all too easy to overlook the distinctive force of that word. It is the key to understanding the geography of Sauvage's poetic world.

The communication of souls is impossible using the tools of human social interaction. When one soul talks to another, indeed, one of its two inevitable topics is the heaviness and soullessness of life as it is inevitably led by humans. Here is a poem in which the mother's soul talks to that of the child within:

Tu tettes le lait pur de mon âme sereine,
Mon petit nourrisson qui n'a pas vu le jour,
Et sur ses genoux blancs elle berce la tienne
En lui parlant tout bas de la vie au front lourd. (55)

[You suck the pure milk of my serene soul,
My little nursling who has not seen the day,
And she on her white knees rocks your own soul
Speaking to her[5] very quietly of heavy-browed life.]

---

4   I shall allow myself to state at this point that I will be avoiding analysis of Sauvage's work as autobiography. The identity and subsequent career of her son are well known; but they are not germane to my argument. I am also, to be honest, conscious of wishing to avoid the general tendency to interpret women's writing as autobiographical.

5   The soul, *l'âme*, is always feminine in French. I would have upset that gender identity if I had translated the mother's soul with a feminine pronoun and the baby's with a masculine or neuter.

I said earlier that the alexandrines that begin the collection were perfect in rhythm and rhyme. These four lines are, too: the syllable count is perfect, the caesura is perfect, the rhymes are perfect... except for the very last letter. I am afraid that to appreciate what Sauvage is doing here, we have to descend into the arcanes of French prosody.

There is a rule, little spoken of but followed religiously by every serious poet writing in French from the sixteenth century to the last third of the nineteenth, concerning the unpronounced last consonant of a line. It is known as 'la règle de la liaison supposée' [the rule of supposed liaison]. It goes like this: in French, many words have a final consonant that is normally unpronounced, but may be pronounced if the following word begins with a vowel. In *quand il est là*, the 'd' at the end of *quand* may well be pronounced; and if it is pronounced, it is pronounced like a 't'. So the word *quand* can only rhyme with words ending with a final consonant that is normally unpronounced, but would be pronounced like a 't' if it were pronounced. Thus, *quand* rhymes with *plant* and with *Gand*, but not with *taon* or *plans*.

According to this rule, Sauvage's otherwise perfect lines end with a false rhyme: *lourd* does not rhyme with *jour*. In 1908, such infringements were not an absolute novelty. Over the previous thirty years, as part of the same loosening of rules that had led to free verse, poets had been increasingly experimenting with such things. But when they had engaged in these experiments, they had done so obviously, insistently, and systematically. Rimbaud's poem 'Honte', for example, written in about 1872 and first published in 1886, rhymes *tant* and *flanc*, which is false in the same way as Sauvage's *jour* and *lourd*; but the entire poem is clearly built from the beginning around false rhymes and other infringements of rules, and that is equally obviously in harmony with the theme of the poem, which is the hatred of adult authority. Krysinska, in the 1880s and 1890s, used rhymes, non-rhymes, false rhymes, assonance, and alliteration in a constant dazzling display of provocative virtuosity. Sauvage, on the other hand, stays within the old rules throughout this quatrain — then abandons them at the very end, for the span of one single consonant that could not be heard. Why? What is the reason for this inaudible inharmony?

L'Âme en bourgeon is about bodies and souls, their essential difference, and their unavoidable interweaving. This poem shows a soul talking to another soul: that of the mother to that of the unborn baby. But talk does not come naturally to souls. We do not find it in nature. Talk is the medium of that which, for Sauvage, is the soul's outcast other: the civilised social life of humans. To the extent that a soul may appear able to talk at all, it cannot do so without reluctantly yoking itself to that life, the life of the social being situating itself relative to others; and that life has a heaviness which always threatens the harmony of the soul.

For the soul is harmony, and only exists in harmony. The rules of poetry are designed to reflect that harmony. The rules governing rhythm and rhyme are all designed to allow us to find similarities of form and sound between verses that have different meanings: to bring harmony to variety. That is what poetry does, and it is what souls do. But it is what life refuses. The rising tide of free verse had always presented itself as driven by the force of life, of a life that, like the child who speaks in Rimbaud's 'Honte', refuses to be bound by old rules. Swimming against that tide, Sauvage tells us, in *L'Âme en bourgeon*, that before what we call life, there is the soul. She had felt that soul within her. It had no need of Rimbaud's revolt. It was not in conflict with authority. She did not exercise authority over her unborn child. Let us note what her soul is doing with the soul of the child: it is rocking, 'elle berce', that archetypal gesture of back and forth which is also the fundamental principle of rhyme as of lullabies, *berceuses*. This we may contrast with the movement of speech, which is linear, not formally repetitive. But life will out, and when it comes out, the lullaby ends.

L'Âme en bourgeon builds up from the beginning a kind of foreboding and suspense that is normally found only in novels and plays, not in collections of poems. The reader feels with the narrator the wonder and beauty of the bond between mother and unborn child. But the genius of Sauvage is to make us sense that this wonder and beauty are dependent on the inwardness, on the separation between the child and life that the mother's body provides.[6] What will happen, we wonder, both to her versification and to her soul's harmony, when the child is born? The logic of the verse leads us to fear that its serenity will not survive that event, that birth will destroy the harmony and the bond. We hope against hope.

The baby is indeed born. His birth is greeted with qualified despair — and another false rhyme, of the same kind, infringing the 'règle de la liaison supposée':

> Te voilà hors de l'alvéole,
> Petite abeille de ma chair,
> Je suis la ruche sans parole
> Dont l'essaim est parti dans l'air.
>
> Je n'apporte plus la becquée
> De mon sang à ton frêle corps;
> Mon être est la maison fermée
> Dont on vient d'enlever un mort. (65)
>
> [Here you are out of the cell,
> Little bee of my flesh,
> I am the wordless hive
> From which the swarm has departed into air.
>
> I no longer feed your frail body
> Like a baby bird with my blood;
> My being is like the shut-up house
> From which a dead body has just been removed.]

That last line is, to me at least, disturbingly cruel. The birth of the poet's son is also his death. He has left her, as decisively as the swarm leaves the hive, or as a dead body leaves a house. There can be no return, and no more communication between their souls. Is it to be the end of poetry?

It is certainly the end of a certain kind of poetry. From this point on, Sauvage never, in any of her poems, returns to the sense of pure joy in communion with

6   What would Lacan have made of Sauvage's poetry? As far as I know he was unaware of its existence.

another being which we find in the earlier poems of *L'Âme en bourgeon*. There is, certainly, love for and happiness with her son, but it is always adulterated with a longing to return to the lost fusion. The last poem in the book suggests again that the birth of her son is also a bitter death which she must accept:

> Il faut que mon cœur se rehausse
> D'un orgueil moins âpre et plus fort,
> Que je laisse aller à la fosse
> Ce qui jette une odeur de mort;
>
> Que je promène sur la plaine
> Des regards moins intransigeants,
> Que je diffuse mon haleine
> Dans l'haleine et l'âme des gens.
>
> Ainsi le veut l'heure éblouie
> De mon nouvel enfant de lait.
> A lui l'audace, la folie,
> La montagne, le serpolet;
>
> A moi l'ivresse retenue
> Comme l'écume qui montait
> Retombe lentement fondue,
> A moi la sobre vérité. (75–76)

> [My heart must lift itself up again
> By means of a stronger and less fierce pride;
> I must allow to fall into the pit of the grave
> That which gives out the smell of death;
>
> I must send wandering over the plain
> Less intransigeant looks,
> I must mingle my breath
> With the breath and the soul of people.
>
> Such is the requirement of the dazzled time
> Of my new suckling child.
> His portion: daring, folly,
> The mountain, wild thyme;
>
> My portion: headiness restrained
> As froth after rising
> Falls back slowly melting.
> My portion: sober truth.]

The only false rhyme in this poem is the very last. Once again, the falseness is subtle, inaudible, contained in a single silent consonant — or its absence. The sober post-partum truth does not rhyme perfectly. But nor does it simply destroy the harmony.

A similar peculiar sleight of versification is used in a poem from a later collection, *Fumées* [Smokes], which she dates from 1910:

> Quelle molle inexistence
> Descend en pâle lueur

De ce bouleau qui balance
Sa ramure de fraîcheur.
Cette fraîcheur endormie
De lumière verte et calme
A la rêveuse harmonie
Et le silence de l'âme. (126–27)

[What a soft inexistence
Comes down in pale glow
From this birch which rocks
Its cooling network of twigs and branches.
This sleepy coolness
Of green calm light
Has the dreamy harmony
And silence of the soul.]

The 'molle inexistence' from which this poem sets out hardly sounds inspiring. And yet, in a typical Sauvage reversal of values, we are led to see that it is perhaps existence, rather than inexistence, and hardness rather than softness, that would be uninspiring. The poet finds in the birch tree that same rocking motion which her soul had shared with her unborn child. There is nothing firm about that motion, nor about the way it reaches us from the tree. Its very existence is problematic. But it shares with the soul two key characteristics: silence and harmony. Having a life but no words, and a rocking motion rather than one aimed at a target, the birch tree can share a certain harmony with our soul.

Sauvage never lets us forget that the very concept of the soul presupposes a duality in us. Not for her, however, the old Christian opposition between the soul and the body. On the contrary, as we saw in *L'Âme en bourgeon*, the body can have a non-verbal life which is not unlike that of the tree, close to the soul. The harmony of the birch tree is actually in the movement of its physical body. Indeed, Sauvage's poetry is shot through, from beginning to end, with the sense that in the physical nature of living things there is a beauty which human language destroys. That is one of the reasons for which she is not an urban poet, for the city is built on words, whereas the countryside allows one to dream of evading them. The soul's other is not the body, but words; the words that break the silence, the dream, and the harmony of the soul. Between the mother and the unborn child, there was a bodily connection, but no words passed. Similarly, between the birch tree and the soul no words pass. Trees do not talk.

Poetry, however, is made of words. Therefore, a poetry that is built on the distinctive value of the non-verbal is bound to question its own medium. In that questioning, one aspect of the French poetic tradition turns out to be on the side of the soul: its harmony, its rocking motion, its repetitions, its to-and-fro. Still, poetry's wordiness is always a discomfort.

Sauvage has two ways of working into her verse the dynamics of that discomfort. The first we see at the beginning of this poem, in the 'molle inexistence'. It is to undermine our faith in the way we receive words. The way that words conventionally value a phenomenon turns out not to correspond to its role in the establishment of harmony. Inexistence and softness, initially unappealing, in fact take us inwards, towards the soul; just as, at the beginning of *L'Âme en bourgeon*, earth, filth, mud, 'la fange', normally in poetry the enemies of ideal beauty, turn out to figure the element of the perfect harmony between mother and unborn child. The very end of 'Quelle molle inexistence' incarnates her other technique for figuring harmony by unsettling words. 'Calme' does not exactly rhyme with 'l'âme'; the 'l' is on the wrong side of the 'a'. How much do we notice this? Who would notice? An informed guess might be that a century ago, readers generally would have been struck by it; today, few would be aware of it. Perhaps it hardly matters. But in the same way, the poem hardly matters. Poems, like rhymes, are made of words, words take us away from harmony, and rhymes, like poems, need tactics to alert us to the unsatisfactory nature of the material from which they are made, at the same time as they lull us into a soft inexistence where we can sense the silence and harmony of the soul.

★   ★   ★   ★   ★

The poems that Sauvage published in book form were written over only six years, from 1905 to 1911 (though some poems written later were published after her death in 1927). We have seen how *L'Âme en bourgeon* follows a narrative arc. If one reads all five of her poetry collections in chronological order, one receives a powerful impression of a wider narrative arc covering the entire body of work. There is, from the moment of the birth of the child, a steadily increasing melancholy and weariness of life. This is accompanied by a gradual shift in thematics, towards a more explicit exploration of the nature of art, and specifically of the relations between poetry, language, gender roles, and music. Towards the end of the last collection she published, *Le Vallon* [The Valley], we find this:

> Voici l'homme chargé
> D'un gros livre broché
> Plein d'assurance et sage.
> Que le monde est divers, mouvant, originel,
> Qu'il est atmosphérique en regard de ces pages
> Qui prétendent fleurir dans le temps éternel
> Et suivront le destin du sable et du nuage.
> Plus haut que la raison s'élève le silence
> Du vallon mélodique où l'âme se balance,
> Où devant la Beauté nue entre les fougères
> L'humanité défile ainsi qu'une étrangère
> Dans le sein de sa propre et divine ambiance. (157–58)

> [Here comes the man weighed down
> By a heavy bound book
> Full of self-assurance and good sense.
> How diverse the world is, how shifting, how original,
> How atmospheric, compared with these pages
> Which claim to flower in an eternal time
> And which will know the fate of sand and cloud.
> Higher than reason rises up the silence

Of the melodic valley where the soul rocks itself,
Where before naked Beauty between the bracken fronds
The ranks of humanity pass as if it were a stranger
Surrounded by its own, its divine ambiance.]

There are many words and themes here we might recognise from *L'Âme en bourgeon*: the soul, the rocking movement associated with it, the opposition between the world of words (here epitomised by the book) and the silence of a natural world which is not to be identified with the conventional beauty of nature. (The 'fougères' mentioned in the third-last line are a recurring presence in her later poetry, as are grasshoppers. The fields of bracken they evoke are not the traditional image of rural beauty.) We find, too, the combination of perfectly versified lines with rhymes that, in subtle ways, subvert convention. Two elements, however, are new. 'Voici l'homme chargé,' the poem begins... certainly, in typical Sauvage style, one can read this as ambiguous. Is 'l'homme' humanity in general? A specific male person? Or men in general, as opposed to women? The French allows for all of these. The modern reader, however, will find it difficult not to hear, in the work of a poet so constantly conscious of gender roles, the last of these meanings. Men rely on, are loaded down by, and are welcome to keep, words consigned in books, heavy words, words that would claim eternity, but are in fact no more eternal than the mineral forms of sand and cloud. What interests Sauvage (and, by implication, women and children rather than adult men) is a quality that she attributes first to the world, and then to the valley after which the collection is named. It has not the weight, fixity, and reason of the man's bound book, with its claim to eternity. Instead, we find it associated with the adjectives 'divers, mouvant, originel' and 'atmosphérique'; then we are told it is silent — and 'mélodique'.

This association of music, through melody, with silence, though perhaps not often as abrupt as it is here, is so ubiquitous in the poetry of the nineteenth and early twentieth centuries in France (as, indeed, elsewhere in Europe) that it hardly strikes the reader, objectively strange though it may be. More obvious is the opposition between the 'vallon mélodique' which is clearly the poem's spiritual home and the disagreeably heavy book with which the poem begins. Sauvage published this poem in a book. Therefore, we are led to conclude that there must be different kinds of book. There is the man's book, weighty and reasonable; and there is hers, silent and melodic like the valley, and the world. This distinction is not entirely original. It reflects in many ways the distinction made by Verlaine in his famous 'Art poétique' between verse which aims to be like music, and 'littérature'. Clearly, the man's book in Sauvage's poem corresponds to the weighty literature that Verlaine considers unpoetic. But Sauvage is here opposing that male wordiness, not to verse, but to world and melodic valley, 'le monde' and 'le vallon mélodique'. She is more radical than Verlaine in appearing to refuse any direct connection between what she values and words. In the valley of melody, no one utters a word, not even the poet. There is only silent music. And Sauvage is correspondingly more radical than Verlaine in affirming that music is present everywhere in nature where plants and animals grow, whereas words are absent. Music must be considered as silent if we look for it through words; although if we know how to listen, we can hear it as sound in nature:

> Langueur pure, douce harmonie
> Des pelouses et des sentiers,
> Les crapauds chantent dans ma vie
> Avec leurs violons mouillés. (86)

> [Pure langour, gentle harmony
> Of lawns and lanes,
> Toads sing in my life
> With their humid violins.]

This little poem, from *Mélancolie* (her first collection after *L'Âme en bourgeon*), is a celebration of the music of toads. Like the beauty of bracken, this is hardly conventional. Birds make music; do toads? But that is precisely the lesson of Sauvage's poetry. She gently herds us away from the belief, encouraged by generations of poets, that there are privileged places in nature, privileged creatures, privileged sights and sounds. She shepherds us towards the intuition that wherever beasts and plants are living according to their natures, there is music. Only humans interrupt this harmony.

The poet herself is party to that interruption. The 'langueur' with which this poem begins is a constant theme, from *Mélancolie* on: the poet, by virtue of the fact that she is a civilised human condemned to live in a world of words, is in a state of permanent nostalgia, melancholy, and world-weariness, which is only relieved by moments of wordless connection with unborn children and quiet country places.

Unborn children and quiet country places; but also with her own soul. Here, too, Sauvage is more radical, more single-minded, more consistent than Verlaine or Mallarmé, indeed than any other poet I know. She separates herself in two. There is the woman who speaks, writes, walks, talks, lives; and there is her soul, who says nothing, as nature says nothing, and lives in the silently musical, rocking time of nature. Mallarmé, certainly, proposes an apparently comparable separation of himself into two: Stéphane Mallarmé as a civilised bourgeois citizen, and his soul. In 'Crayonné au théâtre' [Pencilled in the Theatre], he goes to the theatre with his soul. Bemoaning the superficial state of the dramatic art of his time, he asks his soul what she thinks of it. She responds in words, explaining to him that he was foolish to expect a Parisian theatre to satisfy his artistic needs.[7] Cécile Sauvage's soul, on the contrary, never speaks to her. It has no words. Its only mode of expression is music; music as silent as that of nature:

> Douce chanson, claire chanson,
> Tu sors de mon âme elle-même,
> Comme la rose hors du buisson
> Penche sa pourpre qu'elle sème.
> Tu nais grave comme le jour

---

7   See 'Crayonné au théâtre', where he visits the theatre *'with Psyche, my soul'* (Mallarmé's italics; he is quoting Poe's 'Ulalume'), finds nothing to satisfy her there, and confesses to having made a mistake; Stéphane Mallarmé, 'Crayonné au théâtre', in *Œuvres complètes*, II, 160–61.

Avec un lumineux silence
Où le rêve de ton amour
A le calme d'une eau qui pense,
Et tu rejoins si purement
Les voix de l'ombre de la plaine
Qu'on ne distingue pas le vent
Ni les parfums de ton haleine. (93)

[Sweet song, clear song,
You flow out of my soul herself
Just as the rose out of the bush
Leans her purple which she sows.
You are born as grave as the day
With a luminous silence
In which the dream of your love
Has the calmness of thinking water,
And you join so purely
With the voices of shade and plain
That one cannot distinguish the wind
Or the perfumes from your breath.]

This poem's versification is irreproachable. The subtle incertitude at the end which, in other poems, is generated by a false rhyme, is here created by a syntactic ambiguity instead. One might read: the song's breath cannot be distinguished from the wind and perfumes of nature. Or one might read: the wind and the perfumes of the song's breath cannot be perceived. Does the song have breath? Does it have a fragrance? This cannot be decided, any more than we can decide whether it has a sound, a specific rhythm, or any other tangible physical characteristics. Nothing that belongs to or issues from the soul can be pinned by words to any physical manifestation. If that rule did not apply, there would be no soul; and Sauvage clearly believes, not only that the soul exists, but that there would be no value in poetry or in nature without it.

★   ★   ★   ★   ★

As I said at the outset, everywhere one finds her mentioned, Cécile Sauvage is always presented as the poet of maternity and of nature. My initial instinctive reaction to this is to sigh wearily. It is such a sexist stereotype; we know how poets classified thus will always be relegated to the second rank, as if maternity and nature were secondary considerations. But that is precisely what the poetry of Sauvage invites us to doubt.

If nature and maternity are secondary, what would be primary? I think the answer to this, in the poetic world she knew, can be summed up in one word: Paris. When it is said that Baudelaire was the poet of modernity, this is inevitably linked with the urban character of much of his later poetry. When he added a new section entitled 'Tableaux parisiens' to the second edition of *Les Fleurs du Mal* in 1861, and published a series of prose poems under the title of *Le Spleen de Paris*, he was recognising the centrality of the city of Paris to the contemporary questioning of the nature and status of poetry. He was, of course, right. It was in Paris that prose poetry and free verse in French were developed, and, not much later, that cubism was born. That centrality of Paris is not an adoration of Paris. It is always linked with a sense of alienation. 'Horrible vie! Horrible ville!' wrote Baudelaire, in 'A une heure du matin', remembering a day in the life of a Parisian intellectual.[8] Poetry is not in sympathy with the centre of modern bourgeois life; it marks itself out, it rebels against that centre. But it performs that marking-out, that rebellion, it engages with the centrality of the city to modern life, in order to believe in itself as central. It reflects the structure of bourgeois capitalist modernity in the sense that it has a centre. An invisible one, certainly, as the financial power of capitalism is invisible; but one whose attraction cannot be resisted. Art is exclusive, as snobbery in Proust is exclusive (hence his exhausting fascination with it).

In this totalising modern concept of art, maternity has no place. Baudelaire's poem 'Bénédiction' recounts how the poet's mother curses him at his birth, and vows to make him suffer. The poet grows in spite of his mother's cruelty into a pure idealist with a serene sense of beauty. There is, here, in poetry, a violent refusal of the bond between mother and child. Baudelaire's poetry rejects maternity. No woman, nothing natural, can be involved in the transmission of its essence. Poetry must be a matter between a male God and privileged male humans:

> Vers le Ciel, où son œil voit un trône splendide,
> Le Poète serein lève ses bras pieux
> Et les vastes éclairs de son esprit lucide
> Lui dérobent l'aspect des peuples furieux:
>
> — 'Soyez béni, mon Dieu, qui donnez la souffrance
> Comme un divin remède à nos impuretés
> Et comme la meilleure et la plus pure essence
> Qui prépare les forts aux saintes voluptés!'[9]
>
> [Towards Heaven, where his eye sees a splendid throne,
> The serene Poet lifts up his pious arms
> And the broad lightning of his lucid spirit
> Hides from him the aspect of the peoples in their fury;
>
> — 'Be blest, my God, you who give suffering
> As a divine remedy for our impurities
> And as the best, the purest essence
> Which prepares the strong for the voluptuous pleasures of saintliness!']

A single Poet, with a capital; a single Heaven, with a capital; a single God, with a capital. None of these Baudelairean upper-case singularities will be found anywhere in the poetry of Sauvage. Nor does one find the name of any city. Paris is completely absent. In fact, all place names are absent. Her poetry grows, not from the City of God, nor from any other city, but from the muck of nature. Is nature, then, Sauvage's divinity? Does it deserve a capital N? Once again, Sauvage plays

8   Charles Baudelaire, *Le Spleen de Paris*, ed. by Aurélia Cervoni and Andrea Schellino, Collection Folio (Paris: Gallimard, 2017), p. 58.
9   Baudelaire, *Les Fleurs du Mal* (1857), p. 14.

the subtlest of games with the conventions of the written language she inherits. She places the word 'Nature' at the beginning of the line, in the poem cited above from *L'Âme en bourgeon*; so we cannot tell if it has a capital by virtue of its divinity, or simply by virtue of the position of the word in the poem. Nature never, in her work, has a capital anywhere else.

In one sense, her poetry is supremely that of place. She describes places; places in the countryside, whose character becomes that of her poetry. But none of these places is central. They are humble hills, plains and valleys, not grandiose mountains or infinite oceans. None has a name. We see no cities, towns, or indeed villages in her poetry. It recognises no social centre, as it recognises no religious, artistic, or financial centre. It quietly refuses the very notion of centrality.

Yes, I sigh when I read that Cécile Sauvage is the poet of maternity and of nature. But having been ravished by the power of her poetry, I do not sigh because that is untrue. I sigh because of the implication that it is, for that reason, somehow a lesser poetry. It is not. To me, this poetry of maternity and of nature (which is also a poetry about music, poetry, and many other things, including how a woman perceives her own body) is not just beautiful; it also dances with and illuminates the tradition of French verse in a marvellously delicate manner that allows us to see better than any other what that tradition really contains of value. Does this mean that the poetry of maternity and of nature, Sauvage's poetry, should be given a central place, or at least a more central place, in French poetry? Is it marginalised, and should it be un-marginalised? Centralised, perhaps? To those questions, I have no answer. The very force which sweeps me away into finding it beautiful and fascinating also tells me to refuse to think in terms of centres as desirable, and margins as places from which one needs rescuing. I just want to let her poetry be.

PART V

❖

Between What We See,
What We Hear, and What We Read

I am writing this book for the love of art. Shouldn't I be trying to persuade you to get to know the art I love? After all, I am (or have been) a teacher and a critic. Teachers are generally thought to be distressed (or disgusted) at the thought that their students might never actually read the texts that are being taught. Similarly, critics will generally either write about their favourite works for an intended audience of people who already know them, or else, if they like a book, try to make their public want to read it.

In the final part of this book, however, I will be discussing two works which no student, to the best of my knowledge, has ever read or is likely to read, and which, dear reader, I can be almost certain you have never seen and will never see. They are artist's books: books produced in small print runs, not only as texts, but as art objects in their own right, as works of plastic and visual art. The material form, feeling, and appearance of the book, the visual artwork that accompanies the text, and the way the text is set out, are as indivisible from the book's identity as the wood is from a Stradivarius or the marble from a Michelangelo statue. They were published by Henri Rivière and Tristan Tzara, in 1888 and 1923. They are not particularly famous, and not easy to get hold of. I will be arguing that to appreciate them, you really need to see them, physically.

This may seem a perverse and self-defeating strategy. What could be more pointless than to tell you how wonderful something is, then to say you will never have any access to it, in its wonderfulness? But actually, in the tradition to which this book is dedicated, that strategy is everywhere. In fact, it is the very foundation on which art is built. Keats's 'Ode on a Grecian Urn' is in praise of an urn we will never see, and of the inaudibility of the music played by the pipes figured on that urn:

> Heard melodies are sweet, but those unheard
>   Are sweeter; therefore, ye soft pipes, play on;
> Not to the sensual ear, but, more endear'd,
>   Pipe to the spirit ditties of no tone.

It was a commonplace in Keats's time that we have no clear idea of what the music of the ancient Greeks sounded like, so he could be confident that his readers would be unable to imagine the tunes issuing from those unseen pipes. Proust, in *À la recherche du temps perdu*, ensures that we cannot see or hear the great musical, visual, and literary artworks he evokes and discusses, by the simple expedient of attributing them to fictional creators. Satie's praise of Beethoven's tenth symphony draws, albeit in satirical mode, from the same aesthetic rulebook. So do the endless evocations in late nineteenth-century poetry of music that its readers did not know, played on instruments they had never heard: viols and harpsichords, lyres and lutes. The same applies to the even more endless evocations of silent music, the music of nature, the music of the spheres. None of these is perceptible to our senses. Hence they all allow writers to situate true beauty beyond the reach of those senses. More importantly, they situate the true value of art outside what the artist can actually create or determine. This is what leads, in the end, to Andy Warhol's assertion that his favourite sculpture is a hole in the wall, or John Cage's *4' 33"*, that silent piece of music whose avowed intention is to get the audience to tune in, not to notes provided by the composer, but to the sounds that always surround us.[1] The true artist does not show us, in what he or she makes, the essence of art. The true artist guides our eye or ear towards a different kind of perception.

Surely, though, it takes an artist to do this. Marcel Duchamp (unless it was Elsa von Freytag-Loringhoven), John Cage, and Andy Warhol can work their modernist magic, and make us see art where we might have seen only a urinal or heard background noise in a concert room. Proust can persuade us that the fictional Vinteuil is a genius, and Keats that his non-existent Grecian urn is a thing of beauty. How dare I place myself in their company? What makes me think that I can pull the same trick, and persuade you, my reader, through my own words, that there is art in books you cannot see? The answer to these questions lies partly in the very nature of the artist's book, and partly in the concept of creative criticism, from which the book you are now reading began.

Something between hubris and original sin has led me always to believe, as did Baudelaire, Mallarmé, Ponge, and Derrida, that critical writing must try to emulate the values of the literature it takes as its pretext. They, however, did not write primarily as critics. They were poets, or in Derrida's case, a philosopher. Their readers are generally drawn to their literary critical writings through the more general value of their other publications. I do not have this advantage. I live with the knowledge that my readership will be largely limited to people who are interested in the objects of my criticism. When I write about things which are of no prior interest to anyone, how can I expect to attract readers?

But do I want to attract readers? Perhaps the artist's book teaches us that attracting readers need not be the writer's aim. I said in my introduction to this book that the more I investigated the artistic tradition, the less democratic its values came to appear. Nothing is more undemocratic than the artist's book. If one considers

---

1   Andy Warhol: 'When I look at things, I always see the space they occupy. I always want the space to reappear, to make a comeback, because it's lost space when there's something in it. If I see a chair in a beautiful space, no matter how beautiful the chair is, it can never be as beautiful to me as the plain space. My favourite sculpture is a solid wall with a hole in it to frame the space on the other side' (*The Philosophy of Andy Warhol*, p. 144).

its production values from a sociological point of view, it is appallingly elitist. It is expensive, and deliberately created in a limited number of copies. A painting, of course, is only created in a single copy, and is even more expensive; but the painting can be hung on a wall and seen by many people. The artist's book is designed and fated to be kept in a cupboard and seen by almost no one.

Almost? The first of these two essays is about a book by Tristan Tzara. Many of Tzara's books were originally sold with their pages uncut. To open them, to read them and to see the images within, one had to take a knife to them, and cut the pages. The English artist and collector Roland Penrose bought several of them when they first came out. His collection is now in the library of the Scottish National Gallery of Modern Art. Many of the books have their pages still uncut. Roland Penrose never read them. No one has ever read them. No one, quite probably, ever will, because the library refuses to cut the pages. Its aim is to preserve the works in the state in which they were received by the library: unread, forever. As if that were the ideal state of the book.

This is, admittedly, an extreme case. The two books I will be presenting to you have been read, albeit by tiny numbers of people. I bought my copies second hand, and they were reasonably well worn. Nonetheless, I imagine their previous owners would have been aware both of the exclusivity of the books they had bought, and of that extraordinary sense, which only the artist's book can provide, of secrecy. The book is designed to be kept closed nearly all the time, its beauty invisible. Opening it gives a unique thrill. The most powerful aesthetic emotions of my life have been provided by the moments when, sitting in libraries, I opened Mallarmé's *Le Corbeau* and *L'Après-midi d'un faune* illustrated by Manet (arguably the first ever artist's books), Braque's *Si je mourais là-bas*, Matisse's *Jazz*. The sense that with that gesture of my hand, by opening the cover and turning the pages, I was bringing light to things of such beauty that would soon return to their darkness, the sheer physical proximity to the pages that had been so lovingly and carefully designed and produced by those artists... it gives a peculiar feeling of ghosting the creative process. Still, for me, that was always accompanied by a certain guilt.

Should art not be accessible to all? Do we not now believe that great paintings should be in museums where any art lover can see them, and that great poetry should be similarly accessible? Even critical writing, now, is subjected to the principle of open access. The only exception we tend to make to this principle is copyright: authors need to be able to make money out of what they create. But the artist's book, even when it is out of copyright, knows nothing of open access. Access to it is always closed to almost everyone.

The artist's book seems to want to exist primarily as an object, contained in its own world, which we are only allowed to enter by a special grace which is disturbingly difficult to separate from the social privilege that money or academic status can bring. In its very secrecy, it thus puts on display more clearly than any other genre both the power and the danger of the great artistic tradition. I can neither resist nor deny its beauty. But nor can I blind myself to its obdurate carelessness of inclusivity. I love it; I hate the kind of society that it would seem to stand for. How can I reconcile these two impulses?

I cannot, in fact. However, I can sense a distant point in which they connect. I wrote, quite instinctively, of the artist's book: 'I love it'. Not that I think it is right, or good, or useful, or educational in any way, but: I love it. Now, love is not inclusive, open-access, or democratic. It does not recognise the principle of equal rights for all. Nor does it share the democratic belief that everything must be open to question, to rational analysis. Whether it be a human or a book, what I love is, doubtless, rationally speaking, an object, a thing, a material entity, and it cannot be separated from its materiality; but as I love it, it escapes from that condition.[2] Where to? That I cannot say. All I can do, critically or creatively, is to try to understand the process by which it escapes. This is not a comfortable undertaking. It reveals to me, slowly but mercilessly, how I am myself riven by paradoxes and full of contradictions. To explore one's love of art is to feel the tools of reason losing their grip in a very characteristic way. At least, to me, learning to see how they lose their grip does seem right, good, educational, perhaps even useful. After all, if I say that I hate the kind of exclusive society for which the artist's book seems to stand, that implies I love another kind of society. Indeed I do. But the society I love, like everyone's ideal society, has a problematic relationship with reality, precisely because it is an object of love, and like all objects of love, exclusive. I cannot honestly claim it welcomes all of humanity. How could I? Every society, however imaginary, and whether or not it claims to be democratic, has always defined its polity by excluding from its 'equal rights' certain groups of beings, and those exclusions always seemed natural, until they were successfully contested. Could there be an ideal state of democracy in which there were no such contestable limits? I am sure the answer is no. It will never be clear where humanity begins and ends — if only for the reasons we saw in Part III of this book.

Yes, the love of art is highly problematic, and fraught with moral contradictions. Perhaps if we allowed ourselves to see how and why it is thus, that might help us also to understand, by analogy, why the love of humanity has never been easy.

---

2   Marcel Proust: 'L'œuvre est signe de bonheur, parce qu'elle nous apprend que dans tout amour le général gît à côté du particulier' [The work is a sign of happiness, because it teaches us that in every love the general lies next to the particular] (*Le Temps retrouvé*, in *À la recherche du temps perdu*, ed. by Jean-Yves Tadié, 4 vols, Bibliothèque de la Pléiade (Paris: Gallimard, 1987–89), IV, 483.

CHAPTER 11

❖

Where's the Art?
Tristan Tzara's *De nos oiseaux*

The name of Tristan Tzara (1896–1963) is passably famous in artistic and academic circles. He is always thought of as a Dadaist, and indeed it was with the Dada movement, in the years 1916–23, that he forged his artistic personality. However, his certifiably Dada activities were only a small part of his life's work.

Dada lasted barely seven years. Its other founders — Hans Arp, Hugo Ball, Emmy Hennings, Marcel Janco, and Richard Huelsenbeck — had already abandoned the movement when Tzara proclaimed it dead (for the second time) in 1923. Tzara's career as a poet, on the other hand, lasted forty-five years. Throughout those years, Tzara's preferred and typical form of poetry publication remained the same. He would put together a collection of poems and meanwhile contact a friend who was a visual artist. The friend would provide visual artworks to go inside the book, or occasionally on the cover. Every aspect of the book's physical appearance would be carefully controlled by Tzara and his artist friend, creating a beautiful object that would sit more or less within the tradition of the *livre d'artiste*, the artist's book. Often, the book would be published in a limited edition, or with a small number of more expensive copies containing more elaborate visual art, by the same artist. As we saw in Chapter 7, the list of artists with whom Tzara collaborated thus is astounding. It includes: Arp, Kandinsky, Picasso, Braque, Matisse, Janco, Picabia, Giacometti, Ernst, Dalí, Miró, Sonia Delaunay, Juan Gris, Louis Marcoussis, Suzanne Roger, Camille Bryen, Jean Hugo, Jacques Villon, Fernand Léger, Paul Klee. About forty books of poetry were published in this way.

However, hardly anyone, it seems, has ever read them. They are not at all well known. They are valued in the book market for the visual artworks they contain, not for the poetry. They were not much noticed on first publication. There has been almost no academic critical literature on them. Stephen Forcer has written a pioneering book on Tzara's poetry; but it concentrates on the words of the poetry, not on the book as a physical object, complete with its visual art.[1] Yet the clearest distinguishing feature of Tzara's poetry is that dogged determination always to publish it in something like the artist's book format, in which the book is not merely a container for words, but a physical, visual artwork. He never, in fact, published a

---

1   Stephen Forcer, *Modernist Song: The Poetry of Tristan Tzara* (Cambridge: MHRA, 2006).

book of poetry without visual art, or without careful attention being paid to that physical appearance.

Two plausible explanations suggest themselves for the enduring lack of interest in Tzara's books. Either the poetry they contain is not very good, or too obscure. Or else the books belong to a genre that we have not learned to appreciate. I decided to put my faith in the latter explanation as a result of my own personal experience. I first tried to read Tzara's poetry in the magnificent edition of his complete works, edited with scrupulous care by Henri Béhar, and published between 1975 and 1991.[2] It contains all Tzara's verse, but none of the original visual art. I got nowhere. I could not sense its artistic quality. After a few lines, I lost my ability to concentrate on it. I gave up. Then, when I was studying Dada (working on my book *The Music of Dada*), I saw, in the journals of the movement, how Tzara published his own work when he had control over the printing process. Its physical appearance on the page is always striking, always primordial; and presented thus, it began to make a kind of sense. I managed to find some of his artist's books, and I was engrossed. The verse that had frankly bored me in the edition of his complete work now did something for me. But what?

Meanwhile, I had discovered that nothing is more Dada than this sense of being in the presence of a true work of art, while being totally unable to say why one has that sense. Dada, after all, began from the absolute refusal of any connection between critical reason and artistic quality. I had mapped my own way of dealing with the problem, when looking at Dada as a performing movement. Dada's strategy, I found, building on techniques used by poets since Romantic times, was to use music, conceived of as the art whose value has always been inaccessible to critical reason, to figure the value of its poetry; and it added to that old technique a new one. Abstract visual art, one of whose pioneers was Hans Arp, Tzara's most constant artistic companion, was the demonstration that the non-figurative quality of music could be imported into artistic genres that had previously been representational. If abstract visual art could work, so the argument went, then abstract poetry could work too, abstraction being defined as a composition that represents nothing in the real world outside the work. This was the inspiration behind Dada 'sound poetry', poetry made of nonsense words. It was abstract poetry, to be received as music, not because, like music, it was made of sound, but because, like music, it was an art that did not represent or imitate anything.

I wondered, then, what would happen if I looked for music in Tzara's poetry, and how its figuring of music might relate to abstraction both in poetry and in visual art. I got myself a copy of his book *De nos oiseaux* [Of our Birds], illustrated by Arp and dated 1923, and began by making an inventory of all its references to music.[3]

2   Tristan Tzara, *Œuvres complètes*, ed. by Henri Béhar, 6 vols (Paris: Flammarion, 1975–91).
3   Its publication history is in fact somewhat complicated. Tzara himself, in his own bibliography of his works, dates it from 1923. The book was indeed finished and printed in 1923, but as a result of a disagreement between the author and the publisher, the print run was not released for commercial sale, and very few copies are known to exist. In 1929, another publisher re-issued it (with the same layout and illustrations as in 1923), and this is the edition I have. No date is given in the book, and it is often erroneously assumed by people (including the British Library) who have this second edition

There are certainly a great many. Song is a constant theme. Musical instruments abound. They include violins, cellos, and clarinets, also accordions, mandolins, and pianos. However, while the instruments are often mentioned, inviting us to imagine, doubtless, the music they might play, what we are never told is precisely what music they are playing. Nor are we told who might be listening to them. Similarly, singing is often evoked, but what tune is sung, and who might hear it, we never know.

In the entire collection, I found only one instance of the verb *écouter* [to listen] and one of the verb *entendre* [to hear]. In both cases, the hearing and listening are clearly unconnected with music. In *De nos oiseaux*, then, we are often presented (as we are in the very title of the book) with that which might produce music (do birds not sing?); but we are never witness to its reception. As if we could see where it comes from, but not where it might go.

Nor can we see how it might be shared. In real life, the violin, cello, and clarinet are usually heard in an ensemble, rather than as solo instruments. The piano, mandolin, and accordion are also often parts of an ensemble, or used to accompany song or dance. However, in *De nos oiseaux* the instruments always appear alone. There is never any ensemble; no orchestras, no groups, not even a duo. There are singers and dancers in many poems; but the musical instruments never accompany them.[4] Furthermore, the players of the instruments themselves are never present. They never seem to hear even their own music.

It is as if the poems were giving us the possibility of music by evoking what produces it, but refusing to figure the music itself. The instruments are there, but not the sound they make, nor the effect of that sound on any living being, whether listener or player. We find in the poetry the point of origin of music, but not its point of arrival in concrete musical experience. Every musician, however amateur, knows and appreciates the feeling of being part of the music as we play or sing alone or with others, receiving and living with the music as it is produced. For that lived experience, Tzara's poetry seems to give no space. What, I wondered, is the use of clarinets and violins, of song and of accordions, if there is no one to receive their music? After all, in this sense, Tzara's poetry breaks with a long tradition. From Wordsworth's skylark to Walt Whitman's banjo, from the syrinx of Mallarmé's faun to the flute of Apollinaire's 'musicien de Saint-Merry', poetry as we know it is full of music that, even though we cannot hear it, is presented as it is experienced by the first-person narrator, or by an audience, or at the very least by its player. In eliminating all kinds of audience, even the player as audience, Tzara

---

that it was published in 1923. It is described thus on the front cover: 'Tristan Tzara, *De nos oiseaux*, dessins par Arp'. The publisher is given as Éditions Kra, in Paris.

4   Dance unaccompanied by music was, I feel sure, something Tzara would have learned to think about in discussion with Suzanne Perrottet (1889–1983). Perrottet was one of the core participants in the Zurich Dada soirées. Before she joined the movement, she had already put together an aesthetic rationale for unaccompanied dance, which had led her to a decisive break with the Dalcroze movement. See Suzanne Perrottet, *Ein Bewegtes Leben*, ed. by Giorgio J. Wolfensberger (Bern: Benteli, [n.d.]), p. 93. The question of what sounds, if any, accompanied dance in Zurich Dada soirées is one that will probably forever remain largely unanswered, for lack of evidence. Perrottet, it might be noted, also played improvisations on unaccompanied violin.

seems to be cutting us off from the music itself. Why? What is the point of musical instruments if they do not produce a lived musical experience that we can, at least in imagination, share?

Trying to figure this out, I remembered my original difficulty in receiving Tzara's poetry. The way he presented music in his poetry seemed to me to create an analogous difficulty. In his printed words, poetry was there as an object; but I could not see how it could reach me as a poetic experience. Similarly, in his poetry, music is there, as an object; but it does not seem to reach anyone as a musical experience. Then it occurred to me, in the first place as a vague intuition: perhaps the confrontation between visual art and poetry in Tzara's book offers both a third version of this difficulty, and the way to resolve it.

One thing is consistent across all Tzara's books of poetry: the visual art does not serve to illustrate the poetry. They are juxtaposed, rather than put to work together. Every reader seeks a connection. It is impossible not to desire one, and very difficult not to believe that somewhere, somehow, there is one. But we cannot pin it down, with any sense of security. Sometimes, as we shall see, we fancy we have spotted something, a link, a reason for which a given illustration is placed beside a given poem, perhaps; but before long, we wonder if it is just a coincidence, if we are just making it up, over-interpreting. We are driven to look for something that we feel ought to be given to us, something that any normal poet would give us; and Tzara refuses to let us have it.

This is the exact opposite of the hermeneutic approach to art we are used to. We expect our artistic journey to be one of steadily increasing understanding of, and connection with, the artwork, and through the artwork, with the mindset of the imagined creator. Tzara pushes us in the opposite direction. Instead of inviting us to undertake a journey of interpretation which leads to illumination, he guides us towards abysses we cannot cross, between media and between creators. With the visual art as with the musical instruments, we feel it would be only normal, only fair, for a collaboration with the poetry to usher us into a sense of a shared artistic experience. But that is refused to us. Instead, we are made to contemplate a space between the arts that is also a void. It is indubitably frustrating and baffling. This is hardly surprising. Who could doubt that Tzara, the provocative dadaist, enjoys frustrating and baffling his audience? Still, frustration and bafflement are never the end of the story with Tzara.

> dis: vide pensée
> vite tu sais
> je serai
> violoncelle[5]
>
> [say: empty thought
> quick you know
> I will be
> a cello]

The 'je', the first-person singular, becomes, not music, but a musical instrument.

---

5   Tzara, *De nos oiseaux*, p. 75.

Now this has a famous precedent in the poetic tradition which Tzara acknowledged. Arthur Rimbaud, in both of the 1871 'lettres du Voyant' which are generally taken as his statement of poetic principle, describes the process of becoming a poet precisely as that of becoming a musical instrument. In this process, one becomes, also, a thing, an object. The old poetry in which a human subject speaks is replaced by a new objective poetry, brought to us by an Other, which is an object like a violin or a trumpet: 'votre poésie subjective sera toujours horriblement fadasse. Un jour, j'espère, [...] je verrai dans votre principe la poésie objective [...] Je est un autre. Tant pis pour le bois qui se trouve violon' [your subjective poetry will always be horribly insipid. One day, I hope [...] I will see in your principle objective poetry [...] I is an other. Too bad for the wood which finds itself a violin];[6] 'Car Je est un autre. Si le cuivre s'éveille clairon, il n'y a rien de sa faute' [For I is an other. If brass wakes up as a bugle, you can't blame the brass for that].[7] In Tzara's little poem, we can see the same dynamic. The traditional function of the poetic voice, which is to produce a work in words that we can read, is truncated as the poet becomes a thing that utters no words, no sound, no message we can perceive. However, of course, the poetic *je*, as it becomes a thing, does not become any old thing. It becomes a violin, a bugle, or a cello. Why? Because, arguably unlike any other kind of object in the world, a musical instrument has been created for only one purpose: to project art into real time. To figure the instrument is not to figure any piece of music we can hear. But it is to figure the human drive to experience art in time. Tzara and Rimbaud turn the poet into the object that is the emblem of that drive. At the same time, however, they refuse the essential condition for that drive to realise itself. The trumpet, violin, or clarinet cannot make music without a player.

★ ★ ★ ★ ★

Rimbaud, as is well known, was not able to sustain for long his crusade to create an objective poetry. A few years after writing those 'lettres du Voyant', he gave up writing poetry, replacing it with a life of gun-running action in Africa. Tzara, on the other hand, continued to write poetry all his life. He avoided, it seems, the wall that Rimbaud ran into (which, one might add, was also encountered by all of the other original Dadaists except Arp; Huelsenbeck, Ball, and Hennings all also soon ceased to write poetry). I would like to suggest that the reason for which Tzara was able to do this was his ability to dramatise, to figure in his books the dynamic of instrumentalisation, with all its consequences, including the incomprehension and loss of subjective voice to which it leads, and the unspoken but absolute faith in music on which it is founded.

In *De nos oiseaux*, transformation into a musical instrument is not something that happens only to poets. An elephant's ear can become a piano. Or an aunt's breast can become an accordion:

6   Arthur Rimbaud, letter to Georges Izambard, 13 May 1871, in Arthur Rimbaud, *Œuvres complètes*, ed. by Jean-Luc Steinmetz (Paris: Flammarion, 2010), pp. 91–92.
7   Arthur Rimbaud, letter to Paul Demeny, 15 May 1871, in *Œuvres complètes*, p. 95.

ma tante est accroupie sur le trapèze dans la salle de gymnastique
ses tétins sont des têtes de hareng
elle a des nageoires
et tire tire tire l'acordéon[8] de son sein
elle tire tire tire tire l'acordéon de son sein glwa wawa prohahab[9]

[my aunt is squatting on the trapeze in the gymnasium
her teats are herring's heads
she has fins
and pulls pulls pulls the acordion of her breast
she pulls pulls pulls pulls the acordion of her breast glwa wawa prohahab]

What comes out of the accordion-breast, when the poet's aunt pulls on it? Nothing indicates that it is either music or milk. And if it is words, it is nonsense words: 'glwa wawa prohahab'.

For this poem, 'Saltimbanques' [Acrobats], Tzara gives, in his table of contents, the date 1916. That is, as the early readers of the book would probably have known, a highly significant date in the history of poetry, and of Dada. For it was in 1916 that the Dada movement first produced, and performed live on stage, what came to be known as sound poetry: poetry that was made up of words that could not be understood as meaning anything in particular. This was, indeed, the logical step for Dada poetry to take. The very word 'Dada', as Hugo Ball made clear in his first Dada manifesto, also dating from 1916, was suitable to designate the movement because it had so many different possible meanings in the multiple languages known to and used by the Dadaists; therefore, no one could ever be sure what, if anything, it really meant. It thus reached the audience as a sound, not as a sense. Tzara himself specialised, at the time, in performing poetry that purported to be in African or Oceanic languages, but would certainly have been utterly incomprehensible to his Swiss audience. 'glwa wawa prohahab' is an unmistakeable evocation of this new genre, of poetry made of sounds rather than of comprehensible words.

In the history of Dada, it was a short-lived genre. Within a few years, all its exponents had either stopped writing poetry, or moved on, like Tzara, to writing poetry that was composed at least mainly of words within a language that its readers would recognise and comprehend. I think we can now see why.

Rimbaud and Tzara tell us that when they become poets, they cease to be humans and turn into musical instruments. But the musical instrument cannot actually create music. It cannot make music. It is the human playing the violin or the trumpet that makes the music. We cannot forget this for long. Thus the impulse to make objective poetry leads rapidly to a dead end. The objective poet, like the musical instrument, can only wait for a third party, still human, to come and blow into or bow the instrument that the poet has become. The poet-instrument cannot alone create for us the poetic experience.

8   Tzara here uses only one 'c' in *accordéon*, rather than the usual two. There are several such liberties with French spelling in the book. It would be too easy to suppose that this is due to his imperfect command of French. Elsewhere in the book, he gives *accordéon* with its usual spelling (p. 38).
9   Tristan Tzara, 'Saltimbanques', in *De nos oiseaux*, p. 109.

What Rimbaud did, with such force that his influence on poetry has never waned, is to figure the drama of that situation, of the poet acquiring a conviction that poetry has an inhumanity which stifles him. In many ways, Marcel Duchamp, more slowly and carefully, relived that drama (often as a living death, a life under anaesthetic). The fulguration of sound poetry during the First World War is an iteration of the same drama. The creator or performer of a sound poem could not be speaking in his own voice.[10] He was voicing someone else's language, or a music which was not present in the actual words of the poem. The poetry comes from elsewhere, not from him. He cannot, in fact, create it, any more than the violin can create its tune. This is the double bind of modern art. The artist can no longer create the artwork.

How, then, can the object of art be eased back into human time, so that the poet can continue to write? Rimbaud did not find the answer, and nor did sound poetry. But Tzara did. It relies on a dual mechanism. The first is this: poetry must constantly remind us that we believe in art and we love it, in spite of our modern inability to reason through that faith and that love. It performs this vital task of reminding by evoking the instruments of the ancient artistic tradition from which we have never been weaned. The second part of the mechanism is to transfer the responsibility for playing these instruments, for producing the artistic experience, from the artist to the reader. Tzara as poet does not actually write out for us the work of art. Instead, he gives us, in his books, the elements from which we can construct art — if we have the faith and the courage.

★   ★   ★   ★   ★

What of song? How does that fit into the objective paradigm? When a human being is portrayed as a singer in the act of singing, that, surely, implies a lived, live experience of music, of music proceeding from a human throat. *De nos oiseaux*, as I have said, is full of song. How can Tzara give us song, without that shared experience which his poetics seems to refuse?

There is, in the book, a poem with *chanson* in the title. It is probably Tzara's best-known poem (which is admittedly not saying much): the 'chanson dada'. What, in the poem, makes it a song, rather than a series of words like any other poem? The answer is in the poem's form, its rhythm. It is the only poem in the book which repeats something like the same strophic metrical scheme, three times. This brings to mind the ancient and ever unchanging way in which song has always brought poetry and music together, while respecting their difference. Music works by precise repetition, more than words do. The song allows for this by repeating the same tune, while varying the words; and the indelible trace of this in poetry is the

---

10   In Dada, sound poetry was an overwhelmingly masculine genre. The reasons for this will, I hope, have become clear in this book: the idea of poetry as objective, as a thing, as a created work rather than a living being, was associated with a masculine tradition. Emmy Hennings, who was one of the founders of Dada, and the many other women who worked with it in its early years, including Suzanne Perrottet and Sophie Taeuber, made a vital contribution to the movement; but it was not towards sound poetry that they drew it.

repeated metrical scheme. That scheme is what allows different sets of words to be fitted to the same tune. Every human culture known to me has made use of this principle. So when we see a metrical scheme repeated in a poem with *chanson* in its title, we naturally assume that the scheme corresponds to a tune.

And what might be the tune to the 'chanson dada'? It did, in fact, have one, a lovely little tune, composed by Georges Auric in 1921 (which is also the date Tzara assigns to the poem in *De nos oiseaux*). But it was a well-kept secret. Tzara sang the song once in 1921, in hilarious circumstances, in order to offend André Breton. I know of no evidence that it was ever performed again until forty years later, in 1961, when Tzara recorded it for Hans Richter's film *Dadascope*. Neither Tzara nor Auric ever published the tune.[11] So it is safe to assume that readers of *De nos oiseaux* would not have known that tune, and would have had no access to it. Yet again, what the 'chanson dada' gives us is an evocation of music in its traditional form, defined here by a certain kind of rhythmic structure and repetition, without actually giving us the opportunity to experience that music. Tzara could perfectly well have allowed us access to the tune. He does not.[12] The 'chanson dada' performs the same operation as the many musical instruments we encounter in *De nos oiseaux*. It puts us in mind of music by presenting us with an evocation of a thing whose function is traditionally to allow the production of music; but we are never allowed to feel we are actually witnessing that production. As if the music were frozen into an object.

Freezing is what the poetic voice does in the poem 'autour' [around]:

> jamais jamais je n'oserai
> te donner ma voix gelée
> le vif métal de l'eau
> au fond flûté de ton cerveau[13]

> [never never will I dare
> to give you my frozen voice
> the quickmetal of the water
> at the fluted root of your brain]

And in the penultimate stanza of the same poem, he asks for music itself to be frozen, like an oath on the Bible:

> qu'on gèle la musique sur l'évangile
> et que l'on crève en rêves habiles
> d'une voix forte les reflets
> quitteront la maison mais ce n'est pas de ma faute[14]

> [let music be frozen upon the bible
> and let death explode us into cunning dreams
> of a loud voice the reflections
> will leave the house but it's not my fault]

11   For the history of the tune to the 'chanson dada', see Dayan, *The Music of Dada*, pp. 119–21, 159–61 (I give the tune itself on p. 159).
12   It might be asked why he did give us this access in 1961. The answer is in the visual dimension of the film in which it appears.
13   Tristan Tzara, 'autour', in *De nos oiseaux*, p. 51.
14   Ibid., p. 52.

The poem 'autour' is composed of fifty stanzas. The first forty-nine stanzas, of which the one quoted above is the last, all have four lines. They are followed by a single two-line stanza, which stands apart like the distich at the end of a Shakespearean sonnet: 'mais à quoi bon puisque je t'aime | conquérir les cris du monde' [but what would be the point since I love you | of conquering the cries of the world].[15] As always in Tzara's poems, if one tries to look for a logical sequence of concepts, one rapidly becomes dizzy and discouraged by the apparent disconnects. Still, equally as always, it is worth setting out those disconnects, and speculating on what might have inspired them.

'Je t'aime,' writes Tzara. What could be simpler or more conventional? Is this not what half the world's poetry says? But in half the world's poetry, love and music go together; whereas here, the voice that says 'I love you' seems also to be the one that wants to freeze music. Why? Is not music the food of love? But it is worth examining the famous speech from which that adage has so often been extracted:

> If music be the food of love, play on;
> Give me excess of it, that, surfeiting,
> The appetite may sicken, and so die.
> That strain again! it had a dying fall:
> O, it came o'er my ear like the sweet south,
> That breathes upon a bank of violets,
> Stealing and giving odour! Enough; no more:
> 'Tis not so sweet now as it was before.
> O spirit of love! how quick and fresh art thou,
> That, notwithstanding thy capacity
> Receiveth as the sea, nought enters there,
> Of what validity and pitch soe'er,
> But falls into abatement and low price,
> Even in a minute: so full of shapes is fancy
> That it alone is high fantastical.
> — *Twelfth Night*, 1.1

Thus Duke Orsino describes the experience that Dada turned into an aesthetic principle. Music as it is experienced cannot measure up to love or to art. Only fancy itself — which we might anachronistically interpret either as love, or as imagination — is 'high fantastical'. Here, as in Tzara's poetry, the present artwork 'falls into abatement'.

Duke Orsino, like Tzara, conjures up music, only to stop it from sounding. But for neither of them is that stopped sound the end of the story. It is only the beginning; the creation of a space in which a new music, the music of our imagination, can resound. Tzara engineers that space between those last lines of 'autour', and the page facing them.

Figure 11.1 is the illustration by Arp on that facing page. Some of Arp's illustrations in *De nos oiseaux* are more abstract than others. This illustration to 'autour' is among the least abstract. It seems clearly enough a female figure stopping her ears. Can we relate that to the thematics of the poem? 'autour' can, after all, be

15   Ibid.

FIG. 11.1 Tristan Tzara, *De nos oiseaux*, illus. by Hans Arp (Paris: Kra, [1929]), p. 53.

read as addressed to a female beloved, who is doubtless unable to hear the frozen voice of the poet. However, as soon as we think that, we begin to doubt. Yes, in the illustration as in the poem, the voice does not reach the ear. But in the poem, that is not because the ear is stopped; it is because the voice is frozen. The poem gives us only the male poet's point of view; the illustration shows a female. Are they complementary, then? Perhaps so. But it is for us to fill in the gaps in that complementarity, to bring shapes to fancy. And bringing shapes to fancy is what Arp's illustrations ask us to do.

They are made up of shapes. These shapes are not simply representational, nor simply geometric, nor simply random, nor simply part of any pre-existing artistic vocabulary. They contain elements of all of these, and refuse to settle in any. They need our fancy to make something of them. And then our fancy has a second task to do: relating them to the words around them. That task is ever fanciful, because the relationship between words and images never settles.

That refusal to settle is at the heart of the strategy of Tzara's books. If you look in them for a complete work, you will be frustrated. If you look, not in them, but at them, you will find disparate elements which can inspire you to imagine art, to imagine music, or visual art, or poetry, as it might have been if it could have been there. But it refuses to be there on principle, on the principle that it is wrong to determine your response. What Tzara gives you is an opportunity. He gives it to you by endlessly evoking art, but never allowing any work of art to speak to you in the time of normal human experience. Music is frozen; poetry and visual art interrupt and interrogate each other, and neither gives any sense of completeness. Only art itself is complete, as was fancy for Duke Orsino, and art itself, like fancy, cannot be seen.

No wonder, then, that Tzara's books are not much valued. They are not really works of art in the traditional sense. They are, rather, productions designed to allow us to produce our own sense of art. They never allow us to see the art actually within the poetry.

Concert-goers who love the great Romantic repertoire all know that moment just after the end of a great performance of a great work when one senses its greatness in a unique frisson. The great performance is, indeed, often evoked by reference to a moment of silence before the applause begins. Tzara's books provide their own frisson, in their own moment of silence; but not as one finishes reading them, for one cannot really read them from beginning to end. One dips in and out, wondering and puzzling. The frisson comes as one closes the book. The poems and the illustrations seem to find their home as they meet physically and disappear into the darkness between the pages. It is as they escape from our sight that we feel what they are.

CHAPTER 12

❖

A Window onto the Invisible:
La Tentation de saint Antoine
in Montmartre

This essay is about a blank canvas: an unpainted piece of cloth measuring less than two square metres, stuck over a hole in a wall.

Andy Warhol would have liked that wall with a hole, since his favourite sculpture was 'a solid wall with a hole in it to frame the space on the other side'.[1] Would he have liked the canvas? Perhaps he would. He knew as well as anyone that to appreciate art, one must allow one's thoughts to wander back and forth between holes and what covers them; between blanks and images; between silences and sounds; between muteness and words. I shall begin with the coverings: the images, sounds, and words made to distract an audience from the blankness of the canvas and the emptiness of the hole.

They are to be found in three works all entitled *La Tentation de saint Antoine*, dating from the period 1874–88. Two of them are books. The third was a performance in the shadow theatre of the Chat Noir cabaret in Montmartre, Paris. All three create strange, original, and thought-provoking relationships (real or imagined) between performance, music, and image. I shall begin with the last of the three to be produced, which is also the least famous, the least studied, and the most unique and extraordinary in its format.

La Tentation de saint Antoine by Henri Rivière is a book published in Paris in 1888.[2] It appears at first sight to belong to the category of the *livre d'artiste*, which had been invented not long before, precisely in Paris: the illustrations and the physical quality of the book as an art object are clearly essential production values. It is indeed a strikingly beautiful thing. Images of it can be found by googling on: 'tentation de saint Antoine' Henri Rivière. The cover of the book gives no explicit clue to its genre. On the title page, however, we read:

---

1   Warhol, *The Philosophy of Andy Warhol*, p. 144. See p. 178 n. 1, above.
2   The punctuation of the title is given in three different forms in Rivière's book: with and without the hyphen, with and without the capital on *saint*. I use the form popularised by Flaubert.

Féerie à grand spectacle
en 2 actes et 40 tableaux
par
HENRI RIVIÈRE
représentée pour la première fois sur le théâtre du *Chat Noir*
Le 28 décembre 1887
musique nouvelle et arrangée de
MM ALBERT TINCHANT et GEORGES FRAGEROLLE[3]

The *féerie* was a primarily theatrical, rather than literary, genre, unique, really, to nineteenth-century France, with no exact equivalents elsewhere or at other periods. Its principal ingredients were its spectacular stage-craft, with ingenious scene changes and startling special effects, often involving magical apparitions; its melodramatic and morally simplistic plot, always including magic, supernatural beings, a struggle between good and evil, and the victory of the good; and song and dance. It was universally perceived as a triumph of spectacle over plot, of the visual, musical, and choreographical over the verbal. Whereas other kinds of plays were routinely published and read as literary works in their own right, this made little sense for the *féerie*; generally speaking, when *féeries* were published, they were received, so to speak, as 'books of the play', to remind those who had seen and loved the stage versions of the spectacle they had experienced. (One startling exception to this rule is *Le Château des cœurs* by Gustave Flaubert, which was published as a text, explicitly designated as a *féerie*, and never performed. It is, of all the works he published, the least known. We will shortly come to another, more famous, text by Flaubert which seems, like *Le Château des cœurs*, to quote Mallarmé, 'non *possible au théâtre*, mais *exigeant le théâtre*' [not *possible in the theatre*, but *requiring the theatre*].)[4] Rivière's book, in referencing the theatre at which the *féerie* was performed, seems at first glance to conform to this tradition. Yet, when one goes beyond the title page, what one finds is certainly not a traditional 'book of the play' — any more than it is a traditional *livre d'artiste*.

To begin with: the words that the characters would speak in a *féerie*, which would transmit the plot and define the characters, are almost completely absent. There are, in fact, no words attributed to any protagonist, until p. 34 of the book, which has a total of 88 pages. Indeed, there are few words of any kind. Each double-page spread, in the book, consists of two elements. The right-hand page is entirely taken up by a wordless and untitled illustration, often richly coloured. The left-hand page gives a title which is plainly that of one of the forty *tableaux* that compose the work; then, below that title, a piece of music, either taken from a pre-existing source (as was common practice in a *féerie*), or written in a recognisable popular style. This lay-out is, to my knowledge, unique in the history of the *livre d'artiste*, certainly in that century. The norm, as established by Mallarmé and Manet a decade earlier, was to present poetry and visual art together, but to leave music as an art merely suggested. Rivière, on the contrary, presents music and visual art, and leaves the poetry to the imagination.

3   Henri Rivière, *La Tentation de saint Antoine* (Paris: E. Plon, Nourrit et Cie, 1888), p. 1.
4   Stéphane Mallarmé, *Correspondance. Lettres sur la poésie*, ed. by Bertrand Marchal, Collection Folio classique (Paris: Gallimard, 1995), p. 242.

The story the book tells is, then, not made verbally explicit. But the illustrations show clearly enough what is going on; and in any case, it is a safe bet that the book's intended market was people who had seen the shadow play, or at least knew Flaubert's *Tentation de saint Antoine*, published fourteen years earlier, and unambiguously the inspiration behind Rivière's work.[5] Saint Antoine, presented as the dark figure of a tormented ascetic, dressed in rags, is being subjected to a series of temptations, designed to lead him astray from his Christian faith. He resists, despite great suffering. These temptations begin in the City of Light, contemporary Paris, with its bewildering array of appeals to greed, from fine food to high-society gambling. Then, clearly orchestrated by the Devil (a dark figure, like the saint), comes the temptation of science. After that, the saint is subjected to the temptation of sensuality, embodied by the Queen of Sheba, and by a troop of pretty ballerinas (whom we had already seen on the front cover). Finally, the saint is made to witness a procession of divinities from other religions, who try to persuade him of their superior attractions. He never ceases to resist, of course, despite his agonies, and is rewarded, in true *féerie* style, by a spectacular final apotheosis, when he ascends, surrounded by angels, to a traditional Christian heaven. Apart from the scenes of contemporary Paris, the ballerinas, and the final apotheosis, the themes of these tableaux are taken more or less directly from Flaubert's book.

Most of the illustrations which occupy the right-hand pages depict both a temptation, and the agonised saint, whose difficulty in resisting is always obvious. The temptation is often colourful and attractive; the saint is, in contrast, dark, small, and tormented. We have been informed on the title page that the 'féerie à grand spectacle', first performed at the theatre of the Chat Noir on 28 December 1887, consisted of forty tableaux. The book has forty double-page openings. The reader therefore assumes that each double page corresponds to a tableau in the performance; and equally, doubtless, that the music which occupies the left-hand page, opposite each illustration, represents what was played during the tableau in question.

How does that music relate to the images? The answer appears surprisingly simple. Most of it consists of tunes from well-known operas or other theatrical works of the time. Some of it was composed by Albert Tinchant and Georges Fragerolle, as the title page had informed us; but that, too, is quite conventional in style. And in every case, there is an obvious musical meaning. The music clearly illustrates one aspect of what is happening in the scene pictured on the facing page — but only one aspect. It always represents the temptation. More particularly, it represents what is attractive, tempting, in the temptation. It never represents the torment and anguish of the saint as he resists. Often, as when he is tempted by the food in Les Halles (the great Parisian market) or by the pretty ballerinas, the tune is a light-hearted one taken from a contemporary ballet or comic opera, by composers such as Lecocq or Delibes. Wagner is conscripted to provide the Ride of the Valkyries when the Norse gods appear; Offenbach's comic version of the Orpheus legend provides jaunty tunes to introduce the Greek muses and the gods of Olympus. There is a

5   Gustave Flaubert, *La Tentation de saint Antoine* (Paris: Charpentier, 1874).

striking contrast between this stereotypically Parisian lightness, and the torment and resistance of the saint, which is, after all, the thread that holds the narrative together; as if the music were on the side of the City of Light which provides the first series of temptations, rather than that of the eponymous hero. One might ask why. Indeed, that question, of which side the music is on, turns out, as we shall see, to hold the key to understanding the extraordinary success of Rivière's *Tentation*. But before returning to that question, let us ask where words come in, relative to both music and images.

The only text spoken by a character in Rivière's book also provides the first explicit reference to the book by Flaubert which was clearly the inspiration for Rivière's work. It comes approximately in the middle of the series of temptations, on a left-hand page, just above a line of music which, unusually, is not immediately identified. Here is the text in its entirety:

ANTOINE.

Ah! plus haut! plus haut! toujours!

... Les astres se multiplient, scintillent. La Voie lactée au zénith se développe comme une immense ceinture, ayant des trous par intervalles[;] dans ces fentes de sa clarté, s'allongent des espaces de ténèbres. Il y a des pluies d'étoiles, des traînées de poussière d'or, des vapeurs lumineuses qui flottent et se dissolvent.

Quelquefois une comète passe tout à coup; — puis la tranquillité des lumières innombrables recommence....

(Gustave Flaubert, *La Tentation de saint Antoine*[6]

[Ah! higher! higher! always higher!

... The stars multiply, sparkle. At the zenith, the Milky Way unfolds as an immense belt, with holes at intervals; in these gaps in its clarity, spaces of darkness stretch out. There are showers of stars, trails of gold dust, luminous vapours which float and dissolve.

Sometimes, suddenly, a comet passes; — then the tranquillity of the innumerable lights begins again....

(Gustave Flaubert, *The Temptation of Saint Anthony*]

This text introduces a series, unique in the book, of three tableaux, three double-page spreads, all with the same title: 'Le Ciel' [The Heavens]. On each of the three left-hand pages is a single line of music, a tune which continues across all three. This tune is eventually identified, at the end of the third left-hand page, as 'Rêverie', by Schumann. It is, indeed, a simplified version of the famous tune from Schumann's 'Träumerei', from his *Kinderszenen*, opus 15. The dreaminess which it incarnates is certainly compatible with the otherworldly beauty of the heavens, as it is expressed in the quotation from Flaubert and materialised in the extraordinary illustrations, which represent planets (including, recognisably, the Earth), stars, and the Milky Way seen from space. But what is their relationship with the two dark figures that, in those illustrations, drift across those heavens? One, a black-winged monster with hooves and tail, is the Devil; the other is the saint, dragged by the Devil and looking

---

6   Rivière, *La Tentation de saint Antoine*, p. 34. The closing bracket after '*Antoine*' is missing in the original.

FIG. 12.1. Henri Rivière, *La Tentation de saint Antoine*
(Paris : E. Plon, Nourrit et Cie., 1888), pp. 34–35.

anguished, as usual. Neither Schumann's 'Rêverie', nor Flaubert's words, seem to take any account of this strange couple.

The mystery deepens if one compares these three tableaux in Rivière's book with the scene from Flaubert's *Tentation de saint Antoine* which obviously inspired them. As Flaubert's Devil takes the saint up into the heavens, the first thing to which the saint responds is the beauty of the universe, as shown in the quotation given by Rivière. But then he becomes increasingly distressed by the fact that the three-dimensional universe which the Devil shows him leaves no distinctive place for God's Heaven, no direction in which to seek Him. Antoine had always thought of Heaven as being above him; but in space, as the Devil says, there is no up and no down, only equivalent and ultimately homogenous space, in all directions. Where, then, is God? According to the Devil, He is at once everywhere and nowhere; he is not beyond the material universe, but rather coterminous with it, and Antoine's desire to believe in Him as a loving presence, a father, a great soul, above and beyond the visible world, is foolish nonsense. As the Devil advances this argument, Antoine's suffering steadily intensifies, to the point where he feels he is losing his consciousness of his own being, as the undifferentiated nature of the universe absorbs and destroys him. This suffering is plainly visible in Rivière's startling illustrations, which show the Devil carrying Antoine, like an eagle might carry its prey, steadily further from his home on Earth, and out towards the edges of the solar system. The illustration I give here shows the first of the three images in this series, with Antoine and the Devil quite large, near the centre of the page and also near a clearly recognisable planet Earth (see figure 12.1). In the two subsequent images, Antoine becomes a diminishing black figure, moving as he shrinks, pulled by the Devil towards the edge of a magnificent colourful cosmos from whose meaning he is excluded. His suffering clearly increases as his stature and centrality diminish. But that suffering, that existential distress, expressed both in Flaubert's book and in Rivière's illustrations, is totally absent both from the music and from the words present in Rivière's book.

The music, then, appears to be saying something different from, or at least more limited than, what the pictures say. Perhaps one might be tempted to align the meaning of the music with the meaning of the words from Flaubert's *Tentation* that Rivière quotes; in those words, which are taken from near the beginning of Flaubert's scene, Antoine is still at the stage of being dazzled by the beauty of the cosmos. But anyone who knows Flaubert's text — and surely most of the readers of Rivière's book at the time would have known it — will be acutely aware of what happens in the latter part of that scene, of the way the Devil torments the saint. Thus Flaubert's words, though so few of them are there, seem to echo hauntingly the disharmony between right-hand and left-hand pages: the present words seem to agree with the music, but only absent words fully agree with the illustrations. There is a peculiar tangle of fault-lines between the apparent meanings of the music, of the visible text, of the occluded text, and of the illustrations. Why? That is the question at the heart of this essay. But before we can answer it, we have to take account of a second phantomatic presence behind this work. Just as Flaubert's book is evoked and cited in a way that encourages us to seek parallels with Rivière's book, parallels whose vanishing point appears to be in puzzlement as much as in enlightenment, so the *féerie* in the Chat Noir cabaret is cited and evoked; and readers in 1888, unlike readers in the twenty-first century, would have been aware of that performance, at least as much as of Flaubert's book. What kind of intertext does it provide?

★   ★   ★   ★   ★

The title page of Rivière's book, as we have seen, says that the *féerie* had been performed in the theatre of the Chat Noir. What it does not specify, but what everyone at the time would have been aware of, was the diminutive size of the proscenium of the theatre in question. It was not much larger than a modern domestic flat-screen television. It measured about 1.40 by 1.12 metres. It was a piece of canvas inserted into the back wall of a second-floor room in the cabaret's building in Montmartre.

The Chat Noir cabaret itself was a unique space in many ways. I doubt that any other four walls in the world have ever had between them, in the space of a dozen years, so many great and famous artists, including, for example, Victor Hugo, Émile Zola, Stéphane Mallarmé, Paul Verlaine, Marie Krysinska, Erik Satie, Claude Debussy, Tchaikovsky, Toulouse-Lautrec, Degas, Monet, Renoir, and Rodin, not to mention the Prince of Wales, Clemenceau, Garibaldi, and several characters from Marcel Proust's *À la recherche du temps perdu*. This popularity and wide appeal among the social and artistic elite was not coincidental. The truly unique thing about the Chat Noir was the way it brought together the most absolute unshakeable faith in the high art tradition, the great Romantic belief in art and beauty with its concomitant hatred of philistines and rationalists and materialists, with a truly tremendous sense of irony and sarcasm based on the firm principle that there is a totally unbridgeable gap between the realm of true beauty, and the world we live in. But the world we live in nonetheless (and this is central to the Chat Noir aesthetic) provides the only possible material for art; so that at the heart of the Chat Noir experience is a vertiginous sense of comic distance between what we are currently doing, thinking, desiring, and working with in this world, and what really matters. Anyone who does not have that sense of comic distance, from the Chat Noir point of view, had to be either a bourgeois philistine or else a ridiculous idealistic idiot. The Chat Noir thus created a powerful ideological position which invited those who shared it mercilessly to mock outsiders. Those outsiders included, generally, capitalists and rationalists on the one hand, and believers in established religion on the other. That mockery of both the seriousness of rationalism, and the seriousness of religion, combined with an intense idealism, played beautifully into the French tradition of wit and lightness, as well as into the increasingly forceful idealism of the times; and the pleasures of belonging to a group that could see itself as a very French elite, superior by its wit, and able to laugh at the leaden-footed bourgeoisie, were clearly highly attractive to many of the leading minds of the time.

The cabaret and its house journal, also called *Le Chat Noir*, had a very long list of eminent contributors, but a much shorter list of people who really moulded its character. On that short list figures the now forgotten name of Henri Rivière, master of the shadow theatre where in 1887 and 1888 the *Tentation de saint Antoine* was performed, as a shadow play, over a hundred times. Rivière was not only the creator of the book I have been describing; he was also the technical and artistic mastermind behind the shadow theatre that put on the *féerie*.

Technically, that shadow theatre was an astonishing achievement. The audience sitting in the cabaret theatre, on the second floor of the Chat Noir building, looking at the small canvas screen set into the wall, saw nothing of the stupendous mechanism behind that screen. It was housed in an enormous wooden box, ten metres high, sticking out of the back of the building. At the back of the enormous box, three metres from the screen, was a powerful light source. Between the screen and the light source was a series of about seventy slots, some vertical and some horizontal, through which slides could be moved, up and down or from side to side, by pulling on strings. The back sixty slots were used for slides made of coloured glass or paper; these made the backgrounds. At the front were slides for the characters, which were made out of cut-out zinc. A few of these zinc characters have survived. Some pictures of them may be found by googling on: 'chat noir' Rivière zinc. A character zinc near the front, just behind the cloth screen, would come out as a clear black shadow against the coloured background. A character zinc further back would come out as grey. The zincs and the background slides could all be moved independently to create a dazzlingly complex play of characters and colours. The most characteristic effect was the contrast of static colour, often likened to a stained-glass window, and black for the more mobile and more clearly defined main characters. The spectacle was divided up into a number of tableaux, but within each tableau, there could be more or less movement, particularly of the zincs.

Each tableau lasted for about one minute (so the whole forty-tableau spectacle lasted for forty minutes), and was accompanied both by words and by music. The music was usually provided, as far as I can tell, by the piano, often played by Tinchant (one of the two musicians who arranged and composed the music for the shadow play). Rivière's book shows us what the character of that music was. But what of the words? We have no concrete trace of them. What we do know, from contemporary accounts, is that they were provided by the extraordinary voice of Rodolphe Salis, who spoke all of them from his prominent station in front of the screen.

Rodolphe Salis was the very spirit of the Chat Noir. He founded, owned, and ran the cabaret, he kept his eye on every material, artistic, social, and financial detail of its operation, and he seemed to be present everywhere, running everything and imprinting his character on everything. He welcomed arrivals (and decided who would and would not be allowed into the various rooms in the establishment). But above all, he was the cabaret's *bonimenteur*. This is not an easy word to translate. A *boniment* is usually defined as what a charlatan or a fairground performer would say to attract and dazzle his clientele. It always has an element of wordy excess and hype and telling more or less than the truth. It also implies wit, verbal virtuosity, grandiloquence, bluff, and a certain mocking tone. Salis was universally recognised as a genius in this essentially improvisatory, hyperbolic, comic, and ironic genre; and that is the style in which he provided all the words, as far as one can tell, for all the many hundreds of shadow theatre performances that formed the cultural heart of his cabaret. But of that torrent of words, we have no record at all. Rivière's book contains not the slightest hint of their existence. The few texts in the book are, as we have seen, by Flaubert, not Salis. This evacuation of Salis's words is no chance omission. It is a key symptom of the intermedial relations at the root of the shadow theatre's extraordinary success as an avant-garde theatrical art form.

★   ★   ★   ★   ★

The general principle behind all the Parisian avant-garde art of the time was that art should work by suggesting something absent from the material of the work, something that appeared to come from somewhere else, somewhere outside what we could physically see or hear. This avant-garde art of suggestion was universally defined as an art of idealism, in opposition to naturalism, which was seen as the dominant mode of the despicable bourgeois novel and theatre. The Chat Noir shadow theatre was received from the beginning by critics and by artists as a uniquely successful example of non-naturalist, idealist, suggestive theatrical art. In this, it was truly exceptional. In poetry and painting, idealist suggestive art had had some success by 1887, in the verse of Verlaine and Mallarmé and the paintings we now call 'impressionist'. (It is, of course, no coincidence that many of the poets, painters, and musicians who had been instrumental in creating this aesthetic frequented the Chat Noir, or contributed to its house magazine.) But in the theatre, that aesthetic had struggled to realise itself. The reason for this struggle between the theatre and the new aesthetic was being carefully theorised by Mallarmé in 1887, precisely, in a series of theatre reviews which he subsequently collected and published (in revised form) in his volume *Divagations* under the title 'Crayonné au théâtre' [Pencilled in the Theatre].[7] The fundamental problem is that in the theatre, all the media are physically present together. So suggestion becomes much more difficult. How can music suggest an absent poetry when there is actually poetry present? How can poetry suggest a visual scene when the visual is actually present? Rivière's stroke of genius was to separate the media in space as well as in tonality, while keeping them simultaneously present in time. His shadow theatre separated the images from the sound, so that one came from behind the screen while the other came from in front. They were juxtaposed, but they did not occupy the same space. That aesthetic of juxtaposition is brilliantly materialised in the book by the separation between the music on the left-hand pages and the images on the right; as if the fold in the middle represented the screen in the cabaret. Furthermore, what the music suggests is always related to the images, but is always also very deliberately exceeded by the images. What is missing from the music is that black zinc figure of the saint, and indeed the black zinc figure of the Devil. As they silently move across

---

7   Stéphane Mallarmé, 'Crayonné au théâtre', in *Divagations* (Paris: Eugène Fasquelle, 1897), pp. 153–233.

the screen, they seem to accuse the music of being stuck in the world of meaning, the world in which we believe we can know what things are and what they signify. But the Chat Noir sense of comic distance always tells us at the same time that the meaning of the music, so relentlessly light-hearted, is not to be taken as a full expression of the true artistic value of the work, or of the ideals that it embodies. They go beyond what music can say.

To return to the essential question of situation: in the book, then, the images on every right-hand page go beyond what the music on the left-hand page seems to say. Similarly, in the theatre, the images on the screen would have gone beyond what the music in front of the screen would have been saying; and the physical distance between the piano in front of the screen and the shadow theatre mechanism behind it would have figured that intermedial separation. One might add that just as the shadow play is haunted by Flaubert's work, so the music is haunted by the composers it borrows from, from Offenbach to Haydn, Schumann and Wagner. Behind each is an idealism which is not quite expressed in the other. And what of Salis's words? In the theatre, they, like the music, would have come from in front of the screen. They would, of course, have interpreted for the audience the drama being played out on the screen. But that interpretation would always have presented itself as ironic, never as exhaustive. Salis never saw himself as a poet, as someone whose words had a literary value; he was always a facilitator of art, a *cabaretier*, never a verbal artist himself. (He had for a time been a visual artist; he soon realised his true genius lay elsewhere.) His role as *bonimenteur* was to create, not high art in words, but that sense of comic distance which was the soul of the Chat Noir. In the theatre, this comic distance could be materialised in the physical distance between Rodolphe Salis, in front of the screen, and the zinc characters, behind it. It would have been immediately obvious, of course, that the voice the audience heard was the voice of Salis, not that of Antoine or of the Devil.

In a book, how could this be represented? We are so used to relating printed words directly to the character who is meant to have said them... how could the book have materialised the fact that the words were in Salis's style and voice, and not in the silent, imagined voice of the zinc characters? How could it have reproduced the distance between the place where Salis stood and the screen? It would have been impossible. His improvised comic *boniment*, if printed, would have rooted the characters in their verbal representation, instead of maintaining their separation from it. That would have ruined the ideal suggestiveness of the work. Rivière's solution was to exclude those words totally. Or rather — that is how it appears to us. But in 1888 it is a safe bet that no one would have purchased this book, with its explicit reference to the Chat Noir theatre on the title page, without knowing full well what the Chat Noir style was, without knowing who Rodolphe Salis was, indeed without having either experienced his *boniments*, or having read his comic prose in the house magazine. Haunting Rivière's book, then, we should imagine not only the music and Flaubert's play, but also that hyperbolic verbosity, that *boniment*, never published but always present at every performance of the *féerie* that Rivière's book purports to be. And to the extent that the remembered *boniment* from the performance haunts the book from which it is absent, so, too, does another aspect of the performance which the book occludes: the movement of the images. The fame and effect of the Chat Noir shadow theatre, as constructed by Rivière, was a product of the fact that its tableaux were not static. The zinc characters moved during the scenes; so, too, did the coloured background slides, although, as with the words, we have absolutely no contemporary accounts that tell us exactly how. Anyone reading the book, and having seen or heard about the *féerie* in its original theatrical form, will therefore be drawn not to see the pictures, music, and words in the book as forming a coherent, closed, and mutually referential intermedial unit, but as the stimulus to imagining all the ghostly presences that they suggest, and which escape them. The words of Salis and of Flaubert, the musical world from which Tinchant and Fragerolle borrow, and the moving images of the shadow theatre are all there to be imagined in their absence, as is the inexpressible idealism of the saint at the heart of the work.

★   ★   ★   ★   ★

The Chat Noir shadow theatre really was unique. It was the only theatrical spectacle of those years which was received both as magnificently idealist (and hence anti-naturalist), and magnificently, popularly successful. Zola, the prince of naturalism (who, of course, came to the Chat Noir), had been trying to revolutionise the theatre in the direction of naturalism; his aesthetic enemies rejoiced in the success of the shadow theatre in accomplishing a revolution heading in precisely the opposite direction:

> Pends-toi, Zola! cette révolution [...] s'est réalisée [...] loin des vulgarités de ton naturalisme, dans le domaine de la fantaisie et du rêve, par le théâtre [...] que Rivière vient d'asseoir dans sa forme définitive avec cette *Tentation de saint Antoine* [...]; conception d'artiste et de poète, théâtre idéal [...] théâtre suggestif aussi, où une ligne, un trait, ouvrent à l'imagination du spectateur les horizons insaisissables du rêve.[8]

> [Zola, you may as well go and hang yourself! This revolution [...] has been accomplished [...] far from the vulgarities of your naturalism, in the realm of fantasy and dream, by the theatre [...] that Rivière has established in its definitive form with this *Temptation of Saint Anthony* [...] it is the conception of an artist and a poet, an ideal theatre [...] as well as a theatre of suggestion, where a single line can open up to the imagination the ungraspable horizons of dream.]

This review by Édouard Norès is a perfect example of the intermedial style of the time.[9] To begin with, note how it uses the word *poète*: not to indicate what Rivière did with words — Rivière did nothing with words, he left those to Flaubert and

---

8   Édouard Norès, 'La *tentation de Saint Antoine* de Rivière au Chat Noir', *Les Premières Illustrées*, 1887.

9   Cf. Sophie Lucet, 'Tentation des ombres à l'époque symboliste: l'attraction du Chat Noir', in *Le Spectaculaire dans les arts de la scène du romantisme à la Belle Époque*, ed. by Isabelle Moindrot (Paris: CNRS, 2006), pp. 138–46.

Salis — but to indicate a property of a non-verbal medium, in this case a visual medium, which was opposed to naturalistic representation. A poet in this sense is exactly and precisely *not* someone who writes poetry. On the contrary, a poet is someone who uses non-verbal media to produce that effect of poetry which goes beyond words. That 'going beyond the medium' is also figured here, as it always is, through the emphasis on suggestion, on an opening out onto what cannot be grasped — the ungraspable horizons of dream. And to keep those horizons ungraspable, Norès strategically omits all reference to what really enables this theatre of suggestion to work: its music and the *boniment* of Rodolphe Salis, which carry the work through the forty minutes of its representation and create at once the link to the familiar time of the spectator, and the ironic distance between voice and image that propels us towards 'les horizons insaisissables du rêve'. Norès does not mention the music, Salis's words, or the movement of the slides in the shadow theatre. Nor, as I have said, do any of the other descriptions of the spectacle that have come down to us; not even Rivière's own descriptions, in his wonderfully evocative, posthumously published autobiography.[10] This is no coincidence. What it signifies is that Rivière's contemporaries understood full well the necessity of leaving entire the space of suggestiveness around the work. Just as Rivière does in his book, so all the people who saw and appreciated his achievement knew that they had to leave the *boniment* of Salis, the movement of the images, and the true nature of the music unspoken in print. They were an indispensable part of the spectacle's ideal force and success, but only thanks to the distances that the shadow theatre was able to maintain between them. In the pages of a book or of a journal, those distances must be replaced by silences, and much of what was physically present in the theatre has to be become ghostly.

As well as its house journal, the Chat Noir published a book which became extremely popular: *Les Gaîtés du Chat Noir*. It was largely a collection of the hilarious tales that were told in the cabaret and published in the journal. The book contained none of the words associated with the shadow plays. But in the preface to the second edition, in 1894, Jules Lemaître, one of the leading spirits of the cabaret, paid an appropriate homage to Rivière, to his theatre, and to the idealism of which it was the Chat Noir's purest incarnation: an idealism at the heart of the cabaret, but which its printed words and static images could not capture. After describing the comic force of the cabaret, Lemaître wrote: 'Et, en même temps, le Chat-Noir contribuait au "réveil de l'idéalisme". Il était mystique, avec le génial paysagiste et découpeur d'ombres Henri Rivière. L'orbe lumineux de son guignol fut un œil-de-bœuf ouvert sur l'invisible' [And, at the same time, the Chat Noir was contributing to the 'awakening of idealism'. It was mystical, with Henri Rivière, creator of shadow shapes and landscape painter of genius. The luminous orbit of his puppet theatre was an ox-eye window opening onto the invisible].[11]

---

10   Cf. Henri Rivière, *Les Détours du chemin: souvenirs, notes et croquis, 1864–1951* (Saint-Rémy-de-Provence: Équinoxe, 2004), pp. 46–61.

11   Jules Lemaître, 'Préface', in *Les Gaîtés du Chat Noir*, ed. by Jules Lemaître, 2nd edn (Paris: Paul Ollendorff, 1894), p. vii.

It was not by chance that this idealist shadow theatre flourished in the atmosphere created by the Chat Noir, and nowhere else. When Rodolphe Salis died in 1897, the shadow theatre for which he was the *bonimenteur* died too. It could not work without him and without the theatrical space that he created and animated. Henri Rivière himself lived until 1951, and had a successful career as an artist. But he never tried anything like the shadow theatre again. He knew that it was born of a unique moment, when the music and the words on one side of the screen knew how to entertain their audience while always keeping their respectful distance from the silent images behind them, stiffly moving on that extraordinary series of grooves receding into the distance. Nowhere else, perhaps, have popular music and entertaining banter been so perfectly married in theatrical time with the purest and most silent form of high art; and what enabled this unique moment in artistic time, to which Rivière's lovely book bears witness, was that little cloth screen covering the hole between the source of the sound, in front of the screen, and the source of the images, behind it.

The relationship between words, music, and the moving image in Rivière's *Tentation de saint Antoine* is, then, to be understood in terms of distances, hauntings, absences, ungraspable horizons, and windows onto the invisible, at least as much as in terms of synergies, mutual support, and collaboration. In this, though its genre is unique (as I have said, I know of no other book that combines visual art and music in this way), it represents perfectly intermedial relations as they have defined a certain high art tradition since the days of the Romantic revolution, two centuries ago.

The arts, in their different media, have constructed themselves in relation to each other not by working together in peaceful harmony, but by keeping each other at a certain kind of distance; and it is the quality of that distance that matters. To appreciate the character and value of this distance, my strategy has been to examine how works of art which involve several media actually keep those media apart, in such a way that one cannot properly theorise the relationship between them except as a distance, a gap, a space in which something happens which escapes all media and indeed all theory, including mine. That space is where art lives. What is, to me, uniquely expressive about the Chat Noir shadow theatre is that there, this space can actually be physically localised. It is that hole in the wall covered by a thin piece of blank cloth. Behind it are moving zincs and coloured slides. In front of it are music and words. The spectators in the theatre were actually focusing their eyes on the space between them, the space where they do not quite meet, the screen that is itself nothing but a veil; a veil that we ourselves will never see, but can imagine, as an ungraspable horizon of our dreams.

There lies the truth that is beauty, and the beauty that is truth.

ENVOI

❖

In the early 1970s, I was a pupil at a boys' grammar school. It had a strong practical music tradition. Many of the boys had instrumental lessons and played (as I did) in the school orchestra, or sang in the school choir, with various degrees of interest and pleasure. My social life revolved around music-making.

There were also academic music lessons, though not many. One day, our music teacher asked those boys in the class who played instruments whether they enjoyed it. Yes, several of us replied. He then asked why. What is it, he wanted to know, that you like about making music?

Silence from the class. No one had an answer.

The teacher insisted.

Eventually, one boy said: it's because of the challenge. It's difficult to play an instrument, and when you get something right, that's satisfying. A few others agreed.

What, said the teacher, something like doing a crossword or a jigsaw puzzle?

There was embarrassment in the class. We could feel he wanted us to come up with something else, something different. Nor were we satisfied with what had been said. But none of us knew exactly what he wanted, and we could not think of what else to say.

I said nothing.

After a few long moments of silence, the teacher gave up and moved on to another topic. I remember vividly the weary frustration on his face. As if his reason for being, as a teacher of music, had been shut away in a cupboard.

I cannot remember his name.

BIBLIOGRAPHY OF
WORKS BY PETER DAYAN

❖

Books

The Music of Dada: A Lesson in Intermediality for Our Times (Abingdon: Ashgate Publishing, 2018)

Art as Music, Music as Poetry, Poetry as Art, from Whistler to Stravinsky (Burlington, VT: Ashgate Publishing, 2011)

Music Writing Literature, from Sand via Debussy to Derrida (Aldershot: Ashgate Publishing, 2006)

Lautréamont et Sand (Amsterdam: Rodopi, 1997)

Nerval et ses pères, portrait en trois volets avec deux gonds et un cadenas (Geneva: Droz, 1992)

Mallarmé's Divine Transposition: Real and Apparent Sources of Literary Value (Oxford: Oxford University Press, 1986)

Articles etc.

'Derrida, de Man, Barthes, and Music as the Soul of Writing', in *The Edinburgh Companion to Literature and Music*, ed. by Delia da Sousa Correa (Edinburgh: Edinburgh University Press, 2020), pp. 31–38

'Wagner and French Poetry from Nerval to Mallarmé: The Power of Opera Unheard', in *The Edinburgh Companion to Literature and Music*, ed. by Delia da Sousa Correa (Edinburgh: Edinburgh University Press, 2020), pp. 483–93

'Is There a Life Beyond Lines?', in *Life After Lines: Tim Ingold Across the Humanities*, ed. by Gunhild Moltesen Agger and others, Interdisciplinære kulturstudier (Aalborg: Aalborg Universitetsforlag, 2020), pp. 11–28

'How Musical is Henri Lefebvre's Rhythmanalysis?', in *Rhythms Now: Henri Lefebvre's Rhythmanalysis Revisited*, ed. by Steen Ledet Christiansen and Mirjam Gebauer, Interdisciplinære kulturstudier (Aalborg: Aalborg Universitetsforlag, 2019), pp. 17–31

'Shadow Images Moving to Music: *La Tentation de saint Antoine* in Montmartre', in *Music, Narrative, and the Moving Image: Varieties of Plurimedial Interrelations*, ed. by Walter Bernhart and David Francis Urrows, Word and Music Studies, 17 (Leiden: Brill, 2019), pp. 135–39

'On the Danger of Pushing Poetry Towards Music: The Successes and Failures of Hugo Ball, René Ghil, and Stéphane Mallarmé', in *Dialogues on Poetry: Mediatization and New Sensibilities*, ed. by Dan Ringgaard and Stefan Kjerkegaard (Aalborg: Aalborg Universitetsforlag, 2017), pp. 89–110

'Why the Music of Satie is the Only Genuine Music of Paris Dada', *Hugo-Ball-Almanach*, Neue Folge 8 (2017), 148–61

'The Inaudible Music of Dada', in *Silence and Absence in Literature and Music*, ed. by Werner Wolf and Walter Bernhart, Word and Music Studies, 15 (Leiden: Brill, 2016), pp. 152–65

'Voices From Beyond Paper: Risset's and Kowalski's *L'autre face*', *Contemporary Music Review*, 34.5–6 (2016), 406–15

'Owning People: Human Property in *Indiana*', in *Approaches to Teaching Sand's Indiana*, ed. by David A. Powell and Pratima Prasad, Approaches to Teaching World Literature (New York: MLA, 2015), pp. 54–62

'Which Came First? Nature, Music and Poetry in Mallarmé's "Bucolique"', *Dix-Neuf*, 19.3 (2015), 199–209

'Zurich Dada's Forgotten Music Master: Hans Heusser', *Modern Language Review*, 110.2 (2015), 491–509

'Limiter les "attributions de la science": le refus de la vérité positive en art, de Rameau à Satie', in *Médecine, sciences de la vie et littérature en Europe de la Révolution à nos jours*, ed. by Lise Dumasy-Queffélec and Hélène Spengler, 3 vols (Geneva: Droz, 2014), II, 247–59

'Zurich Dada, Wagner and the Union of the Arts', *Forum for Modern Language Studies*, 50.4 (2014), 426–52

'Apollinaire's Music/ La Musique d'Apollinaire', *Apollinaire*, 14 (2013), 81–100

'Losing Sense, Making Music: What Erik Satie's Music and Poetry Do for Each Other', in *Words and Notes in the Long Nineteenth Century*, ed. by Phyllis Weliver and Katharine Ellis (Woodbridge: Boydell Press, 2013), pp. 21–33

'Different Music, Same Condition: Hofstadter and Lyotard', *thinking verse*, 2 (2012), 9–26

'Erik Satie, *Uspud*, et la mystification au service de l'art', *Romantisme, revue du dix-neuvième siècle*, 156 (2012), 101–10

'Intermediality and the Refusal of Interdisciplinarity in Stravinsky's Music', in *Intermedial Arts: Disrupting, Remembering, and Transforming Media*, ed. by Leena Eilitta, Liliane Louvel, and Sabine Kim (Newcastle: Cambridge Scholars Publishing, 2012), pp. 159–71

'Pour un comparatisme entre les arts', in *Vers un nouveau comparatisme*, ed. by Antonio Domínguez Leiva and Sébastien Hubier, *Revue d'Études Culturelles Online* (2012), 375–89 <http://etudesculturelles.weebly.com/nouveau-comparatisme.html> [accessed 21 November 2021]

'Seeing Words and Music as a Painter Might: The Interart Aesthetic', in *Word and Music Studies: Essays on Performativity and on Surveying the Field*, ed. by Walter Bernhart, Word and Music Studies, 12 (Amsterdam: Rodopi, 2012), pp. 265–77

'Apollinaire's Music', *Forum for Modern Language Studies*, 47.1 (2011), 36–48

'L'Absence de la polyphonie dans les romans de George Sand', in *George Sand: intertextualité et polyphonie*, ed. by Nigel Harkness and Jacinta Wright, 2 vols (Oxford: Peter Lang, 2011), II, 93–109

'Medial Self-reference between Words and Music in Erik Satie's Piano Pieces', in *Self-reference in Literature and Music*, ed. by Walter Bernhart and Werner Wolf, Word and Music Studies, 11 (Amsterdam: Rodopi, 2010), pp. 51–64

'Pas de vérité en art? Quelques pensées de Satie, Braque, Mallarmé et Derrida', in *Le Mensonge: Multidisciplinary Perspectives in French Studies*, ed. by Kate Averis and Matthew Moran (Newcastle: Cambridge Scholars Publishing, 2010), pp. 101–14

—— and Carolina Orloff, 'Finding Rhythm in Julio Cortazar's *Los Premios*', *Paragraph*, 33.2 (2010), 215–29

—— and David Evans, 'Rhythm in Literature after the Crisis in Verse', *Paragraph*, 33.2 (2010), 147–57

'The Time for Poetry', *Oxford Literary Review*, 31.1 (2009), 1–14

'Truth in Art, and Erik Satie's Judgement', *Nineteenth-century Music Review*, 6.2 (2009), 91–107

'Whistler et la poésie du son', *Revue Silène* (April 2009) <http://www.revue-silene.com/images/30/extrait_131.pdf> [accessed 21 November 2021]

'Erik Satie's Poetry', *Modern Language Review*, 103.2 (2008), 409–23

'Interart Contraband: What Passed between Garcia, Sand, and Liszt in *Le Contrebandier*', in *Essays on Word/ Music Adaptation and on Surveying the Field*, ed. by David Francis Urrows, Word and Music Studies, 9 (Amsterdam: Rodopi, 2008), pp. 115–34

'The Force of Music in Derrida's Writing', in *Phrase and Subject*, ed. by Delia da Sousa Correa (Oxford: Legenda, 2006), pp. 45–58

'Nature, Music, and Meaning in Debussy's Writings', *19th-Century Music*, 28.3 (2005), 214–29

'L'Obscurité, entre Mallarmé et Proust', in *Visions/ Revisions: Essays on Nineteenth-century French Culture*, ed. by Nigel Harkness and others (Oxford: Peter Lang, 2004), pp. 261–74

'Derrida Writing Architectural or Musical Form', *Paragraph*, 26.3 (2003), 70–85

'La Musique et les lettres chez Barthes', *French Studies*, 57.3 (2003), 335–48

'On the Meaning of "Musical" in Proust', in *Word and Music Studies: Essays in Honor of Steven Paul Scher and on Cultural Identity and the Musical Stage*, ed. by Suzanne M. Lodato, Suzanne Aspden, and Walter Bernhart, Word and Music Studies, 4 (Amsterdam: Rodopi, 2002), pp. 143–58

'Do Mallarmé's *Divagations* Tell Us Not to Write about Musical Works?', in *Word and Music Studies: Essays on the Song Cycle and on Defining the Field*, ed. by Walter Bernhart and Werner Wolf in collaboration with David Mosley, Word and Music Studies, 3 (Amsterdam: Rodopi, 2001), pp. 65–80

'De la traduction en musique chez Baudelaire', *Romance Studies*, 18.2 (2000), 145–55

'Mallarmé and the *siècle finissant*', in *Symbolism, Decadence, and the Fin de Siècle*, ed. by Patrick McGuinness (Exeter: Exeter University Press, 2000), pp. 19–28

'What Can Music Express of Consuelo?', in *Women Seeking Expression: France 1789–1914*, ed. by Rosemary Lloyd and Brian Nelson, Monash Romance Studies, 6 (Melbourne: Monash University, 2000), pp. 146–58

'De la traduction en musique chez Sand', *George Sand Studies*, 17.1–2 (1998), 29–42

'Lautréamont's Literary Life', in *The Process of Art: Essays on Nineteenth-century French Literature, Music, and Painting in Honour of Alan Raitt*, ed. by Michael Freeman and others (Oxford: Clarendon Press, 1998), pp. 25–42

'Looking for Life in Lautréamont', *New Comparison*, 25 (1998), 40–51

'Mallarmé et Philomène', in *Verlaine 1896–1996*, ed. by Martine Bercot (Paris: Klincksieck, 1998), pp. 105–14

'Who is the Narrator in *Indiana*?', *French Studies*, 52.2 (1998), 152–61

'Baudelaire at his Latrine: Motions in the *Petits poèmes en prose* and in George Sand's Novels', *French Studies*, 48.4 (1994), 416–24

'L'Admirable Inconséquence de George Sand', in *Actes du Xe Colloque International George Sand* (Debrecen: Debrecen University Press, 1993), pp. 49–54

'The Romantic Renaissance' and 'Poetry Dies Again', in *Poetry in France: Metamorphoses of a Muse*, ed. by Keith Aspley and Peter France (Edinburgh: Edinburgh University Press, 1992), pp. 139–53, 169–83

'Working on Word-processed French', *ReCALL*, 4.7 (1992), 27–28

BIBLIOGRAPHY OF WORKS CITED

❖

AURIC, GEORGES, *Quand j'étais là* (Paris: Grasset, 1979)

BAKHTIN, MIKHAIL, *Problems of Dostoevsky's Poetics*, trans. by Caryl Emerson (Manchester: Manchester University Press, 1984)

BARTHES, ROLAND, *Image, Music, Text*, ed. and trans. by Stephen Heath (London: Fontana, 1977)

BATTERSBY, CHRISTINE, *Gender and Genius: Towards a Feminist Aesthetics* (London: The Women's Press, 1989)

BAUDELAIRE, CHARLES, 'À Arsène Houssaye', *La Presse*, August 1862

———*Les Fleurs du Mal* (Paris: Poulet-Malassis, 1857)

———*Les Fleurs du Mal* (Paris: Garnier, 1961)

———*Œuvres complètes*, ed. by Claude Pichois, 2 vols, Bibliothèque de la Pléiade (Paris: Gallimard, 1975–76)

———*Petits poëmes en prose (Le Spleen de Paris)*, ed. by Robert Knopp (Paris: Gallimard, 1973)

———*Le Spleen de Paris*, ed. by Aurélia Cervoni and Andrea Schellino, Collection Folio (Paris: Gallimard, 2017)

BEAUVOIR, SIMONE DE, *Le Deuxième Sexe II*, Collection Folio (Paris: Gallimard, 1976)

BEETHOVEN, LUDWIG VAN, *Briefwechsel Gesamtausgabe*, ed. by Sieghard Brandenburg, 7 vols (Munich: G. Henle, 1996–98)

———*The Letters of Beethoven*, coll., trans., and ed. by Emily Anderson, 3 vols (London: Macmillan, 1961)

BENJAMIN, WALTER, *Gesammelte Schriften. Band 1 Teil 2* (Frankfurt: Suhrkamp, 1980)

———'L'Œuvre d'art à l'époque de sa réproduction mécanisée', trans. by Pierre Klossowski, *Zeitschrift für Sozialforschung*, 5.1 (1936), 40–68

BENSON, STEPHEN, 'For Want of a Better Term? Polyphony and the Value of Music in Bakhtin and Kundera', *Narrative*, 11.3 (2003), 292–311

BENSON, STEPHEN, and CLARE CONNORS, eds, *Creative Criticism: An Anthology and Guide* (Edinburgh: Edinburgh University Press, 2014)

BORDAS, ÉRIC, 'La Contre-polyphonie sandienne de *Consuelo*', in *Lectures de 'Consuelo, la comtesse de Rudolstadt' de George Sand*, ed. by Michèle Hecquet and Christine Planté (Lyon: Presses universitaires de Lyon, 2004), pp. 22–37

BRAQUE, GEORGES, *Cahier* (Paris: Maeght, 1994)

BROOKS, PETER, SHOSHANA FELMAN, and J. HILLIS MILLER, eds, *The Lesson of Paul de Man* (= *Yale French Studies*, 69 (1985))

CARTER, A. E., *Paul Verlaine*, Twayne's World Authors (New York: Twayne, 1971)

CHARBONNIER, GEORGES, *Monologue du peintre: entretiens avec Braque* [and others] (Neuilly-sur-Seine: Durier, 1980)

CHOPIN, FRÉDÉRIC, *Correspondance de Frédéric Chopin*, ed. and trans. by Bronislas Edouard Sydow and others, 3 vols (Paris: Richard-Masse, 1953–60)

COMTE, AUGUSTE, *Discours sur l'esprit positif* (Paris: Vrin, 1995)

COOPER, BARRY, 'Beethoven's Tenth Symphony', *Journal of the Royal Musical Association*, 117.2 (1992), 324–29

DARWIN, CHARLES, *The Autobiography of Charles Darwin*, ed. by Nora Barlow (New York & London: W. W. Norton, 1993)

——*The Descent of Man, and Selection in Relation to Sex* (London: Penguin, 2004)

——*The Expression of the Emotions in Man and Animals*, ed. by P. Ekman (London: Harper Perennial, 2009)

——*On the Origin of Species* (London: John Murray, 1859)

DERRIDA, JACQUES, *La Dissémination* (Paris: Seuil, 1972)

——*La Vérité en peinture* (Paris: Flammarion, 1978)

——*The Truth in Painting* trans. by Geoffrey Bennington and Ian McLeod (Chicago: University of Chicago Press, 1987

——*The Work of Mourning*, ed. by Pascale-Anne Brault and Michael Naas (Chicago: University of Chicago Press, 2001)

EVANS, DAVID, *Théodore de Banville: Constructing Poetic Value in Nineteenth-century France* (Oxford: Legenda, 2014)

FÉTIS, FRANÇOIS-JOSEPH, *Biographie universelle des musiciens et bibliographie générale de la musique*, 8 vols (Brussels: Leroux, 1835–44)

FEYNMAN, RICHARD, *The Feynman Lectures on Physics* <http://www.feynmanlectures.caltech.edu/III_01.html>

FLAUBERT, GUSTAVE, *Extraits de la correspondance ou Préface à la vie d'écrivain*, ed. by Geneviève Bollème (Paris: Seuil, 1963)

——*La Tentation de saint Antoine* (Paris: Charpentier, 1874)

FORCER, STEPHEN, *Modernist Song: The Poetry of Tristan Tzara* (Cambridge: MHRA, 2006)

HELMHOLTZ, HERMANN VON, *Théorie physiologique de la musique fondée sur l'étude des sensations auditives*, trans. by M. G. Guéroult (Paris: Masson, 1868)

HURET, JULES, *Enquête sur l'évolution littéraire* (Paris: Charpentier, 1891)

JANKÉLÉVITCH, VLADIMIR, *L'Ironie* (Paris: Flammarion, 1964)

LAUTRÉAMONT, ISIDORE DUCASSE, COMTE DE, *Les Chants de Maldoror, Poésies I et II* (Paris: Flammarion, 1990)

LEMAÎTRE, JULES, ed., *Les Gaîtés du Chat Noir*, 2nd edn (Paris: Paul Ollendorff, 1894)

LEPELLETIER, E., *Paul Verlaine: sa vie — son œuvre* (Paris: Mercure de France, 1907)

LUCET, SOPHIE, 'Tentation des ombres à l'époque symboliste: l'attraction du Chat Noir', in *Le Spectaculaire dans les arts de la scène du romantisme à la Belle Époque*, ed. by Isabelle Moindrot (Paris: CNRS, 2006), pp. 138–46

MACDONALD, MARGARET, ed., *Whistler's Mother: An American Icon* (London: Lund Humphries, 2003)

MALLARMÉ, STÉPHANE, *Correspondance. Lettres sur la poésie*, ed. by Bertrand Marchal, Collection Folio classique (Paris: Gallimard, 1995)

——*Divagations* (Paris: Eugène Fasquelle, 1897)

——*Œuvres complètes*, ed. by Bertrand Marchal, 2 vols, Bibliothèque de la Pléiade (Paris: Gallimard, 1998–2003)

MARCHAL, BÉATRICE, *Les Chants du Silence* (Paris: Delatour, 2013)

——*Écrits d'amour* (Paris: Cerf, 2009)

NORÈS, ÉDOUARD, 'La *tentation de Saint Antoine* de Rivière au Chat Noir', *Les Premières Illustrées*, 1887

PERROTTET, SUZANNE, *Ein Bewegtes Leben*, ed. by Giorgio J. Wolfensberger (Bern: Benteli, [n.d.])

PROUST, MARCEL, *À la recherche du temps perdu*, ed. by Jean-Yves Tadié, 4 vols, Bibliothèque de la Pléiade (Paris: Gallimard, 1987–89)

RABATEL, ALAIN, 'La Dialogisation au cœur du couple polyphonie/ dialogisme chez Bakhtine', *Revue Romane*, 41 (2006), 55–80

RIMBAUD, ARTHUR, *Œuvres complètes*, ed. by Jean-Luc Steinmetz (Paris: Flammarion, 2010)

RIVIÈRE, HENRI, *Les Détours du chemin: souvenirs, notes et croquis, 1864–1951* (Saint-Rémy-de-Provence: Équinoxe, 2004)

——*La Tentation de saint Antoine* (Paris: E. Plon, Nourrit et Cie, 1888)

SAND, GEORGE, *Consuelo; La Comtesse de Rudolstadt*, 3 vols (Meylan: L'Aurore, 1983)

——*Œuvres autobiographiques*, ed. by Georges Lubin, 2 vols, Bibliothèque de la Pléiade (Paris: Gallimard, 1970–71)

SATIE, ERIK, *Correspondance presque complète* (Paris: Fayard/ IMEC, 2003)

——*Ecrits, réunis par Ornella Volta* (Paris: Champ libre, 1981)

——*A Mammal's Notebook*, ed. by Ornella Volta, trans. by Antony Melville (London: Atlas Press, 1996)

——*The Writings of Erik Satie*, ed. and trans. by Nigel Wilkins (London: Eulenburg Books, 1980)

SAUVAGE, CÉCILE, *Œuvres complètes*, ed. by Claude-Jean Lannay, with a preface by Olivier Messiaen (Paris: La Table Ronde, 2002)

SCHINDLER, ANTON, *Biographie von Ludwig van Beethoven* (Münster: Aschendorff, 1860)

SCHOR, NAOMI, *George Sand and Idealism* (New York: Columbia University Press, 1993)

TARUSKIN, RICHARD, *The Danger of Music and Other Anti-Utopian Essays* (Berkeley: University of California Press, 2010)

TZARA, TRISTAN, *De nos oiseaux*, illus. by Hans Arp (Paris: Kra, [1929])

——*Lampisteries, précédées des sept manifestes dada, quelques dessins de Francis Picabia* (Paris: Jean-Jacques Pauvert, 1963)

——*Œuvres complètes*, ed. by Henri Béhar, 6 vols (Paris: Flammarion, 1975–91)

VERDET, ANDRÉ, *Entretiens, notes et écrits sur la peinture: Braque, Léger, Matisse, Picasso* (Paris: Galilée, 1978)

VERLAINE, PAUL, *Confessions (Paris: Magnard, 2002)*

——*Œuvres poétiques complètes*, Bibliothèque de la Pléiade (Paris: Gallimard, 1962)

——*Les Poètes maudits* (Paris: Vanier, 1888)

VERLAINE, EX-MADAME PAUL, *Mémoires de ma vie*, ed. by Michael Pakenham (Seyssel: Champ Vallon, 1992)

WARHOL, ANDY, *The Philosophy of Andy Warhol* (London: Penguin, 2007)

WHISTLER, JAMES MCNEILL, *The Gentle Art of Making Enemies* (London: Heinemann, 1994)

WHITING, STEVEN MOORE, *Satie the Bohemian* (Oxford: Oxford University Press, 1999)

WINTER, ROBERT S., 'Beethoven's Tenth Symphony', *Journal of the Royal Musical Association*, 117.2 (1992), 329–30

WOOLF, VIRGINIA, *A Room of One's Own; Three Guineas*, World's Classics (Oxford: Oxford University Press, 1992)

WYN JONES, DAVID, *Beethoven: Pastoral Symphony* (Cambridge: Cambridge University Press, 1995)

ZWEIG, STEFAN, *Paul Verlaine*, trans. by O. F. Theis (Boston, MA: Luce, 1913)

INDEX

❖

www.ingramcontent.com/pod-product-compliance
Lightning Source LLC
Chambersburg PA
CBHW080542090426
42734CB00016B/3177